The Avid Assistant Editor's Handbook

The go-to-guide for assistant editors learning about Avid and their jobs

Kyra Coffie

The Avid Assistant Editor's Handbook: The go-to-guide for assistant editors learning about Avid and their jobs

ISBN: 978-0615487755

Questions, comments, or additional information?
Contact: Kyra@AvidAsstEditor.com
www.AvidAsstEditor.com

Cartoons: David Fletcher
Author Photo: ©2011 Jennifer Berkowitz
Copy Editing, Indexing, and Interior Design: Jill Cooper

ACKNOWLEDGEMENTS

THIS BOOK IS A culmination of years of learning and teaching, and I couldn't have written a single word without the tutelage of my early influencers, my parents, Larry and Linda Payne, and U.S. Army CPT Michael Newman. Thanks so much for supporting me and Mike for answering every single one of my crazy questions. I couldn't have done it without you guys!

Writing a book is frequently a solo journey, but my experience was an exception because I had Jennifer Berkowitz at my side for any request. Her googling skills are unparalleled, an art even, and she took many tasks off of my hands to give me a break or to just lend a helping hand. I absolutely could not have done the book without you. Thank you forever and a day.

Along the way, I have received guidance from Alex Palatnick and Josh Petok, who let me dissect their brains about every little facet of Avid. All questions were laboriously answered until I had complete understanding and any new Avid tidbit was selflessly shared with me at every available opportunity. I am forever indebted to you two.

Many thanks to my editor Jill Cooper. She took my coal of a book and chiseled, polished, and set my unrefined manuscript into the gem that you see today. Her ability to assimilate unfamiliar material and transform it into a cohesive, flowing book is unparalleled, and I am so fortunate to have her in the book's corner. I absolutely couldn't have done this without her and her tireless dedication and attention to detail.

Additionally, thank you to the numerous kind souls who have held my hand throughout this journey. My support system of Rona Cohen, Jennifer Seibel, Anthony Zaldivar, Ralik Amir, Brian Shackelford, and Lewis Avramovich was the best a writer could ever have. I may not have said it enough, but your daily support, kind words, and unwavering friendship pulled me through some of the more difficult moments writing this book. I humbly thank you all.

To all of you that I have crossed paths with over the years: each of you were wonderful in your own way, and I am forever grateful. And to all of the companies that made this book possible, thank you.

Elvis Payne	Avid Technology	Mike Zaldivar
Tanitah Tanudech	Terrance Payne	Joseph Harrison
Santiago Chillari	Bella Berkowitz	Larry Payne II

Leslie Davis	Stephan Kiessling	Joy Berkowitz
Sandra Oliver	Norma Moody	Charlene Cook
Jocelyn Borgner	Vahid Brignoni	Galen Christy
Natalie Longoria	Athanas Berkley	Kelly Vars
Alyssa Loveall	Lyric Ramsey	Sushila Love
Aja Smith	Trey Johnson	Hector De Leon
Shannon Hollins	Stephanie Herrera	Mira Browne
Sara Hillner	Chapen Hayslett	Eric Wilson
John Ramsey	Michelle Ivan	Lori Calvillo
Melissa Brown	Jerome Allen	Drew Whitaker
Ryan Flinn	Mike Noble	David Bailey
Charlotte Hendrix	Erin Dowgiert	Emily Storer
Mike Jones	Patrick Hale	Dan McCarthy
Matt Juaregui	Kyle Gildea	Nico Agostino
Doug Bay	Brian Weiss	Maciej Ochman
Ryan Smith	Nick Kiraly	John Beyer
Greg Faber	Greg Price	Bryan Fantinelli
Mica Scott	Jenny Utterback	David Sous
Regi Allen	Pete Scott	Christine Gottschalk
Paige Gold	Jeff Smith	Barbie Gilardi
Brad Phillips	Brandon Bradford	Ian Arwas
Tracey Vail	Lynsey O'Brien	Tina Krohn
Jessica Sherlock	Kevin Ryan	Dawn Taylor
James Oh	Edwin Rivera	Leslie Bolton
Jesse McGill	Livio Linares	Cynthia Davis
Lou Wilkins	Lara Ruth	Robyn Miner
Mike Skvarla	Microsoft	Mark Jones
John Benedetto	Twitter Followers	Discovery Communications
Harry Bond	51 Minds Entertainment	Facebook Fans
Story House Productions	Swift River Productions	Devlin Charlton-Dennis
Nick Warren-Mordecai	U.S. Army	

Last and definitely not least, to all of you who read this book. Together we are creating a community of knowledge that will elevate the postproduction field to new heights. Thank you for your dedication to our field and helping to make it grow and flourish.

Kyra

November 2011

CONTENTS

TASKS

INTRODUCTION

THIS BOOK WILL TEACH you concepts, provide you with step-by-step tasks in Avid, and guide you around common editing pitfalls all serving to enhance your skillset, broaden your knowledge, and make your assistant editing in Avid faster and more efficient. The information provided to you in this book will facilitate your rise from an assistant editor position to a coveted editor role. Take these lessons to heart, and you will reap the rewards throughout your editing career.

This book is a distillation of concepts and best practices gained through more than 10 years of hands-on editing for many well-known companies. The lengthy list of people and companies in the Acknowledgements evidences the depth and breadth of the knowledgebase at the foundation of this book. While each postproduction office operates a little differently, the concepts and practices presented here will hold true and firm withstanding any company-specific adaptations that may be required.

A few tips that will allow this book to be as beneficial to you as possible are as follows:

Master a concept/technique completely before moving on to the next. Each concept/technique builds upon its predecessors and incomplete knowledge can lead to costly and time-consuming errors down the line.

The purpose of this book is to get you started. This book does not contain every infinitesimal detail of assistant editing processes or Avid. There is a lot of on-the-job learning that can never be replaced by a book; however, this book can give you confidence in those newly learned concepts and techniques. Allow this book to get you moving with confidence as you find your way around Avid and your job.

Ask questions of your coworkers. The people who succeed are the ones who ask questions, remember the answers, and put those solutions to work. Be that person! The ASSISTANT EDITOR CHECKLIST is provided as a framework for those questions and as a place to store critical information.

Have fun! Assistant editing is a rewarding experience that will pay dividends when you make the jump to editing. Enjoy yourself and all you are learning because it will make you a better editor.

Teach others. Knowledge is power—power that is meant to be shared. You will encounter people who jealously guard what they know, but that behavior is counterproductive because by trying to make things harder for others, they are only making things harder for themselves. Don't be that person. Teach a new concept to someone just as you would like someone to teach one to you.

Mac vs. PC. This book is written from the perspective of an Apple-based Avid. To apply this book to a PC-based Avid, when a shortcut instructs you to press Apple, press Ctrl instead. Don't worry, there are reminders throughout the book!

Avid version. Avid 3.0.5 is the basis for this book. As with all technology, newer versions are released all the time, but the concepts presented in this book hold true through later versions of Avid in that the later versions will simply make things easier through enhanced menus, updated naming, and so on. Using a different version of Avid with this book, should not impact your learning experience.

There are different Avid software products, and you may come across Avid NewsCutters, Adrenalines, Media Composers, or Symphonys. The software you use will determine the name displayed in some of the windows you'll see in your editing application, and consequently, the figures in this book. In this book, those naming differences indicate the name of the software used and aren't a cause for concern.

Tips, notes, and cautions. Useful tips and extra information is provided throughout the book. There are also cautions to keep you from losing or corrupting your data. Keep an eye out!

How to Use This Book

CHAPTER 1 gets you started by introducing the main Avid windows—the Project window, Composer window, and Timeline window—and guiding you through creating user profiles and projects.

CHAPTERS 2–11 are each divided into three sections: Settings Needed, Task Breakdowns, and Did I Do This Correctly?

SETTINGS NEEDED—This section helps you navigate the numerous settings in Avid by listing and defining those needed to complete the tasks for that chapter. You will need to modify your user profile to match the settings needed for each chapter. There will be chapters that do not list settings. In those instances, make sure you have modified your user profile according to the settings listed in all of the previous chapters. Some chapters require you to consider how you will handle certain issues—for example, the naming conventions you will use to name projects, bins, files, sequences, clips, etc.—and these issues are addressed in this section.

TASK BREAKDOWNS—This section provides detailed, step-by-step guides to completing the tasks for that chapter. Addressing both the how and the why, the task breakdowns are filled with explanations, tips, and notes.

DID I DO THIS CORRECTLY?—This section encourages you to question yourself about how well you understand the concepts/techniques presented in that chapter and how comfortable you are with completing the tasks.

APPENDICES 1–7 contain quick-reference guides to some of the tools, configurations, mappings, concepts, and techniques that you will encounter in this book. APPENDIX 8 is the ASSISTANT EDITOR CHECKLIST that will accommodate any Avid editing environment you encounter.

Book Conventions

> Tip | Provides practical but nonessential information related to the current discussion (for example, an alternative method of performing a function).

> Note | Provides information that emphasizes or supplements important points.

> Caution! | Highlights information that if not understood or followed will result in data loss or data corruption.

A Series of Menu Selections—Chevrons indicate consecutive menu selections. For example: Select File≫New Bin.

Text That You Type—Quotation marks enclose text that you type: do not type the quotation marks. For example: Type "15".

Keyboard Shortcuts—There are two types of keyboard shortcuts.

The first type of keyboard shortcut is the result of either default keyboard mapping (see TABLE APPENDIX 3-1 on page 324) or customized keyboard mapping: Avid-specific shortcuts that you customize by mapping Avid commands/functions to your keyboard. For example, in CHAPTER 4: *Multigrouping*, you are instructed to map the F2–F10 keys on your keyboard to commands that facilitate multigrouping, such as mapping the Add Edit command to the F8 function key (see pages 76–78), and then a step in a task will instruct you to insert an add edit point in a timeline with the following: Add Edit (press F8).

You are already familiar with the second type of keyboard shortcut. Mac users know them as ⌘+Key, and PC (Windows) users know them as Ctrl+Key. For example, Mac: ⌘+V | PC: Ctrl+V is the keyboard shortcut for the Paste command (see TABLE INTRODUCTION 1-1 on page 4).

TABLE INTRODUCTION 1-1.   KEYBOARD SHORTCUTS

Command	Keyboard Shortcut
Add an audio track	Mac: ⌘+U | PC: Ctrl+U
Add a video track	Mac: ⌘+Y | PC: Ctrl+Y
Copy	Mac: ⌘+C | PC: Ctrl+C
Copy from bin to bin	Mac: Option+Drag | PC: Alt+Drag
Create a bin	Mac: ⌘+N | PC: Ctrl+N
Create a sequence	Mac: Shift+⌘+N | PC: Shift+Ctrl+N
Deselect all	Mac: Shift+⌘+A | PC: Shift+Ctrl+A
Duplicate	Mac: ⌘+D | PC: Ctrl+D
Get Current Sequence	Mac: ⌘+G | PC: Ctrl+G
Get Sequence Info	Mac: ⌘+I | PC: Ctrl+I
Open Audio tool	Mac: ⌘+1 | PC: Ctrl+1
Open Avid Calculator	Mac: ⌘+2 | PC: Ctrl+2
Open Capture tool	Mac: ⌘+7 | PC: Ctrl+7
Open Command palette	Mac: ⌘+3 | PC: Ctrl+3
Open Effect palette	Mac: ⌘+8 | PC: Ctrl+8
Paste	Mac: ⌘+V | PC: Ctrl+V
Save	Mac: ⌘+S | PC: Ctrl+S
Save a title	Mac: Shift+⌘+S | PC: Shift+Ctrl+S
Scrub through a sequence	Mac: ⌘+Drag | PC: Ctrl+Drag [1]
Select all	Mac: ⌘+A | PC: Ctrl+A
Snap to the head of a clip	Mac: ⌘+Click | PC: Ctrl+Click
Solo/Unsolo an audio or a video track	Mac: ⌘+Click | PC: Ctrl+Click
Sort in ascending order	Mac: ⌘+E | PC: Ctrl+E
Sort in descending order	Mac: ⌘+Option+E | PC: Ctrl+Alt+E
Stop spinning wheel	Mac: ⌘+. | PC: Ctrl+. [2]
Undo	Mac: ⌘+Z | PC: Ctrl+Z
Zoom in	Mac: ⌘+] | PC: Ctrl+]
Zoom out	Mac: ⌘+[| PC: Ctrl+[

[1] Enable Caps Lock on keyboard to hear the audio during scrubbing.
[2] Press period key.

CHAPTER 1:
Getting Started in Avid

Tasks in This Chapter

THE ÆDVENTURES OF KARS & GRETIG

I N THIS CHAPTER, YOU will learn to create two essential elements for working in Avid: user profiles and projects. You will also be introduced to the three main components of the Avid user interface: the Project window, Composer window, and Timeline window.

Creating User Profiles

To use Avid, you must have a user profile on the computer that you want to use. If you do not have a user profile on that specific computer, you have three options: you can import a user or user profile, use a preexisting user profile, or create a user profile.

Avid has numerous settings/options that are stored in your user profile that are task dependent. Importing a user or user profile is preferred (if you have a profile saved on another computer) because you may not need to reconfigure the relevant settings/options for the task at hand. Using a preexisting user profile isn't the best option because you shouldn't configure someone else's settings, and it is possible that the changes they have made to their profile won't make sense to you. If you create a new profile, you will definitely have to configure your settings/options, but those changes will help you as you work with Avid. Since you are just getting started in Avid, let's create your user profile.

To create a user profile

1. In the Select Project dialog box (which opens when you start Avid), in the User Profile menu, select Create User Profile.

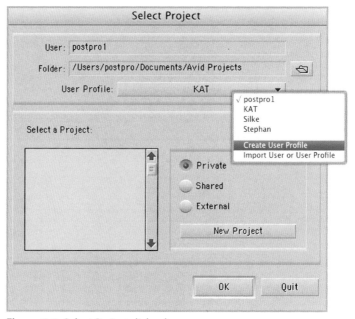

Figure 1-1. Select Project dialog box.

2. In the Create User Profile dialog box, in the Profile Name box, type a user name, and then click OK.

Figure 1-2. Create User Profile dialog box.

The next time you use that computer, you can access your user profile by choosing it from the User Profile menu.

Creating Projects

Projects serve to keep media organized and separate from other media. Finding media is easier when you know exactly where it is because of project creation and organization.

To create a project and then open it

1. In the Select Project dialog box (which opens when you start Avid), in the User Profile menu, select a user profile.

2. In the Select a Project area, click New Project.

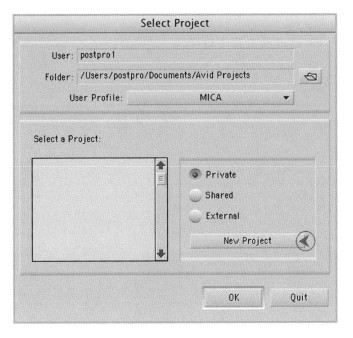

3. In the New Project dialog box that appears, do the following, and then click OK.

(a) In the Project Name box, type a name for the project.

(b) In the Format menu, select a project format.

Figure 1-3. New Project dialog box.

> **Tip** | To open a project, in the Select Project dialog box, you can also double-click its name in the Project list.

4. In the Select Project dialog box, in the Project list, click the name of the newly created project to open it, and then click OK.

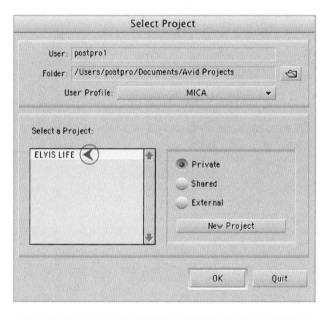

> **Note** | In the Select Project dialog box, click Browse (button to the right of the Folder box), and the Project Directory (Mac)|Browse for Folder (PC) dialog box appears.
>
> The Project Directory (Mac)| Browse for Folder (PC) dialog box allows you to select projects in different locations, and it is used in conjunction with the project options.

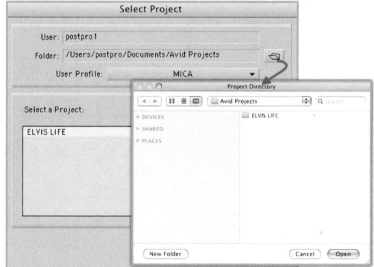

Opening a project causes the Project window, Composer window, and Timeline window to open with the selected user profile settings loaded.

Introducing the Avid User Interface

When you start Avid, the Avid Media Composer window appears displaying the default setup of the Project window on the left and the Composer window stacked above the Timeline window on the right.

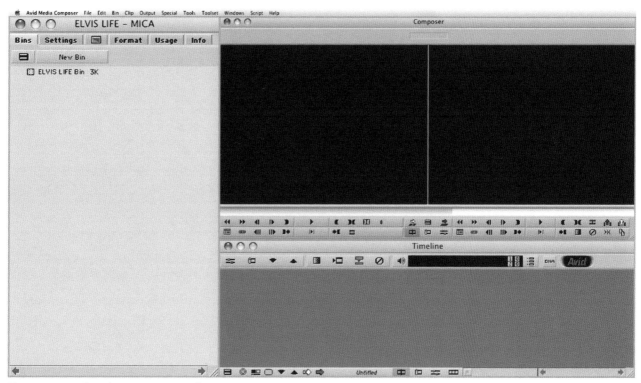

Figure 1-4. Avid Media Composer window.

Project Window

The Project window is a key user interface component that contains the tools and information required to work on a project. These tools and this information are located within the Project window's six tabs: Bins, Settings, Effects, Format, Usage, and Info. The Project window title bar displays the project name and the user profile name.

The Project window tabs are described as follows:

■ **Bins**—The default view that displays project bins and folders. This is where you create and open bins.

■ **Settings**—Lists project and user settings that can be modified.

Tip | You can also access these effects via a separate window within the Effect palette.

- **Effects**—Lists the effects available for use.

- **Format**—Displays information about the project format.

- **Usage**—Displays information about the work session usage.

- **Info**—Displays information about system memory usage and system hardware configuration.

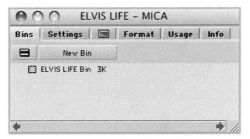

Figure 1-5. Project window | Bins tab.

The two tabs that you will use most frequently are the Bins tab for navigating within a project and the Settings tab for modifying the settings.

Bins Tab

The Project window defaults to the Bins tab. The Bins tab is used to navigate within a project. It displays an alphabetical list of all of the project bins and folders.

To create a bin

- Select File≫New Bin.

To open a bin

Tip | You can also create a bin by doing the following: in the Project window, on the Bins tab, click New Bin (Mac: ⌘+N | PC: Ctrl+N).

Note | A bin icon that appears dimmed indicates an open bin.

A diamond (Mac) or an asterisk (PC) preceding the bin name in a bin's title bar indicates that changes have been made to the bin and you need to save it.

- In the Project window, on the Bins tab, double-click the bin icon to the left of the bin name, and the bin opens in a separate window.

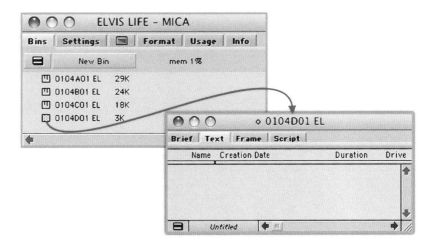

SETTINGS TAB

The Project window Settings tab alphabetically lists all of the settings that can be modified. Through these settings, you can customize a project to the demands of the project and to the personal preferences of the assistant editor or editor.

If you accidentally select a user profile other than your own, you don't have to exit Avid to select your user profile. On the Settings tab, click the User Profile menu and select your user profile.

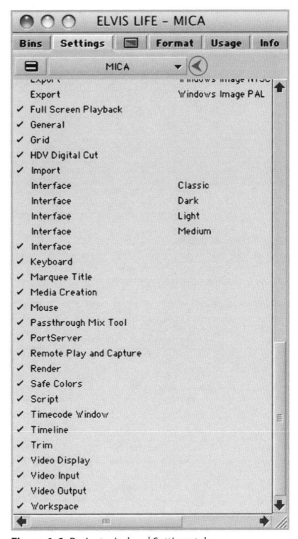

Figure 1-6. Project window | Settings tab.

Settings are task dependent. In CHAPTERS 2–11, all of the settings required for the tasks in each chapter are presented in *Settings Needed* at the beginning of each chapter. You will be guided through changing the settings in a step-by-step manner. There will be chapters that do not list settings. In those instances, make sure you have modified your user profile according to the settings listed in all of the previous chapters.

To practice changing settings, let's modify the Interface settings. The Interface settings control the appearance of Avid windows and buttons.

To change the Interface settings

1. In the Project window, on the Settings tab, double-click Interface (there will be a check mark next to it).

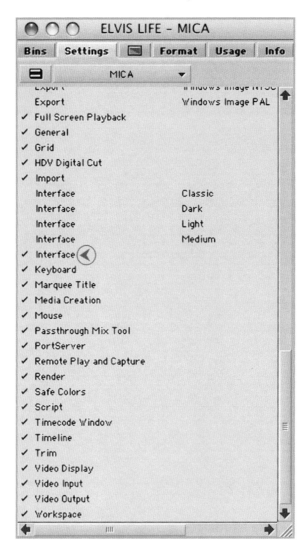

2. In the Interface dialog box that appears, do the following, and then click OK.

   (a) On the Appearance tab, click the color box to the left of the Background check box.

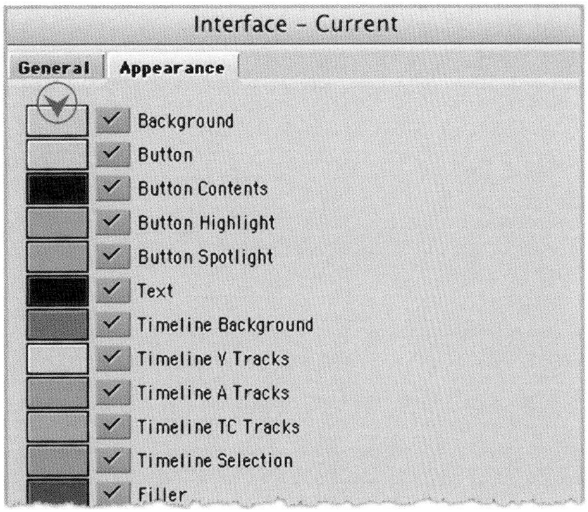

Figure 1-7. Interface dialog box | Appearance tab.

(b) Select a color, click Apply, and then notice that the background of the Avid interface elements change to the selected color.

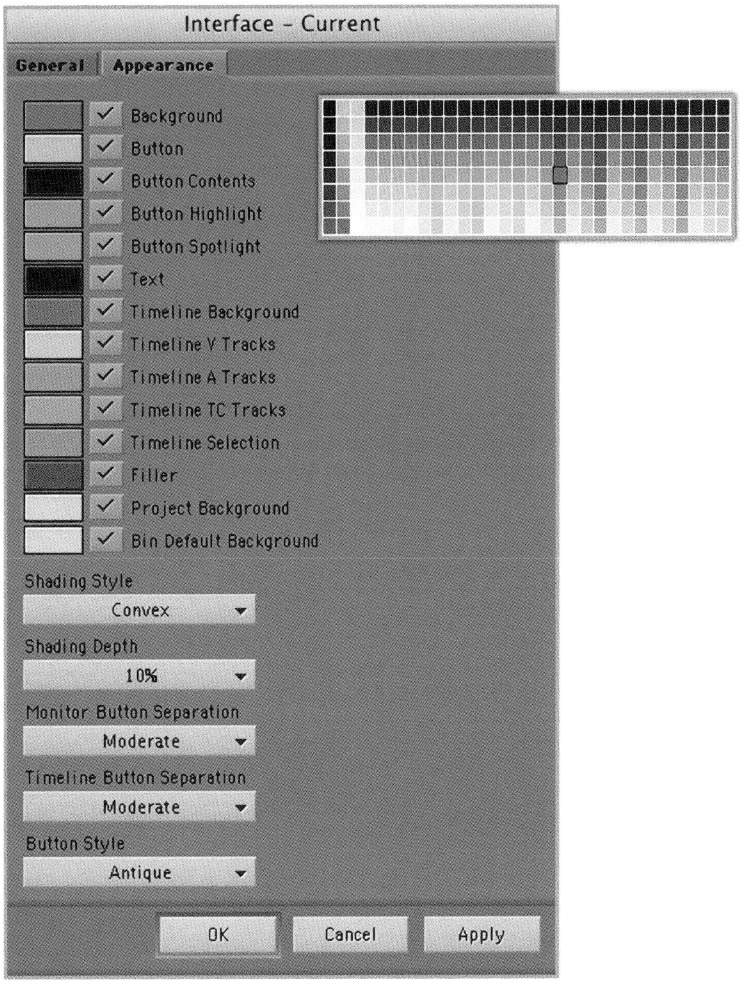

Composer Window

The Composer window consists of two monitors: the Source monitor on the left and the Record monitor on the right.

The Source monitor displays all the material that can be brought into Avid. This material includes video clips, music files, images, and graphics. The Source monitor displays the elements used to create a sequence being built in the Timeline window.

The Record monitor displays the sequences that are loaded in the Timeline window.

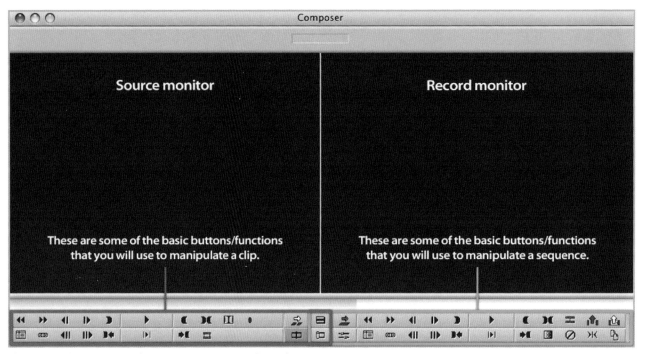

Figure 1-8. Composer window = Source monitor + Record monitor.
Source monitor: Shows the elements used to create a sequence | Record monitor: Shows the sequence being edited.

Timeline Window

The Timeline window displays clips and sequences allowing you to track and manipulate sequence elements. The Timeline window also displays controls at the lower-left corner—the Timeline bottom toolbar—allowing for efficient navigation through a sequence and configuring the details displayed in the tracks.

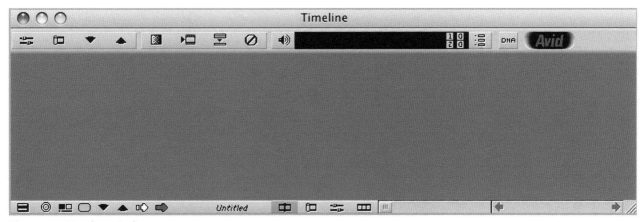

Figure 1-9. Timeline window.

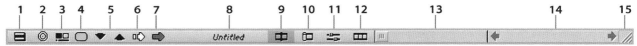

Figure 1-10. Timeline bottom toolbar with numbered components (see Table 1-1).

	Component	Function
	TABLE 1-1. TIMELINE BOTTOM TOOLBAR COMPONENTS/FUNCTIONS (SEE FIGURE 1-10)	
	Component	Function
1	Timeline Fast Menu button	Displays a list of Timeline commands such as Zoom In and Zoom Back.
2	Focus button (press H)	Zooms in to the Timeline focusing on a few seconds to either side of the position indicator.
3	Toggle Source/Record in Timeline button	Switches the Timeline window view from the sequence to whatever is loaded in the Source monitor.
4	Video Quality Menu button	Changes how the quality of the video is displayed.
5	Step In/Step Out buttons	◆ Steps in to a nested effect in the sequence. ◆ Steps out of a nested effect in the sequence.
6	Segment Mode (Extract/Splice-in) button	Selects and moves clips in a sequence.
7	Segment Mode (Lift/Overwrite) button	Selects and replaces clips in a sequence and leaves a hole.
8	View Menu button	Allows you to name, save, and select Timeline views from the View menu.
9	Source/Record Mode button (press Y)	Default editing mode. Creates new sequences from source clips.
10	Trim Mode button (press U)	Editing mode where edit points are modified.
11	Effect Mode button	Editing mode where effects are modified.
12	Color Correction Mode button	Editing mode where clips are color corrected.
13	Scale bar	Zooms in and out of a sequence.
14	Timeline scroll bar/position bar	A scroll bar that allows you to quickly reposition yourself in the Timeline.
15	Resize box	Drag to resize the window (found at the lower-right corner of most windows).

CHAPTER 2:
Capturing

Tasks in This Chapter

THE ÆDVENTURES OF KARS & GRETIG

M OST POSTPRODUCTION FACILITIES FILM show footage on some type of tape/disc such as DVCPRO HD, Betacam SP, IMX, or mini DV. Despite their different sizes and filming lengths, these tape/disc formats share a common denominator: a video deck is needed to get the video off of the tape/disc and into digital format for import into Avid. The process of converting information from a tape/disc into digital format is called *capturing* in Avid, and that term is used throughout this book; however, within the industry, it is frequently called *digitizing*.

Video decks can be hooked up to tapes/discs via composite, component (YRB), FireWire, or serial digital interface (SDI). This is important to know because it affects the Capture tool setup. Sometimes decks are labeled with the hook-up information, so you will not have to go behind the system to check. If you are in doubt, ask a seasoned assistant editor or your company's video engineer. Your coworkers will appreciate your questions, but make sure you write down those answers because they won't want to tell you twice!

There are two tasks in this chapter: *To capture an entire tape/disc* and *To capture by logging clips*. Capturing is an easy process, but it is important that you understand the steps to complete the process and the reasoning behind them; therefore, throughout the task breakdowns, significant explanations are provided.

Settings Needed

Configure the following settings before beginning the tasks in this chapter.

CAPTURE SETTINGS DIALOG BOX

General Tab

Navigation: Project window | Settings tab | Select Capture from the Settings list | Capture Settings dialog box | General tab

- **Force unique clip names (select check box)**—When capturing, Avid assigns the names of the clips based on the bin name. When this option is selected, captured clips will have unique names. In the event of a timecode break, Avid assigns ".01," ".02," ".03," etc., to subsequent clips to differentiate among them.

- **Activate bin window after capture (default selection)**—When this option is selected, the bin is automatically selected, so you can immediately work with the bin.

- **Capture across timecode breaks (select check box)**—When this option is selected, Avid captures to the point of the timecode break, keeps the clip recorded before the break, and scrolls past the timecode break and continues capturing. This is a great time saver.

■ **Stop capture if a bad frame is detected (clear check box)**—When this option is selected, Avid stops capturing every time there is a bad frame—bad frames occur when there is a camera glitch or a wrinkle on the tape—so if the tape/disc is not being monitored, a lot of time could be wasted.

■ **Ignore Detected Media Read Errors (default selection)**—When this option is selected, Avid ignores any dropouts on the tape/disc and captures everything it can from the tape/disc.

■ **Ask before discarding a canceled clip (default selection)**—When this option is selected, Avid asks if you want to discard the canceled clip or keep it.

■ **Ask for name when a new tape is seen (default selection)**—When this option is selected, Avid prompts you to name the tape/disc or to select the tape/disc name if it already exists. Otherwise, the tape/disc inserted into the video deck may not have the correct name assigned to it.

■ **Display incoming video in the client monitor (select check box)**— When this option is selected, the video of the tape/disc is displayed in the client monitor (an external display monitor) letting you know that there is incoming video.

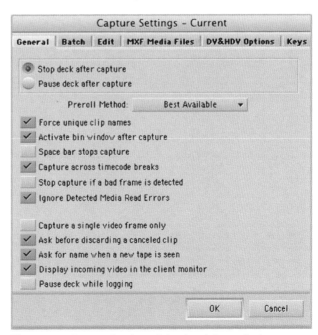

Figure 2-1. Capture Settings dialog box | General tab.

MXF Media Files Tab

Navigation: Project window | Settings tab | Select Capture from the Settings list |
Capture Settings dialog box | MXF Media Files tab

■ **Maximum (default) capture time (enter 190 minutes or more)**—You may have to capture a tape/disc that is longer than the 70-minute default for this setting, and if this setting is not increased, Avid will stop capturing at the 70-minute mark. Since it is unlikely that there will be a tape/disc more than 3 hours long (180 minutes), 190 minutes should be sufficient for the majority of tapes/discs. Better to set it at a high mark and lessen the risk of Avid not completely capturing a tape/disc.

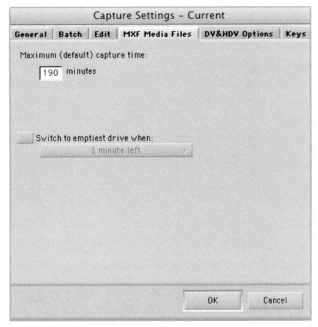

Figure 2-2. Capture Settings dialog box | MXF Media Files tab.

Capturing Entire Tapes/Discs

To capture an entire tape/disc

1. In the Project window, click the Bins tab.

2. Create a bin (Mac: ⌘+N | PC: Ctrl+N).

> **Note** | The bin automatically created when a new project is created can also be used as a new bin—you just have to rename it.

3. Name the new bin exactly the same as the tape/disc to be captured (or according to your company's naming conventions), and then press Enter.

Tape/discs are named on set, and the names are typically a composite of the date, camera, tape/disc load, and the name of the show. For example, the name of a tape/disc filmed on January 4, for the show "Elvis Life," on B camera's first tape/disc could be 0104B01 EL. This naming convention keeps the tapes/discs organized by show because without the show's initials, there is a possibility that another B01 tape/disc from January 4 could exist and cause confusion. Naming conventions differ from company to company, but no matter how the tapes/discs are named, make sure that the bins are named according to your company's naming conventions.

❶ Bin Views

There are four bin views: Brief, Text, Frame, and Script. For capturing, select the Text view (Text tab) because it displays important information about captured tapes/discs.

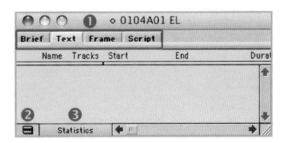

❷ Bin Fast Menu button (aka Hamburger menu)

Fast menus offer context-sensitive options and are found throughout Avid. All Bin menu commands are available in the Bin Fast menu.

❸ Bin View menu

Located on the Text tab, the Bin View menu displays several options. Statistics is one of the default views.

Figure 2-3. Bin components.

4. In the Bin window, click the Text tab.

5. On the Bin View menu, select Statistics.

Note | In Statistics view, it is easy to see if a tape/disc is caught in a capture loop because the clips being captured have duplicating start and end times.

A capture loop occurs because a tape/disc was recorded to the very end, and as a result, Avid captures the same section of the tape/disc over and over again from the last timecode break.

Name	Tracks	Start	End	Duration	Mark IN	Mark OUT	IN-OUT	Tape	Video
0104A01 EL.08	V1 A1-2	13;07;29;21	13;08;04;22	34;29				0104A01 EL	DV
0104A01 EL.07	V1 A1-2	13;07;03;06	13;07;13;25	10;19				0104A01 EL	DV
0104A01 EL.06	V1 A1-2	13;05;40;13	13;05;57;14	17;01				0104A01 EL	DV
0104A01 EL.05	V1 A1-2	13;05;00;04	13;05;06;05	6;01				0104A01 EL	DV
0104A01 EL.04	V1 A1-2	13;04;26;07	13;04;32;08	6;01				0104A01 EL	DV
0104A01 EL.03	V1 A1-2	13;03;32;25	13;03;50;19	17;24				0104A01 EL	DV

◊ 0104A01 EL

Brief | Text | Frame | Script

Statistics

Figure 2-4. Bin in Text view displaying Statistics chosen from the Bin View menu.

6. Drag the Resize box (lower-right corner of the Bin window) to display more columns.

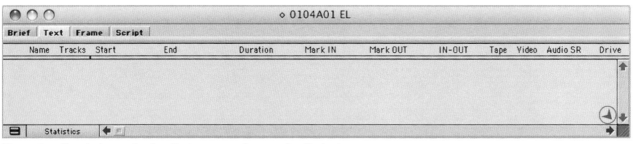

Figure 2-5. Bin window resized to display more columns using Resize box.

In Statistics view, the column headings that pertain to capturing are as follows:

- **Tracks**—Displays the tracks present in a clip. (Example: V1 A1-A2)

- **Start**—Displays the start time of a clip. (Example: 01;00;35;02)

- **End**—Displays the end time of a clip. (Example: 01;00;50;15)

- **Duration**—Displays the duration of a clip. (Example: 15;13)

- **Tape**—Displays the name of the tape/disc the clip was captured from. (Example: 0104B01 EL)

- **Drive**—Displays the drive the media files are on. (Example: 0104 (P:))

7. Open the Audio tool (Mac: ⌘+1 | PC: Ctrl+1).

The Audio tool displays the audio levels coming into Avid.

Figure 2-6. Audio tool.

Tip | This is a good time to take a look at APPENDIX 1: *Capture Tool* on page 307.

Caution! | If the Select Tape dialog box appears after opening the Capture tool, click Cancel to close the Select Tape dialog box.

8. Open the Capture tool (Mac: ⌘+7 | PC: Ctrl+7).

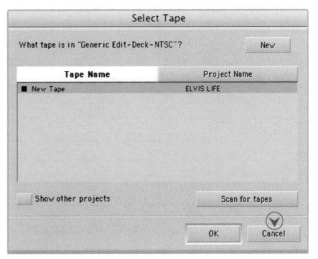

Figure 2-7. Select Tape dialog box.

You will typically work in an environment with multiple edit suites. Multiple decks can be connected to Avid in those suites. Since Avid retains the Capture tool settings of the last setup, if a different deck is connected, the Capture tool will have the settings for the previous deck.

It is a bad practice to select a tape/disc name when the wrong deck is connected. If you are certain that the video deck is correctly connected to Avid and the Capture tool is displaying that video deck's name in the Deck Selection menu, proceed to Step 9. Otherwise, see APPENDIX 2: *Deck Configuration* on page 311 to make sure that the video deck connected to Avid is recognized by the Capture tool.

9. Ensure that the Capture tool is set up correctly by checking the following nine components (see FIGURE 2-8 on page 24):

   (a) **Channel Selection buttons**—Click the channels to be captured.

   (b) **Video (Input) menu**—Select the correct video input settings depending on the deck hookup.

   (c) **Audio (Input) menu**—Select the correct audio input settings depending on the deck hookup.

   (d) **Bin menu**—Ensure that the bin is named correctly.

   (e) **Res (Resolution) menu**—Select the correct video resolution.

   The final video product should be at a high resolution. Since high-resolution files take up a lot of server space, some postproduction facilities work in low-resolution files and then bring in the clips for the final product at a high resolution. Therefore, resolutions must be set correctly to prevent running out of server space and to prevent low-resolution files from being in the final product. Re-capturing is a time-consuming process that most postproduction schedules do not allow for.

(f) **Target Drive menu**—Select the correct drive for the tape/disc.

(g) **Time Remaining on Target Drives display**—Before capturing, ensure that there is enough disk space to capture an entire tape/disc. The numbers represent hours, minutes, seconds, and frames available at that resolution.

(h) **Deck Selection menu**—Displays the name of the deck Avid believes is connected to the computer. (If the deck name is displayed in italics, the deck is offline.)

(i) **Source Tape display**—Displays the tape/disc name. The bin should be named the same as the tape/disc (or in accordance with your company's naming conventions).

> **Note |** The Source Tape display will not display a name because a tape/disc has not been inserted. However, once you become more familiar with capturing, it is not uncommon to perform these steps in a different order, and as a result, a tape/disc may already be in the deck and its name will be displayed.

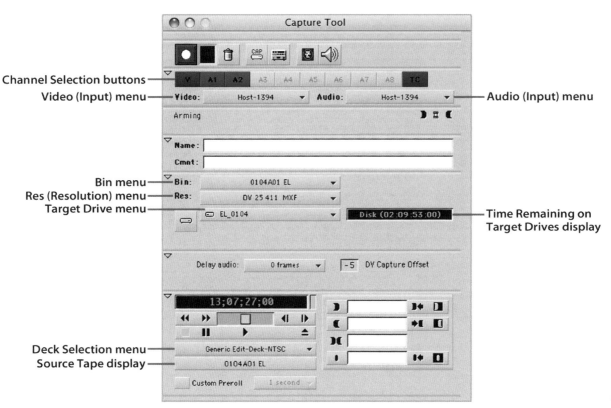

Figure 2-8. Capture Tool window.

10. Insert the tape/disc, and then do one of the following:

   (a) If the Select Tape dialog box appears, proceed to Step 11.

   –or–

   (b) If the Select Tape dialog box does not appear, read APPENDIX 2: *Deck Configuration* on page 311. Once you have completed the steps in APPENDIX 2, proceed to Step 11.

11. In the Select Tape dialog box, click New.

12. In the Tape Name column, name the tape/disc correctly.

Note | Avid retains the names of tapes/discs that have already been captured. Be careful not to select a tape/disc name that has already been entered. (Unless that is the name of your tape/disc!)

13. Press Enter twice: once to enter the name and once to close the dialog box. The tape/disc name will update in the Capture tool.

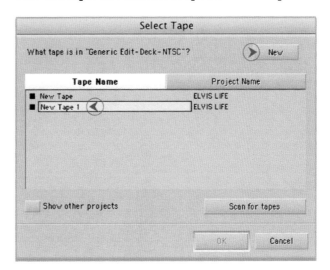

14. On the Capture tool, click Rewind to rewind the tape/disc to the beginning.

   Clicking Rewind on the Capture tool will not rewind the tape/disc if the deck is in local (the deck needs to be in remote to control it through the Capture tool). Either put the deck in remote and click Rewind on the Capture tool, or press Rewind on the deck.

Tip | The tape/disc should run before the capture process begins (this is called *preroll*) for at least five seconds. Later in the editing process, these captured clips are re-captured at a higher resolution (this is called *uprezzing*) and letting the tape/disc preroll allows Avid to correctly re-capture the tape/disc.

15. Click Play on the tape/disc via the Capture tool, and then wait for the tape/disc to get up to speed.

16. On the Capture tool, click Record.

17. Check if the tape/disc is being captured by confirming the following:

   (a) The Capture indicator is flashing.

(b) There is video in the Record monitor.

(c) There are audio levels in the Audio tool—if video and audio were both recorded.

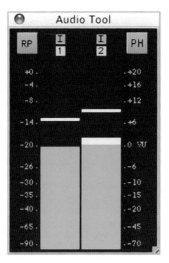

18. Do one of the following:

(a) If the tape/disc is being captured, proceed to Step 19.

–or–

(b) If the tape/disc is not being captured, click Trash to abort the capture process, and repeat Step 9 (Capture tool setup) and Steps 14–17, and then proceed to Step 19.

19. (Optional) Once capturing begins, on the Capture tool, in the Clip Name text box, type a name for the clip.

20. Let the tape/disc run until all of the footage on the tape/disc is completely captured and the clips are displayed in the bin.

Not every tape/disc is entirely recorded. Some may have 5 minutes and some may have 30 minutes. The clips in this bin had approximately 3 minutes on the entire tape/disc (Start: 13;01;12;01 and End: 13;08;04;22). Avid will automatically stop recording at the end of a tape/disc, or you can click Record on the Capture tool to stop the capturing process.

21. When the tape/disc has finished capturing, fast forward the tape/disc using the Capture tool to ensure that there is no additional footage on it. (The timecode numbers only advance if there is more footage on the tape/disc, so if the timecode numbers do not advance, then there is no additional footage on the tape/disc.)

22. Rewind the tape/disc almost to the beginning.

    It is important to rewind the tape/disc onto timecode (rewind the tape/disc so that the playhead of the deck is resting at a spot where there is timecode before or after that moment) after capturing because the tape/disc may be used later. A deck can "hold" on to the timecode of the last tape/disc inserted into the deck, and it can temporarily assign this "ghost" timecode to a newly inserted tape/disc that is sitting on the first (or last) bit of timecode. Since the deck cannot determine if a tape/disc is at the beginning or end, when you instruct Avid to find timecode X, it may try to fast forward/rewind a tape/disc when the opposite is required.

23. Eject the tape.

24. Mark the tape/disc with a colored circle, an "X," or a check mark (or how your company wants a tape/disc to be marked) to indicate to other assistant editors that the tape/disc has been captured.

25. Double-click one of the clips in the bin and then confirm that there is video, audio, or both on the clip (depending on what was captured).

26. Save the bin (Mac: ⌘+S | PC: Ctrl+S).

Name	Tracks	Start	End	Duration	Mark IN	Mark OUT	IN-OUT	Tape	Video
0104A01 EL.08	V1 A1-2	13;07;29;21	13;08;04;22	34;29				0104A01 EL	DV
0104A01 EL.07	V1 A1-2	13;07;03;06	13;07;13;25	10;19				0104A01 EL	DV
0104A01 EL.06	V1 A1-2	13;05;40;13	13;05;57;14	17;01				0104A01 EL	DV
0104A01 EL.05	V1 A1-2	13;05;00;04	13;05;06;05	6;01				0104A01 EL	DV
0104A01 EL.04	V1 A1-2	13;04;26;07	13;04;32;08	6;01				0104A01 EL	DV
0104A01 EL.03	V1 A1-2	13;03;32;25	13;03;50;19	17;24				0104A01 EL	DV

◇ 0104A01 EL

Brief | Text | Frame | Script

Statistics

27. Close the bin.

28. If there are additional tapes to capture, create a bin (Mac: ⌘+N | PC: Ctrl+N).

29. Name the new bin exactly the same as the tape/disc to be captured (or according to your company's naming conventions), and then press Enter.

30. In the Bin window, click the Text tab.

31. On the Bin View menu, select Statistics.

32. Drag the Resize box (lower-right corner of the Bin window) to display more columns.

33. Repeat Steps 9–27.

Logging Clips

In some situations, only a few of the clips on a tape/disc require capturing. The Capture tool has a function that allows you to log those clips and Avid will capture them automatically.

To capture by logging clips

1. In the Project window, click the Bins tab.

2. Create a bin (Mac: ⌘+N | PC: Ctrl+N).

3. Name the new bin exactly the same as the tape/disc that needs to be captured (or in accordance with your company's naming conventions), and then press Enter.

4. In the Bin window, click the Text tab (if it isn't already selected).

5. On the Bin View menu, select Statistics.

6. Drag the Resize box (lower-right corner of the Bin window) to display more columns.

7. Open the Audio tool (Mac: ⌘+1 | PC: Ctrl+1).

8. Open the Capture tool (Mac: ⌘+7 | PC: Ctrl+7).

9. Insert the tape/disc.

10. In the Select Tape dialog box, click New.

11. Name the tape/disc correctly.

> **Note |** The Capture tool must be set up correctly to log clips from a tape/disc.
>
> Ensure that the deck is in remote and the Capture tool recognizes the deck connected to Avid. If the video deck's name isn't displayed in the Deck Selection menu, read Appendix 2: *Deck Configuration* on page 311.

12. Press Enter twice: once to enter the name and once to close the dialog box. The tape/disc name will update in the Capture tool.

13. On the Capture tool, click Rewind, and then rewind the tape/disc to the beginning.

14. Click Capture/Log Mode (to toggle to Log mode).

    The Capture/Log Mode button toggles between Capture mode (for capturing) and Log mode (for logging clips). The appearance of the Capture/Log Mode button toggles between the two icons shown in FIGURE 2-9.

Figure 2-9. Capture Tool window—Top: Capture mode and Bottom: Log mode.

15. Just as when capturing an entire tape/disc, when logging clips, the Capture tool must be set up correctly. Check the following four components of the Capture tool:

    (a) **Channel Selection buttons**—Select the channels to be captured.

    (b) **Bin menu**—Ensure that the bin is named correctly.

    (c) **Res (Resolution) menu**—Select the correct video resolution.

    (d) **Source Tape display**—Displays the tape/disc name. The bin should be named the same as the tape/disc (or in accordance with your company's naming conventions).

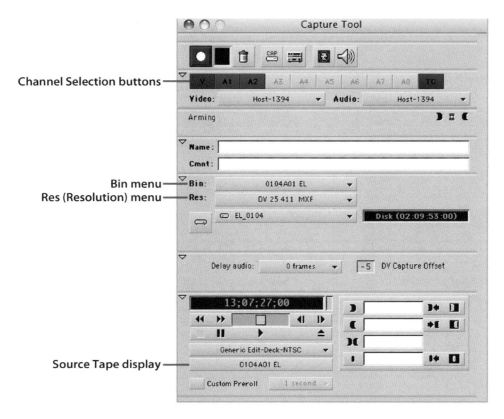

Channel Selection buttons

Bin menu
Res (Resolution) menu

Source Tape display

16. Click Play or click Shuttle to find the first timecode.

Click Mark IN and the timecode will display in the box to the right of the button (see FIGURE 2-10).

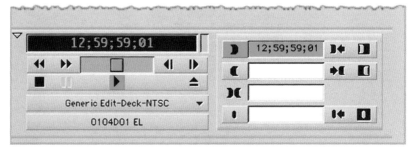

Figure 2-10. Capture Tool window displaying Mark IN timecode and the following buttons (from left): Shuttle, Play, and Mark IN.

17. Click Play or click Shuttle to find the last timecode.

Click Mark OUT and the timecode displays in the box to the right of the button, and the duration between the Mark IN and Mark OUT timecodes displays in the Duration display (see FIGURE 2-11).

Note | If an incorrect Mark OUT timecode is entered, you can either type a new timecode or press Clear OUT and repeat Step 17 on page 30.

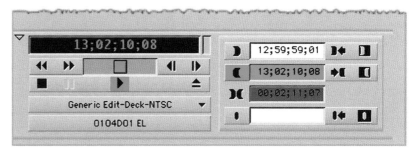

Figure 2-11. Capture Tool window displaying Mark OUT timecode and duration.

18. (Optional) On the Capture tool, in the Clip Name text box, type a name for the clip.

19. Click Log Clip ✐ and a clip appears in the bin with its name, tracks, start, and Capture Tool settings.

20. Repeat Steps 16–19 until the tape/disc is logged.

21. Save the bin (Mac: ⌘+S | PC: Ctrl+S).

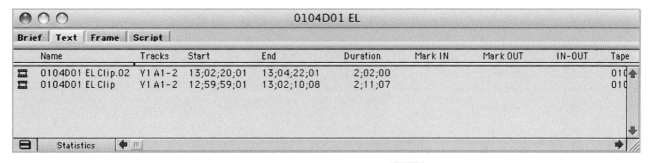

22. Click Capture/Log Mode 🄻🄾🄶 to return to the default Capture tool.

23. Confirm that the Capture tool is set up correctly.

    It is possible to select different video and audio track combinations when logging clips, and the Capture tool will only capture those tracks. Also, if you mistakenly select or deselect the tracks, you can delete the clip and start over.

24. Click the bin.

25. Select all of the clips in the bin (Mac: ⌘+A | PC: Ctrl+A).

Note | Once Avid starts to capture the logged clips, you will not be able to modify the Capture tool settings. *Setting up the Capture tool correctly before capturing the clips is very important.* You do not want to cause the Batch Capture function to abort.

26. Select Clip≫Batch Capture.

27. In the Batch Capture dialog box, do the following, and then click OK.

    (a) Select Offline media only.

If there are already captured clips in a bin, selecting the Offline media only option causes Avid to ignore those clips and capture the offline clips.

(b) Ensure that the Extend handles beyond master clip edges check box is not selected.

Avid captures the exact timecodes you chose. If those timecodes are near a timecode break and the Extend handles beyond master clip edges option is selected, the new extended timecodes may cross over those timecode breaks, and Avid cannot complete a batch capture when there are timecode breaks.

If footage is present on the tape/disc, selecting the Extend handles beyond master clip edges option causes Avid to add extra frames to the beginning and the end of the clip.

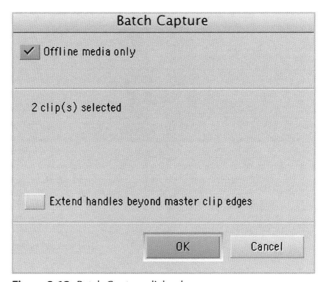

Figure 2-12. Batch Capture dialog box.

It is common to log several tapes/discs and then batch capture them all at once. In these situations, Avid may prompt you to insert a different tape/disc even though a tape/disc may be present in the deck.

28. Insert the correct tape/disc, if needed. (If you have not been logging more than one tape/disc, the tape/disc in the deck is used.)

29. The Avid Media Composer dialog box appears when you log more than one tape/disc at a time. In the Avid Media Composer dialog box, click Mounted, and Avid begins capturing the clips in the bin according to the settings given to the clips.

Figure 2-13. Avid Media Composer dialog box prompting you to insert the correct tape/disc if you have been logging more than one tape/disc at a time.

Note | Batch Capture is a great timesaver if you do not want to capture an entire tape/disc, but be aware that if there are any timecode breaks in between the set timecodes, Avid aborts the Batch Capture process.

Once the Batch Capture process is finished, a message displays saying that the Batch Capture is complete or incomplete.

If the Batch Capture is incomplete, the message lists the number of clips correctly captured.

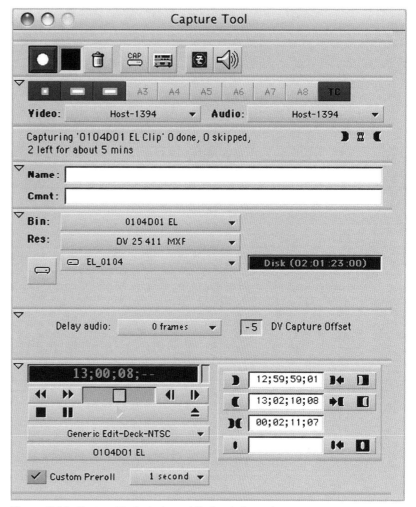

Figure 2-14. Capture Tool window while Batch Capturing.

30. Double-click one of the clips in the bin and confirm there is video, audio, or both on the clip (depending on what was captured).

31. Save the bin (Mac: ⌘+S | PC: Ctrl+S).

32. Close the bin.

33. Rewind the tape/disc almost to the beginning.

34. Eject the tape/disc.

35. Mark the tape/disc with a colored circle, an "X," or a check mark (or how your company wants a tape/disc to be marked) to indicate to other assistant editors that the tape/disc has been captured.

Did I Do This Correctly?

■ **Were tapes/discs rewound to the beginning before capturing?**

If tapes/discs are not rewound to the beginning before capturing, all of the footage will not be captured and those tapes/discs will have to be re-captured.

■ **After capturing, were tapes/discs fast forwarded to the end?**

Fast forwarding ensures that there is no more footage on the tapes/discs letting you know that all of the footage has been captured. The end timecode of the last clip in the bin should be the last timecode on the tape/disc.

■ **Were tapes/discs captured at the correct video resolution?**

Before closing the bin, look at the resolution beneath the Video column heading in the bin and make sure the desired resolution is displayed.

■ **Were tapes/discs captured to the correct drive?**

Before closing the bin, look at the Drive column heading and make sure that all of the footage is on the correct drive.

■ **Were tapes/discs and bins correctly labeled?**

Look at the name on the physical tape/disc and the bin name and the tape/disc name in Avid. All of them should adhere to your company's naming conventions.

■ **Were all tapes/discs captured?**

There should be a master tape/disc list that shows all of the tapes/discs that were received or needed to be captured. Compare this list against all of the bins that have been captured and verify that all the tapes/discs listed are present in Avid.

■ **Was Capture across timecode breaks chosen in the Capture Settings dialog box?**

Check the Capture settings on all of your Avid computers and ensure that the Capture across timecode breaks option is selected. In the Project window, click the Settings tab, and then select the Capture setting and verify that this option was selected. Don't assume that once Avid stops capturing, the tape/disc has finished capturing. This mistake can be avoided by having this setting selected and fast forwarding on a tape/disc to make sure no footage was missed.

■ **If a tape/disc stopped in the middle of the capturing process and continued to roll without capturing footage, was the tape/disc rewound to the timecode of the last clip?**

Avid sometimes hiccups while capturing and instead of capturing across a timecode break, it will stop capturing but the tape/disc will continue playing. When this happens, look at the end timecode of the last clip captured, rewind the tape/disc to that point, and continue capturing. Don't forget to let the tape/disc preroll for five seconds!

■ **Were tapes/discs marked to indicate that they were captured?**

If a tape/disc is properly marked, then it will not be captured twice. Checking the project's bins is another way to determine if a tape/disc has been captured.

CHAPTER 3:
File-Based Media

Tasks in This Chapter

THE ÆDVENTURES OF KARS & GRETIG

T HERE ARE CAMERAS THAT shoot on formats other than tape. These cameras can record video to file-based media such as Secure Digital (SD) cards, CompactFlash® (CF) cards, and XDCAM® discs. This file-based media is recorded in a variety of formats including QuickTime® movies.

Bringing file-based footage into Avid differs from tape-based footage because unlike tape-based footage that has to be captured and converted into a digital file format that Avid can read prior to bringing it into Avid, file-based footage is already in digital format and only requires conversion prior to bringing it into Avid.

File-based footage comes with a huge bonus: metadata. *Metadata* is information that a camera can attach to a clip—such as when the footage was shot, the cameraperson's name, the episode filmed, and the location. This metadata is extremely useful when it is available in a database. Through metadata, companies can create searchable catalogs of all of their footage from all of their video shoots. This is a big departure from tape-based media because although tape logs may accompany a tape from a video shoot, finding a particular shot isn't as easy or as fast as it is with file-based media.

In typical Avid fashion, there are several ways to ingest file-based media such as capturing (as discussed in CHAPTER 2: *Capturing* on page 17) and importing. Importing includes workflows such as Avid Media Access (AMA)—a plug-in that allows you to view file-based footage without importing the media into Avid—and the Import command.

Settings Needed

Configure the following settings before beginning the tasks in this chapter.

AMA SETTINGS DIALOG BOX

Bins Tab

Navigation: Project window | Settings tab | Select AMA from the Settings list | AMA Settings dialog box | Bins tab

■ **Use active bin (select option)**—When this option is selected, you have greater control over the media going into the bins.

Figure 3-1. AMA Settings dialog box | Bins tab.

Volume Mounting Tab

Navigation: Project window | Settings tab | Select AMA from the Settings list | AMA Settings dialog box | Volume Mounting tab

> **Caution!** | If Enable AMA Volume Management was not previously selected, you must restart the application for the setting to take effect.

■ **Enable AMA Volume Management (select check box)**—When this option is selected, AMA is turned on.

■ **When mounting previously mounted volumes, do not check for modifications to the volume (clear check box)**—When not selected, this acts as a check because if file-based footage was already accessed through Avid, it prevents the media from being loaded in a bin.

To load the same file-based footage multiple times within a project, select the check box; however, *that is not the case for this chapter*.

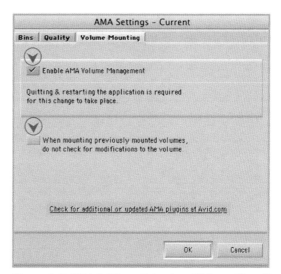

Figure 3-2. AMA Settings dialog box | Volume Mounting tab.

NAMING CONVENTIONS

Ensure that the folder and file names of the file-based footage adhere to your company's naming conventions and contain no more than the Avid-allowed 27 characters. You must do this before the footage is brought into Avid.

Naming folders and files is not a trivial matter. Accessing poorly named folders/files is frustrating and time consuming not only for the person who named them but also for that person's coworkers for months and even years into the future. If your company has a naming convention in place, follow it to the character. And if it does not, make it a point to practice good file management by choosing a naming convention that provides useful information and by using it consistently.

Folder/file names also have to fit within the allowed number of characters of the programs where they are used. Avid restricts the names of bins and folders to 27 characters (this does not include the period and the three-character file extension). Since cameras can assign names that are more than 27 characters, at minimum you must shorten the file names from cameras to no more than 27 characters to bring those files into Avid.

A popular naming convention uses 22 characters. Its components are described below. Note that an underscore (_) character is added between each component.

- 2-character show abbreviation
- 4-character location abbreviation
- 4-character sublocation abbreviation

    (Optional, but if a camera shoot spans several sublocations within one location, it is a useful differentiating element.)
- 2-character camera and card/disc abbreviation
- 6-character date abbreviation

18 characters + 4 underscores = 22 characters

For example, the 22-character folder name EL_KIMD_PARK_A1_101410 is based on the following components:

- **EL:** Show abbreviation (Elvis Life)
- **KIMD:** Location abbreviation (Kent Island, Maryland)
- **PARK:** Sublocation abbreviation (dog park)
- **A1:** Camera and card/disc abbreviation (camera A, disc 1)
- **101410:** Date abbreviation (mmddyy)

CROSSOVER CLIPS

When shooting tape, a cameraperson can only shoot a certain amount of footage before the tape has to be changed; however, in a card environment, it is possible to shoot for longer periods of time. Some digital video cameras support having multiple cards in them at the same time. These cameras automatically split the media between two cards (for example, card 2 and card 3) if the file size becomes too large for one card, so the cameraperson can continue recording.

> **Caution!** | It is important to mount all of the folders from a file-based shoot in bins at the same time to prevent "crossover clips" from being half online and half offline.

It is important that assistant editors accommodate this possibility in their workflow because when the time comes to look at that file in Avid, to see it completely, the folders containing the media from card 2 and card 3 must have been mounted (placed) in bins at the same time; otherwise, the clip that "crossed over" from card 2 to card 3 will be half online and half offline.

Bringing File-Based Footage into Avid Using AMA

Avid Media Access (AMA) is a plug-in that allows you to view file-based footage without bringing the media into Avid.

To bring file-based footage into Avid using AMA

1. Connect the drive containing the file-based footage to the Avid computer.

2. Double-click the drive that contains the file-based footage and check the names of the folders and files (see *Naming Conventions* on page 40).

> **Note** | For details on creating user profiles and creating projects, see CHAPTER 1: *Getting Started in Avid* on pages 6 and 7, respectively.

3. Start Avid, and in the Select Project dialog box that appears, do the following, and then click OK.

    (a) In the User Profile menu, select an existing user profile.

    (b) In the Project list, select a project.

4. In the Project window, on the Format tab, ensure that the Project Type menu is at the correct setting.

    This is an important choice that determines the options available in the Target Video Resolution menu in the Consolidate/Transcode dialog box in *To transcode clips*, Step 4(d), page 52.

    ■ If the file-based media is shot in an HD resolution, and the HD resolution is to be preserved for edit, set the Project Type to the correct HD setting (this varies depending on the HD format of the file-based footage).

■ If the file-based media is shot in an HD resolution, but the edit is to be performed in SD, set the Project Type to an SD setting.

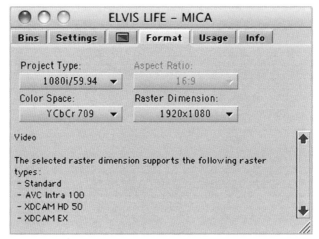

Figure 3-3. Project window | Format tab.

5. Create a bin (Mac: ⌘+N | PC: Ctrl+N).

6. Copy the name of any file-based media folder on the drive (Mac: ⌘+C | PC: Ctrl+C).

7. Paste the folder name as the bin name (Mac: ⌘+V | PC: Ctrl+V), and then type "FB" (for file-based) at the end of the bin name.

   Appending "FB" (file-based) to the end of a bin name differentiates bins/folders linked to cards/discs from bins/folders linked to Avid's shared media storage.

8. Press Enter.

9. Select File≫Link to AMA Volumes.

10. In the Select the root of the virtual volume dialog box that appears, click the file-based media folder name on the drive, click Choose, and then wait for the clips to load in the bin.

    When the clips load in the active bin, they are automatically highlighted yellow and columns for the clip metadata are automatically created in the bin.

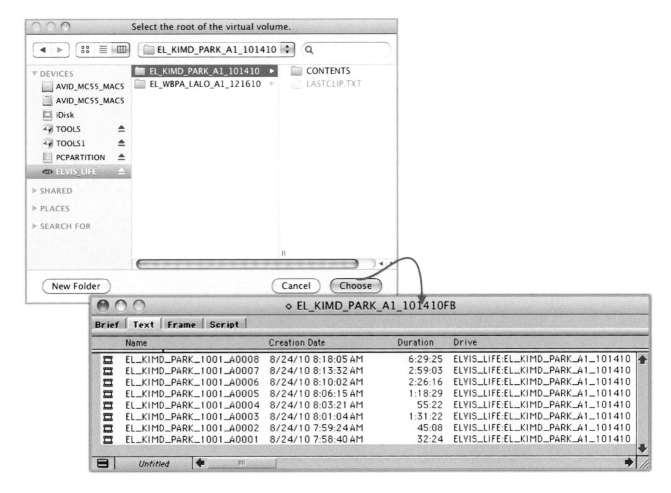

11. Drag the Resize box to the right to view the clip metadata in the bin.

If the metadata is not present, it may need to be added.

Figure 3-4. Project bin displaying the Text tab showing clip metadata.

12. Click the Bin Fast Menu, and select Headings.

13. In the Bin Column Selection dialog box that appears, click All/None twice to clear all previous column selections.

> **Note** | Notice in the Bin Column Selection dialog box, in the Select the columns to display list that all of the current column headings (including the metadata columns that were automatically added) are available for use.
>
> While the metadata columns will be removed from display on the Text tab of the Bin window for the next process, the information remains available for use.

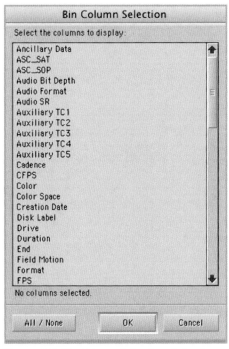

Figure 3-5. Bin Column Selection dialog box.

14. From the Select the columns to display list, select Drive and Format, click OK, and then the Drive and Format columns appear.

> **Note** | If you intend to consolidate/transcode these files, it's a good practice to display the Format column and take a quick look at the file format to see if it is compatible with the project format.
>
> This ensures that Avid can read the files and is able to consolidate/transcode them. For example, a PAL project format will not work with NTSC footage.
>
> If the file format isn't compatible, change the format on the Format tab of the Project window.

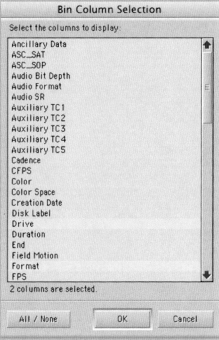

The purpose of Steps 15–23 is to preserve critical information in an easily accessible format.

■ **Clip File Paths**—There are occasions when the Drive column displays information other than the original location of the footage. For example, after consolidating, the Drive column displays the project name. If you need to find the original location of the footage, preserving the file path information of the Drive column will allow you to do so.

The procedure is to duplicate the Drive column information and place it in a newly created column (Folder Name column) to preserve the original file path information.

■ **Clip Names**—There are occasions when the clip names will be a series of numbers that won't make sense to you. While it is better to change clip names before they are brought into Avid, you can change clip names once they are in the bin, but it is important to retain the original information in the bin to cross reference with the original media on the cards/discs.

The procedure is to duplicate the Name column information (the original clip names as a series of numbers) and place it in a newly created column (Clip Name column) to preserve the original-name information.

> **Note** | Column headings can contain a maximum of 14 characters (including spaces).

15. In the Bin window, on the Text tab, create two columns:

    (a) Click in the empty area to the right of the column headings (that is, to the right of the Drive column), type "Folder Name" and then press Enter.

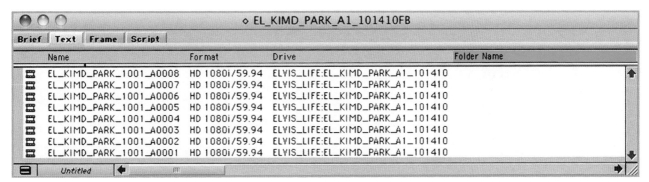

Figure 3-6. Project bin: creating a column.

    (b) Click in the empty area to the right of the Folder Name column, type "Clip Name" and then press Enter.

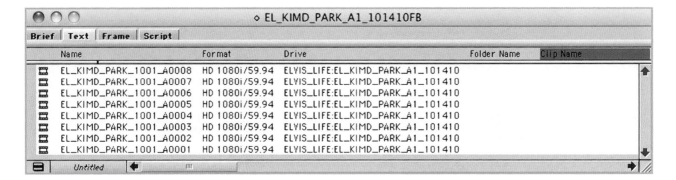

16. Click the Bin View menu, and select Save As.

17. In the View Name dialog box that appears, type "File Based View" in the Name of this view box, and then click OK.

Figure 3-7. View Name dialog box.

18. Drag the Resize box to the right until all column headings are visible.

19. Duplicate the Name column information by clicking the Name column heading, and then pressing Mac: ⌘+D | PC: Ctrl+D.

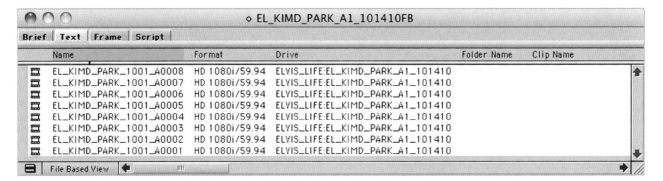

20. In the Select dialog box that appears, from the Copy 'Name' column to list, select Clip Name, and then click OK.

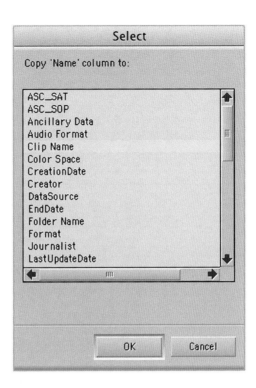

21. Duplicate the Drive column information by clicking the Drive column heading, and then pressing Mac: ⌘+D | PC: Ctrl+D.

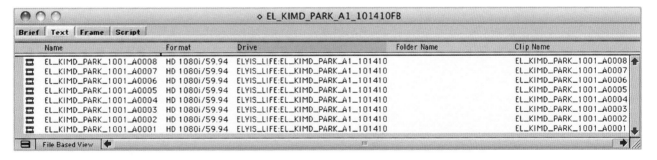

22. In the Select dialog box that appears, from the Copy 'Drive' column to list, select Folder Name, and then click OK.

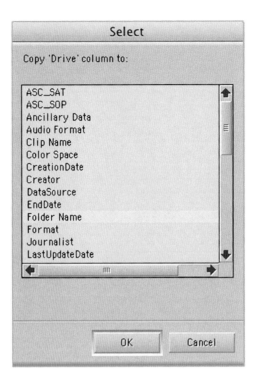

23. Repeat Steps 5–22 until all of the folders from the shoot are mounted in separate bins.

All folders from a file-based shoot must be mounted in bins at the same time to prevent crossover clips from being half online and half offline. See *Settings Needed: Crossover Clips* on page 41 for the full discussion.

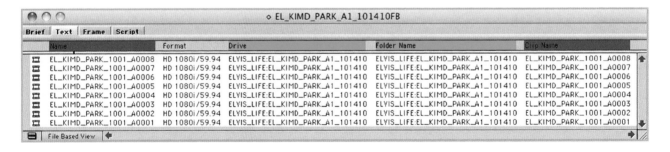

Consolidating and Transcoding

Consolidating and transcoding perform two different functions. Consolidating creates copies of clips to a target drive that you specify while preserving the native resolutions. Transcoding creates copies of clips to a target drive that you specify while changing the native resolutions. Choose the process that is best suited for the task at hand.

Consolidating

To consolidate clips

1. Select all of the clips in the bin (Mac: ⌘+A | PC: Ctrl+A).

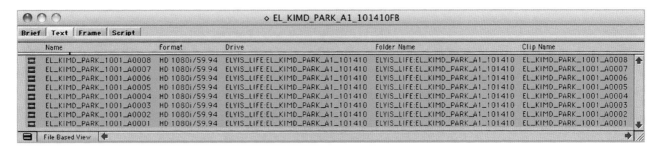

Tip | You can also right-click one of the clips, and then select Consolidate/Transcode.

2. Select Clip≫Consolidate/Transcode.

3. In the Consolidate/Transcode dialog box that appears, do the following:

   (a) Select Consolidate.

   (b) In the Target Drive(s) area, select the Video, audio, and data on same drive(s) check box.

   (c) In the Video/Data list, select the target drive (that is, the drive the media will copy to).

   (d) Clear the Delete original media files when done check box.

   (e) Clear the Skip media files already on the target drive check box.

   (f) Click Consolidate.

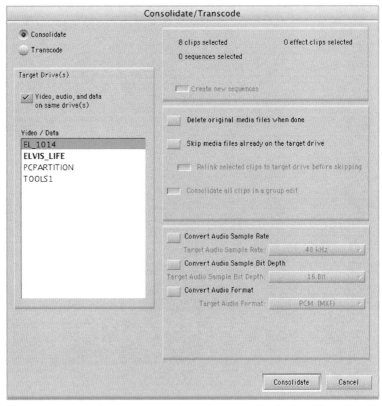

Figure 3-8. Consolidate/Transcode dialog box displaying Consolidate settings.

4. In the Copying Media Files dialog box that appears, select Relink Master clips to media on the target drive, and then click OK.

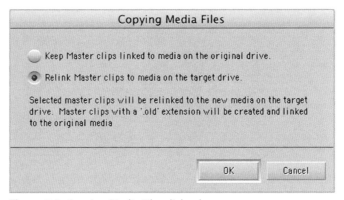

Figure 3-9. Copying Media Files dialog box.

When Relink Master clips to media on the target drive is selected in the Copying Media Files dialog box, Avid creates new clips that link to media copied to the target drive. To differentiate between the original and the new clips, Avid appends ".old" at the end of the original clip names.

> **Note |** In Figure 3-11, notice that the Drive column shows the ELVIS_LIFE drive as the location (file path) of the consolidated clips.
>
> If the information in the Drive column had not been copied into the Folder Name column (see *To bring file-based footage into Avid using AMA*, Steps 21–22, page 47), it would be very difficult to find the location of the original footage.

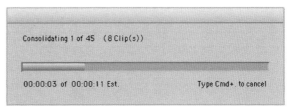

Figure 3-10. Consolidating status.

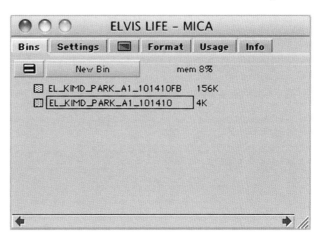

Figure 3-11. Project Bin window displaying offline clips (yellow highlight) and online clips (blue highlight) after consolidating.

5. In the Project window, copy the name of the bin with "FB" at the end of its name (Mac: ⌘+C | PC: Ctrl+C).

6. Create a bin (Mac: ⌘+N | PC: Ctrl+N).

7. Paste the name into the new bin name (Mac: ⌘+V | PC: Ctrl+V), delete "FB" from the end of the bin name, and then press Enter.

> **Note |** After consolidating and the clips are copied to the target drive, when the drives are disconnected from the system, the original file-based clips appear offline.
>
> It is a good practice to separate the original file-based clips from the consolidated clips by creating a bin for the consolidated clips because it will prevent editors from thinking that their media is offline.

8. Drag the consolidated clips into the new bin.

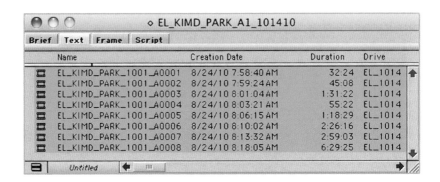

9. Close both bins.

Transcoding

To transcode clips

1. In the Project window, on the Format tab, in the Project Type menu, select the project type that you want to change the clips to.

2. Click on the bin, and then select all of the clips in the bin (Mac: ⌘+A | PC: Ctrl+A).

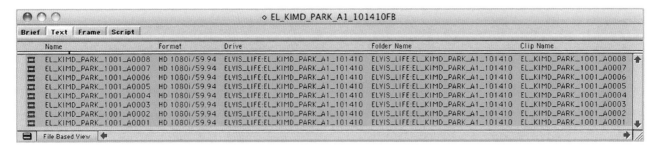

> **Tip** | You can also right-click one of the clips, and then select Consolidate/Transcode.

3. Select Clip≫Consolidate/Transcode.

4. In the Consolidate/Transcode dialog box that appears, do the following:

   (a) Select Transcode.

   (b) In the Target Drive(s) area, select the Video, audio, and data on same drive(s) check box.

> **Note** | Remember, when consolidating, the clips are copied in their original format to the new target drive, and when transcoding, the clips are copied at the resolution you select in the Target Video Resolution menu, in the Consolidate/Transcode dialog box to the new target drive.

   (c) In the Video/Data list, select the target drive (that is, the drive the media will copy to).

   (d) In the Target Video Resolution menu, select the target video resolution.

   (e) Click Transcode.

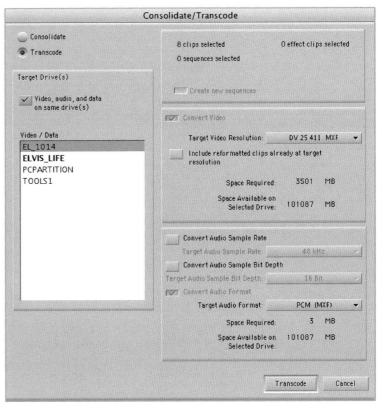

Figure 3-12. Consolidate/Transcode dialog box displaying Transcode settings.

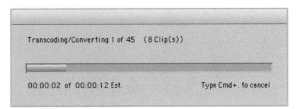

Figure 3-13. Transcoding status.

> **Note |** For this section (for example), the project type was set at 30i NTSC in Step 1, page 52, and these are the corresponding options available in the Target Video Resolution menu in the Consolidate/Transcode dialog box.
>
> If, for example, the project type was set to be 1080i/59.94, there would be different options in the Target Video Resolution menu.

5. In the Project window, copy the name of the bin with "FB" at the end of its name (Mac: ⌘+C | PC: Ctrl+C).

6. Create a bin (Mac: ⌘+N | PC: Ctrl+N).

7. Paste the name into the new bin name (Mac: ⌘+V | PC: Ctrl+V), delete "FB" from the end of the bin name, and then press Enter.

8. Drag the transcoded clips into the new bin.

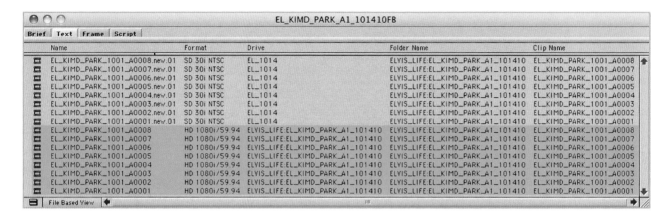

9. Close both bins.

Mounting Drives

Avid retains the names of the folders that you mount and will prevent you from mounting those folders over and over again to avoid consolidating/transcoding the same clips. If you try to access a previously mounted folder, the following message appears:

"AMA Manager - This volume was already processed. To mount this volume again, change your Volume Mounting options in the AMA Settings to always mount the volumes."

To mount a previously accessed folder, in the AMA Settings dialog box, on the Volume Mounting tab, select the check box for When mounting previously mounted volumes, do not check for modifications to the volume.

Bringing XDCAM Footage into Avid

As mentioned in the beginning of this chapter, XDCAM® discs are another type of file-based media. Unlike file-based media that exists on a card or a hard drive, XDCAM discs can be brought into Avid like tape (capturing), from a hard drive (importing), or a combination of the two. The choice you make is dependent on the resources at your disposal.

To bring XDCAM footage into Avid, you can use either a deck or a disc drive (for example, a Sony PDW-F70 or a Sony PDW-U1, respectively). Whether using a deck or a disc drive, the instructions are the same—the main difference is the use of AMA:

■ Enable AMA to immediately view the clips. Once the clips are viewed, consolidate or transcode them to your storage system to have access without the deck/disc drive and the disc.

  Follow the instructions in *To bring XDCAM footage into Avid using AMA.*

■ Disable AMA if you want to immediately import the full-resolution or proxy footage.

  Proxy files are lower-resolution copies of the full-resolution clips that were created while recording. They allow you to quickly bring in XDCAM footage.

  Follow the instructions in *To bring XDCAM footage into Avid with AMA disabled* on page 61.

Work through the options in TABLE 3-1, and read through the rest of this section to determine the workflow appropriate for your situation.

TABLE 3-1. XDCAM INGEST OPTIONS (OTHER FILE-BASED MEDIA FORMATS MAY APPLY)

AMA	Footage Immediately Viewable	Consolidate/ Transcode	Import	Result
Enabled	Yes	Consolidate	No	◆ Slower and more drive space needed to preserve the native resolution, but the files will not need to be uprezzed later.
Enabled	Yes	Transcode	No	◆ Faster and less drive space needed to transcode to lower resolution, but the files will need to be uprezzed later.
Disabled	No	Unnecessary	Yes Full-Resolution Files	◆ Slower and more drive space needed to preserve the native resolution, but the files will not need to be uprezzed later.
Disabled	No	Unnecessary	Yes Proxy Files	◆ Faster and less drive space needed to transcode to lower resolution, but the files will need to be uprezzed later.

To bring XDCAM footage into Avid using AMA

1. Connect the XDCAM deck/disc drive to the computer.

2. Turn on the XDCAM deck/disc drive.

3. In the Project window, on the Settings tab, double-click AMA, and the AMA Settings dialog box appears.

4. Click the Bins tab, and confirm that Use active bin is selected.

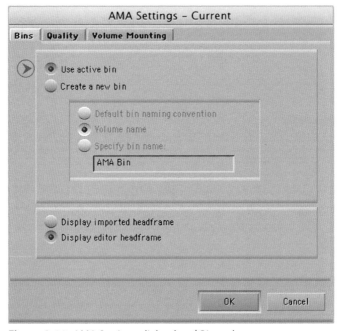

Figure 3-14. AMA Settings dialog box | Bins tab.

5. Click the Volume Mounting tab, and confirm that Enable AMA Volume Management is selected.

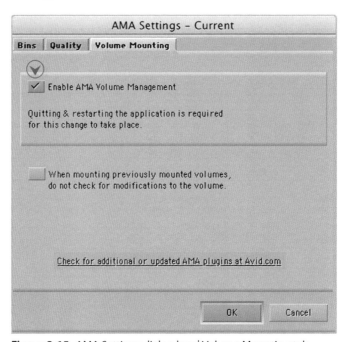

Figure 3-15. AMA Settings dialog box | Volume Mounting tab.

6. Click OK.

7. In the Project window, click the Bins tab.

8. Create a bin (Mac: ⌘+N | PC: Ctrl+N).

Note | If you consolidate/ transcode the clips, there needs to be separation between the bin that contains the XDCAM clips and the bin that contains the consolidated/transcoded clips.

9. Name the new bin exactly the same as the disc to be imported (or according to your company's naming conventions), add "XDCAM" to the end of the bin name, and then press Enter.

10. In the Bin window, click the Text tab.

11. On the Bin View menu, select Statistics.

12. Insert the XDCAM disc into the deck/disc drive, and an XDCAM disc icon appears on your desktop, and the clips appear in the bin.

Figure 3-16. AMA linking clips status (left) and XDCAM disc icon on the computer's desktop (right).

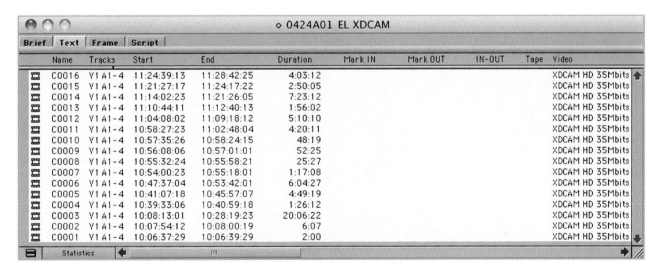

13. Do one of the following:

    (a) If the clips automatically appear in the bin, proceed to Step 14.

    –or–

    (b) If the clips do not appear in the bin, do the following and then proceed to Step 14.

(i) Select File≫Link to AMA Volumes.

(ii) In the Select the root of the virtual volume dialog box that
     appears, click the XDCAM disc icon, click Choose, and then
     wait for the clips to load in the bin.

14. Select all of the clips in the bin (Mac: ⌘+A | PC: Ctrl+A).

Note | You can work with these clips, but for the clips to be accessible to multiple users in a shared environment, they should be consolidated/transcoded to a shared media storage.

	Name	Tracks	Start	End	Duration	Mark IN	Mark OUT	IN-OUT	Tape	Video
	C0016	V1 A1-4	11:24:39:13	11:28:42:25	4:03:12					XDCAM HD 35Mbits (1080i/60)
	C0015	V1 A1-4	11:21:27:17	11:24:17:22	2:50:05					XDCAM HD 35Mbits (1080i/60)
	C0014	V1 A1-4	11:14:02:23	11:21:26:05	7:23:12					XDCAM HD 35Mbits (1080i/60)
	C0013	V1 A1-4	11:10:44:11	11:12:40:13	1:56:02					XDCAM HD 35Mbits (1080i/60)
	C0012	V1 A1-4	11:04:08:02	11:09:18:12	5:10:10					XDCAM HD 35Mbits (1080i/60)
	C0011	V1 A1-4	10:58:27:23	11:02:48:04	4:20:11					XDCAM HD 35Mbits (1080i/60)
	C0010	V1 A1-4	10:57:35:26	10:58:24:15	48:19					XDCAM HD 35Mbits (1080i/60)
	C0009	V1 A1-4	10:56:08:06	10:57:01:01	52:25					XDCAM HD 35Mbits (1080i/60)
	C0008	V1 A1-4	10:55:32:24	10:55:58:21	25:27					XDCAM HD 35Mbits (1080i/60)
	C0007	V1 A1-4	10:54:00:23	10:55:18:01	1:17:08					XDCAM HD 35Mbits (1080i/60)
	C0006	V1 A1-4	10:47:37:04	10:53:42:01	6:04:27					XDCAM HD 35Mbits (1080i/60)
	C0005	V1 A1-4	10:41:07:18	10:45:57:07	4:49:19					XDCAM HD 35Mbits (1080i/60)
	C0004	V1 A1-4	10:39:33:06	10:40:59:18	1:26:12					XDCAM HD 35Mbits (1080i/60)
	C0003	V1 A1-4	10:08:13:01	10:28:19:23	20:06:22					XDCAM HD 35Mbits (1080i/60)
	C0002	V1 A1-4	10:07:54:12	10:08:00:19	6:07					XDCAM HD 35Mbits (1080i/60)
	C0001	V1 A1-4	10:06:37:29	10:06:39:29	2:00					XDCAM HD 35Mbits (1080i/60)

Tip | You can also right-click one of the clips, and then select Modify.

15. Select Clip≫Modify.

16. In the Modify dialog box that appears, from the Modify Options menu, select Set Source.

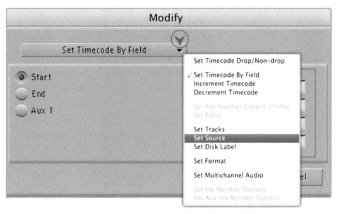

Figure 3-17. Modify dialog box displaying the Modify Options menu with Set Source selected.

Note | Avid retains the names of tapes/discs that have already been captured/imported. Be careful not to select a tape/disc name that has already been entered. (Unless that is the name of your disc!)

17. In the Select Tape dialog box that appears, click New.

18. In the Tape Name column, name the disc correctly.

Tape names are added to the clips because clips from XDCAM discs are labeled C0001.MXF, C0002.MXF, C0003.MXF, etc., and if you have multiple clips from multiple XDCAM discs within the same bin or sequence, it is difficult, if not impossible, to know which XDCAM disc the clip came from. If you add a tape name, the XDCAM disc will appear during CHAPTER 11: *Onlining: To gather source tapes*, Step 21, page 292, and this will allow you to generate a complete tape/disc EDL (edit decision list) of all of the tapes/discs associated with your project.

Figure 3-18. Select Tape dialog box.

19. Press Enter twice: once to enter the name and once to close the dialog box.

20. In the Modify dialog box, notice that the tape name is displayed, and then click OK.

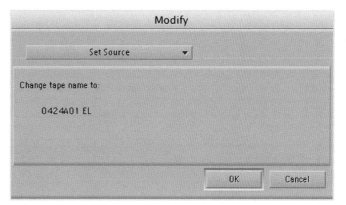

Figure 3-19. Modify dialog box displaying the tape name.

21. In the Avid Media Composer dialog box that appears, click OK.

Figure 3-20. Avid Media Composer dialog box prompting you to confirm that you want to change the tape name.

22. In the Avid Media Composer dialog box that appears, click OK, and the assigned tape name appears in the Tape column of the bin.

Figure 3-21. Avid Media Composer dialog box displaying additional information regarding changing the tape name.

	Name	Tracks	Start	End	Duration	Mark IN	Mark OUT	IN-OUT	Tape	Video	Au
	C0016	V1 A1-4	11:24:39:13	11:28:42:25	4:03:12				0424A01 EL	XDCAM HD 35Mbits (1080i/60)	
	C0015	V1 A1-4	11:21:27:17	11:24:17:22	2:50:05				0424A01 EL	XDCAM HD 35Mbits (1080i/60)	
	C0014	V1 A1-4	11:14:02:23	11:21:26:05	7:23:12				0424A01 EL	XDCAM HD 35Mbits (1080i/60)	
	C0013	V1 A1-4	11:10:44:11	11:12:40:13	1:56:02				0424A01 EL	XDCAM HD 35Mbits (1080i/60)	
	C0012	V1 A1-4	11:04:08:02	11:09:18:12	5:10:10				0424A01 EL	XDCAM HD 35Mbits (1080i/60)	
	C0011	V1 A1-4	10:58:27:23	11:02:48:04	4:20:11				0424A01 EL	XDCAM HD 35Mbits (1080i/60)	
	C0010	V1 A1-4	10:57:35:26	10:58:24:15	48:19				0424A01 EL	XDCAM HD 35Mbits (1080i/60)	
	C0009	V1 A1-4	10:56:08:06	10:57:01:01	52:25				0424A01 EL	XDCAM HD 35Mbits (1080i/60)	
	C0008	V1 A1-4	10:55:32:24	10:55:58:21	25:27				0424A01 EL	XDCAM HD 35Mbits (1080i/60)	
	C0007	V1 A1-4	10:54:00:23	10:55:18:01	1:17:08				0424A01 EL	XDCAM HD 35Mbits (1080i/60)	
	C0006	V1 A1-4	10:47:37:04	10:53:42:01	6:04:27				0424A01 EL	XDCAM HD 35Mbits (1080i/60)	
	C0005	V1 A1-4	10:41:07:18	10:45:57:07	4:49:19				0424A01 EL	XDCAM HD 35Mbits (1080i/60)	
	C0004	V1 A1-4	10:39:33:06	10:40:59:18	1:26:12				0424A01 EL	XDCAM HD 35Mbits (1080i/60)	
	C0003	V1 A1-4	10:08:13:01	10:28:19:23	20:06:22				0424A01 EL	XDCAM HD 35Mbits (1080i/60)	
	C0002	V1 A1-4	10:07:54:12	10:08:00:19	6:07				0424A01 EL	XDCAM HD 35Mbits (1080i/60)	
	C0001	V1 A1-4	10:06:37:29	10:06:39:29	2:00				0424A01 EL	XDCAM HD 35Mbits (1080i/60)	

Brief | Text | Frame | Script |

◇ 0424A01 EL XDCAM

Statistics

Figure 3-22. Bin window displaying the newly assigned tape name in the Tape name column.

23. Do one of the following:

> **Note** | If you intend to keep the clips in their native format, another option is to import the clips with AMA disabled.

(a) To bring in the clips from the XDCAM disc and retain their resolution, follow the instructions in *To consolidate clips* on page 49.

–or–

(b) To bring in the clips from the XDCAM disc and change their resolution, follow the instructions in *To transcode clips* on page 52.

24. Right–click the XDCAM disc on the desktop to eject the media from the deck/disc drive.

25. Repeat Steps 8–24 to import additional discs.

To bring XDCAM footage into Avid with AMA disabled

1. Connect the XDCAM deck/disc drive to the computer.

2. Turn on the XDCAM deck/disc drive.

3. In the Project window, on the Settings tab, double-click AMA, and the AMA Settings dialog box appears.

4. Click the Volume Mounting tab.

5. Confirm that Enable AMA Volume Management is not selected.

Caution! | If Enable AMA Volume Management was previously selected, you must restart the application for the setting to take effect.

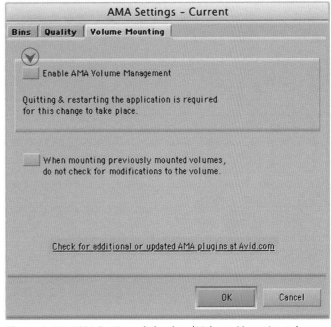

Figure 3-23. AMA Settings dialog box | Volume Mounting tab.

6. Click OK.

7. In the Project window, on the Settings tab, double-click Import, and the Import Settings dialog box appears.

8. Click the XDCAM tab, select the settings appropriate for your situation, and then click OK.

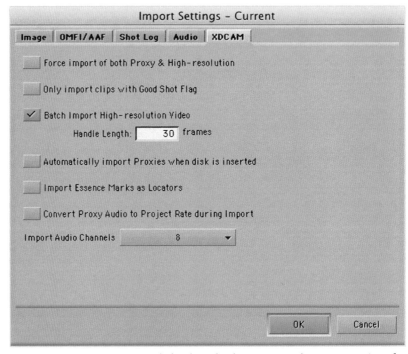

Figure 3-24. Import Settings dialog box displaying example import settings for importing XDCAM clips.

Force import of both Proxy & High-resolution (not selected)—When this option is selected, the proxy and high-resolution files are imported. When this option is not selected, you have to choose which files to import.

Only import clips with Good Shot Flag (not selected)—When this option is selected, any clips marked with the OK or KP (Keep) flag (using proxy software) are imported. When this option is not selected, all selected clips are imported.

Batch Import High-resolution Video (selected)—When this option is selected, the Batch Import function automatically imports high-resolution files to replace proxy files. When this option is not selected, the Batch Import function imports proxy files, unless you manually select the high-resolution files.

> **Handle Length box**—Type the number of frames to add as extra frames to the beginning and the end of the batch imported clip (30 frames is the default value).

Automatically import Proxies when disk is inserted (not selected)— When this option is selected, the proxy files are automatically imported. When this option is not selected, only selected files are imported.

Import Essence Marks as Locators (not selected)—When this option is selected, markers created during filming or using proxy software are imported into Avid as locators. When this option is not selected, the Essence Marks are not imported as locators.

Convert Proxy Audio to Project Rate during Import (not selected)— When this option is selected, Avid converts the proxy's sample rate (8 kHz) to your project's sample rate. When this option is not selected, the proxy's sample rate is not converted.

Import Audio Channels menu—Choose 2, 4, 6, or 8 as the maximum number of audio channels to import.

9. In the Project window, click the Bins tab.

10. Create a bin (Mac: ⌘+N | PC: Ctrl+N).

11. Name the new bin exactly the same as the disc to be imported (or according to your company's naming conventions), and then press Enter.

12. In the Bin window, click the Text tab.

13. On the Bin View menu, select Statistics.

14. Insert the XDCAM disc into the deck/disc drive, and then wait for the XDCAM disc icon to appear on the desktop.

15. Click on the bin.

16. Select File≫Import.

> **Tip** | You can also right-click in the bin, and then select Import.

17. In the Select files to Import dialog box that appears, navigate to the XDCAM disc, and then click it.

18. In the Avid Media Composer dialog box that appears, click OK.

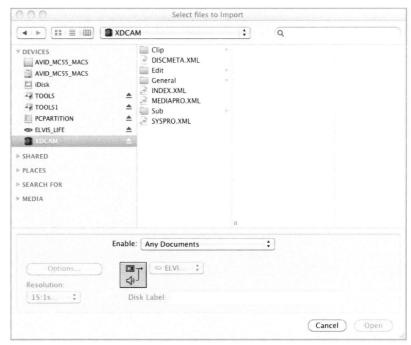

Figure 3-25. Select files to Import dialog box.

19. In the Disk Label box, enter a disk label.

The disk label is important because it allows you to differentiate between the same-named clips from different discs.

If these clips are batch imported during the online process, you will be prompted to insert the correct disc, but only if the disk label is inserted during the initial import.

To learn more about batch importing XDCAM clips, see Chapter 11: *Onlining: To batch import graphics into the sequence at full resolution* on page 298.

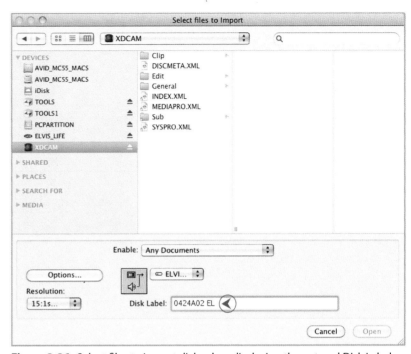

Figure 3-26. Select files to Import dialog box displaying the entered Disk Label.

Note | The clips can be imported at full-resolution or using proxy files. *Proxy files* are lower-resolution copies of the full-resolution clips that were created while recording. They allow you to quickly bring in XDCAM footage.

When using the Import function for proxy files, there is a neat upside when uprezzing the video. Avid remembers the file path of imported clips, and when using the Batch Import function, you are prompted for the correct disc, and the file path will point to the full-resolution file and not the proxy file.

20. Do one of the following:

   (a) Click the Clip folder to bring in the *full-resolution clips*.

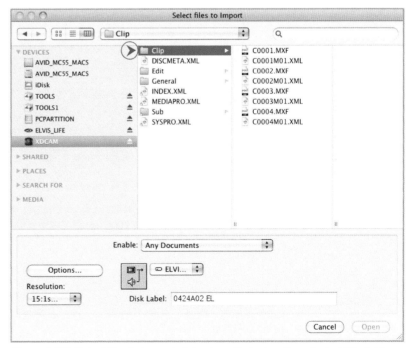

Figure 3-27. Select files to Import dialog box displaying the selected Clip folder.

–or–

   (b) Click the Sub folder to bring in the *proxy files*.

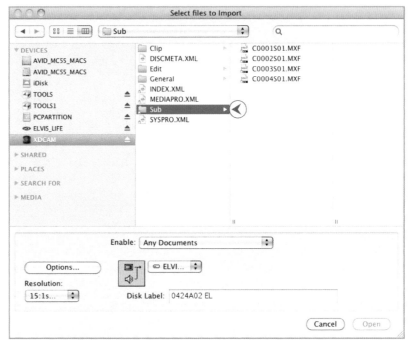

Figure 3-28. Select files to Import dialog box displaying the selected Sub folder.

21. Select the files with the .MXF file extension *not* the .XML files.

22. In the Video Drive menu, select the correct drive, and then click Open.

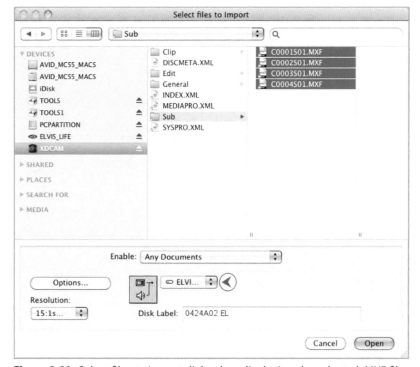

Figure 3-29. Select files to Import dialog box displaying the selected .MXF files within the Sub folder.

Figure 3-30. Importing XDCAM Proxy file status.

Figure 3-31. Avid Media Composer dialog box prompting you to insert the 0424A02 EL XDCAM disc during the Batch Import function.

While importing, be mindful that you can't import XDCAM files at a different resolution than what exists on the XDCAM disc. If you choose the full-resolution files, the file will be imported at full-resolution and override the project's settings—assuming the full-resolution file is compatible with the project's format. Conversely, if you are in a full-resolution project, you won't need to change the project's format because the proxy files will import at the lower proxy resolution. If you want to choose the resolution of the clips, you should use *To bring XDCAM footage into Avid using AMA* on page 55; otherwise, you will need to transcode the newly imported clips.

23. Select all of the clips in the bin (Mac: ⌘+A | PC: Ctrl+A).

24. Select Clip≫Modify.

<aside>
Tip | You can also right-click one of the clips, and then select Modify.
</aside>

25. In the Modify dialog box that appears, from the Modify Options menu, select Set Source.

26. In the Select Tape dialog box that appears, click New.

27. In the Tape Name column, name the disc correctly.

<aside>
Note | Avid retains the names of tapes/discs that have already been captured/imported. Be careful not to select a tape/disc name that has already been entered. (Unless that is the name of your disc!)
</aside>

During importing, you can't add a tape name, you can only add a disk label. While disk labels are crucial for batch importing, they aren't helpful when creating EDLs. If you add a tape name, the XDCAM disc will appear during CHAPTER 11: *Onlining: To gather source tapes*, Step 21, page 292, and this will allow you to generate a complete tape/disc EDL of all of the tapes/discs associated with your project.

28. Press Enter twice: once to enter the name and once to close the dialog box.

29. In the Modify dialog box, notice that the tape name is displayed, and then click OK.

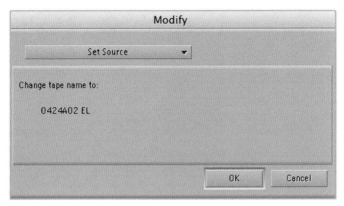

Figure 3-32. Modify dialog box displaying the tape name.

30. In the Avid Media Composer dialog box that appears, click OK.

31. In the Avid Media Composer dialog box that appears, click OK, and the assigned tape name appears in the Tape column of the bin.

   When dealing with XDCAM footage, importing the proxy files takes the least amount of time. It is a toss-up between importing the full-resolution files and consolidating/transcoding AMA-accessed XDCAM files because it is largely dependent on the size of the clips on the XDCAM disc, the speed of your computer, and the deck/disc drive you are using. The different methods discussed aren't about time but how you want the clips to be brought into Avid. If you want greater control regarding the resolution, use AMA. If the clips can be brought in at their native resolutions, whether full-resolution or proxy, then importing may be more appropriate.

32. Right-click on the XDCAM disc on the desktop to eject the media from the deck/disc drive.

33. Close the bin.

34. Repeat Steps 10–33 to import additional discs.

Did I Do This Correctly?

■ **Was the copied media at the correct resolution?**

   Depending on the needs of the project, the media may be consolidated into the project at the original resolution, or it may be transcoded into a different, and usually lower, resolution.

■ **Were the original clip name and file path preserved?**

Preserving the original clip name and file path allows future users to locate the media.

■ **Were all of the folders mounted in bins at the same time?**

All of the folders from a particular shoot must be mounted in bins at the same time. If they are not, crossover clips will cause the consolidation/transcode process to not finish correctly resulting in clips that are half online and half offline.

■ **Were tape names added to the XDCAM discs?**

It is important to add a tape name to an XDCAM disc to identify which XDCAM disc a clip came from for two reasons. One, XDCAM clips are labeled C0001.MXF, C0002.MXF, C0003.MXF, etc., and if there are multiple clips from multiple XDCAM discs, it would be difficult, if not impossible, to know which XDCAM disc the clip came from. Two, when gathering source material to online a sequence, an EDL won't generate a complete list unless the discs have tape names or the clips have descriptive clip names. Tape names on the XDCAM discs is especially helpful during batch importing because you will have the discs you need when prompted to insert the correct XDCAM disc.

CHAPTER 4:
Multigrouping

Tasks in This Chapter [1]

[1] This list represents the main tasks for this chapter. For the full list, see *Tasks* on page vii.

VERITE, STUDIO PRODUCTIONS, INTERVIEWS, and concerts can be filmed with several cameras rolling at the same time. All of those camera angles can be viewed at the same time in a split-screen. Linking these clips to one another so they can all be viewed at the same time is called *grouping*. A bunch of groups combined together is called a *multigroup*.

Multigrouping is an unavoidable part of television. As little as two and up to nine (or more) cameras can be rolling on the same action getting various angles. It is important in the pre-editing process to group these cameras correctly and completely. Through multigrouping, you become very familiar with the footage making it easier to find that perfect shot for a time-crunched editor.

Multigrouping is a repetitive process, and once you learn a concept, it will be repeated over and over until it is time to move on to the next. So master a concept before moving on to the next or it will wreak havoc on the final multigroup.

The main components of the multigrouping process are as follows:

- **All Camming the Day's Clips**—Accumulating all of the day's clips from all cameras and placing them into a bin.

- **Producing the Layout**—Laying out all of the clips into a sequence.

- **Syncing**—Syncing the clips in the sequence to one another.

- **Add Editing**—Assigning the clips new (auxiliary) timecode and dividing them into groups.

- **Subclipping**—Creating smaller clips from the master clips.

- **Creating Multigroups**—Linking the subclips into groups.

- **Checking and Fixing Multigroups**—Verifying that all of the footage from the shoot is within the multigrouping and in the proper locations.

You should read through the chapter to familiarize yourself with the concepts and terms before fully diving in.

Settings Needed

Configure the following settings before beginning the tasks in this chapter.

The last setting in this section—*Timeline Fast Menu Settings: Track Color* on page 81—cannot be set before you begin the chapter because it is dependent on something that occurs in the chapter; therefore, at the appropriate time, you will be instructed to return to this section to modify your user profile accordingly.

The settings needed for *Checking and Fixing Multigroups* are within that section on page 130. You do not need to configure them until then.

GENERAL SETTINGS DIALOG BOX

Navigation: Project window | Settings tab | Select General from the Settings list | General Settings dialog box

In the General Settings dialog box, in the Default Starting TC box, change the colons (non-drop-frame timecode) to semicolons (drop-frame timecode) or vice versa depending on the format your company uses. Default Starting TC is displayed as HH:MM:SS:FF (Hours:Minutes:Seconds:Frames).

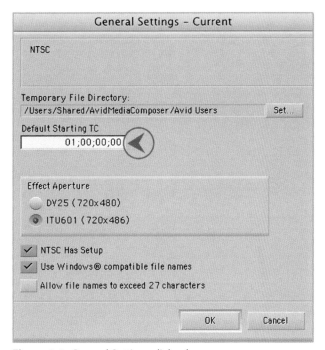

Figure 4-1. General Settings dialog box.

DROP-FRAME VS. NON-DROP-FRAME TIMECODE

Timecode is simply labeling each frame with a number so that each frame is uniquely identified. There are two types of timecode—drop-frame (DF) and non-drop-frame (NDF). Both types of timecode label every frame, but each follows a different labeling method. DF does not mean that any frames of video are dropped or left out. A sequence in DF is identical cut for cut and frame for frame to a sequence in NDF. An easy way to tell DF from NDF is by the separator character used within the timecode: DF uses semicolons and NDF uses colons.

DF and NDF timecode are just two different ways of numbering each frame in a video.

Drop-Frame Timecode

■ Counts 30 frames per second.

■ Every minute (except for every tenth minute), two frame numbers are dropped (skipped), so the frame numbering goes from 29 to 02 to 03, etc.—that is, 00 and 01 are dropped (29 | $_{00}$ | $_{01}$ | 02 | 03).

Clock time (electricity) operates at 60 Hz (cycles per second). A television operates at 59.94 Hz, or it can display 59.94 frames per second, which is 29.97 frames per second when halved. With DF, 30 frames are counted each second, when the television is only capable of displaying 29.97 frames per second. Over time, the 0.03 frame per second difference adds up causing the elapsed time displayed in the timecode to drift further away from the real elapsed time of the video. By skipping a few numbers here and there, DF stays in sync with real time.

Non-Drop-Frame Timecode

■ Counts 30 frames per second.

■ After frame 29, frame 00 is the next frame from the next second, so the frame numbering goes from 29 to 00 to 01 to 02 to 03, etc.

Composer Settings Dialog Box

Window Tab

Navigation: Project window | Settings tab | Select Composer from the Settings list | Composer Settings dialog box | Window tab

■ **First (lower) Row of Info (selected)**—When this option is selected, one row of information is displayed above the Source and Record monitors in the Composer window that can show the duration, timecode, and other useful information about the clip or sequence loaded in the Source and Record monitors.

■ **Second Row of Info (selected)**—When this option is selected, a second row of information (above the first row of information) is displayed that can show the duration, timecode, and other useful information about the clip or sequence loaded in the Source and Record monitors.

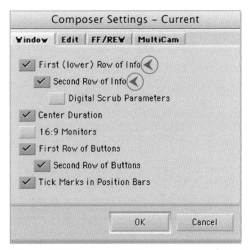

Figure 4-2. Composer Settings dialog box | Window tab.

Figure 4-3. Composer window displaying the First and Second Row of Information.

KEYBOARD SETTINGS

It is possible to change the function of the buttons of the physical keyboard to your own specifications. Changing (mapping) the Keyboard settings of the F2–F10 function keys as described makes multigrouping easier.

To map the keyboard settings of the F2–F10 function keys for multigrouping

1. In the Project window, on the Settings tab, double-click Keyboard, and the Avid Keyboard appears.

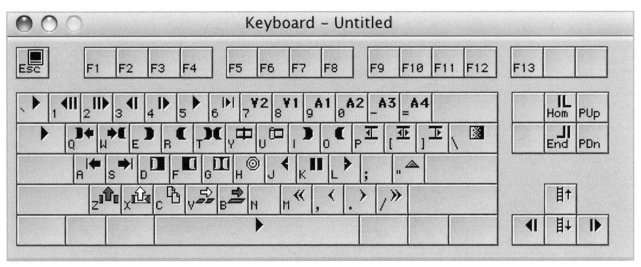

Figure 4-4. Avid Keyboard: default.

2. Open the Command palette (Mac: ⌘+3 | PC: Ctrl+3).

3. On the Command palette, select 'Button-to-Button' Reassignment.

Figure 4-5. Command palette with 'Button to Button' Reassignment selected.

4. Drag a shortcut from any tab of the Command palette to a key on the Keyboard, and the shortcut icon appears on the mapped Keyboard key. To prepare for multigrouping, map the F2–F10 keys as follows:

    (a) **F2 ➤ Mark Clip (Command palette: Edit tab)**—Sets IN and OUT points at the very beginning and very end of a clip. When this button is pressed, the entire clip is selected.

    (b) **F3 ➤ Go to IN (Command palette: Move tab)**—Moves the position indicator to an IN point.

    (c) **F4 ➤ Match Frame (Command palette: Other tab)**—Finds the exact frame of a clip. It takes the frame the playhead is on, opens the clips it came from in the Source monitor, finds the exact same frame, and then sets the IN point on that frame.

    (d) **F5 ➤ Go to OUT (Command palette: Move tab)**—Moves the position indicator to an OUT point.

    (e) **F6 ➤ Mark OUT (Command palette: Edit tab)**—Marks the end of a section of a clip or sequence, and it is known as an OUT point. That frame may not necessarily be at the end of a clip.

    (f) **F7 ➤ Make Subclip (Command palette: Edit tab)**—Uses IN and OUT points to mark a portion of a larger clip and make it into its own smaller clip, or subclip, to save in a bin.

    (g) **F8 ➤ Add Edit (Command palette: Edit tab)**—Divides sequences and clips in a sequence into smaller parts. Similar to a slice or razor cut in other editing applications.

    (h) **F9 ➤ Nine Split (Command palette: MCam tab)**—Displays nine cameras at a time in a multigroup. This is not enabled by default, so each time a multigroup is loaded, this key will have to be pressed. (You can also select Quad Split—if there are fewer cameras, the clips will display larger in the Source monitor.)

    (i) **F10 ➤ Add Locator (Command palette: More tab)**—Places a reference marker on a clip to which you can add comments. It is an oval shape of different colors, and it doesn't affect the video or audio.

5. Close the Avid Keyboard and Command palette.

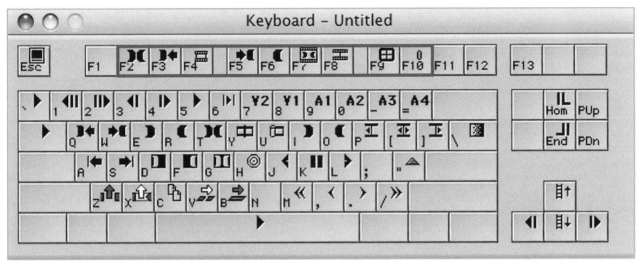

Figure 4-6. Avid Keyboard with F2-F10 function keys mapped for multigrouping highlighted.

TIMELINE SETTINGS DIALOG BOX

Display Tab

Navigation: Project window | Settings tab | Select Timeline from the Settings list | Timeline Settings dialog box | Display tab

- **Show Marked Waveforms (select check box)**—When this option is selected, only the waveforms, or audio patterns, between the Mark IN and OUT points are displayed (that is, the waveforms, or audio patterns, over the entire sequence are not displayed).

Figure 4-7. Timeline Settings dialog box | Display tab.

Edit Tab

Navigation: Project window | Settings tab | Select Timeline from the Settings list | Timeline Settings dialog box | Edit tab

- **Auto-Patching (clear check box)**—When selected, this option automatically patches enabled source tracks to enabled tracks in the sequence, which can be a nuisance while trying to group. This option is unnecessary and potentially problematic for multigrouping.

- **Auto-Monitoring (clear check box)**—When selected, this option automatically monitors the track you patch to, which can be a nuisance while trying to group. This option is unnecessary and potentially problematic for multigrouping.

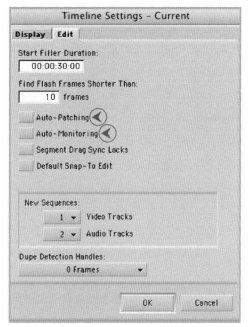

Figure 4-8. Timeline Settings dialog box | Edit tab.

Timeline Fast Menu Settings

Navigation: Timeline window | Fast menu (leftmost button on the bottom toolbar)

- **Wrap Around (not selected)**—When this option is not selected, it zooms in to the portion of the sequence where the position indicator is. When this option is selected, it zooms in to a sequence and wraps the sequence in the window so every portion of the sequence is visible.

- **Dupe Detection (selected)**—When this option is selected, it alerts you to the presence of duplicated clips by displaying colored lines above them in the tracks—even if the duplicated clips are on separate tracks. For example, if there is one dupe, there will be one set of orange lines, and if there are two dupes, there will be one set of orange lines and one set of green lines. Up to 10 color sets can be seen during a single detection process.

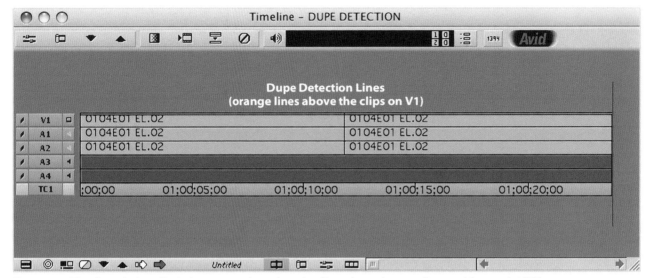

Figure 4-9. Timeline window displaying orange dupe detection lines above the two clips on video track 1 (V1).

- **Clip Color (Source selected)**—When this option is selected, the clip icon in the bin is the same color as the clip in the Timeline.

To change source colors

1. Click on a clip or sequence in a bin.

2. Select Edit≫Set Clip Color.

3. Select a Clip Color.

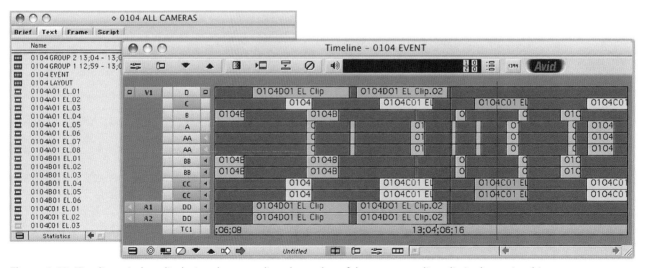

Figure 4-10. Timeline window displaying the same clip color as that of the corresponding clip in the project bin.

■ **Clip Color (Offline selected)**—When this option is selected, it alerts you to the presence of offline clips in the sequence by coloring them red. (Red is the default color. The clip icon in the bin does not appear red.)

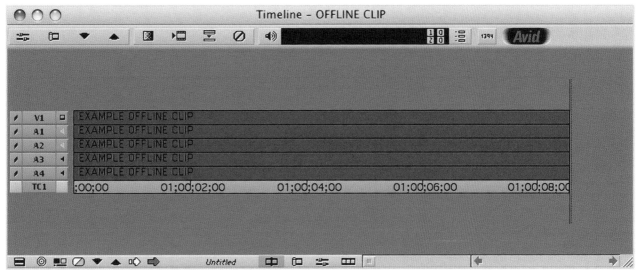

Figure 4-11. Timeline window displaying offline clips in red (default color).

LOCATORS FAST MENU SETTINGS

■ **Disable Locator Popup Always (selected)**—When this option is selected, the Locator dialog box does not open each time a locator is created thereby speeding up the multigrouping process (you can add comments to locators later if you choose).

To select the Disable Locator Popup Always option

1. Select Tools≫Locators.

2. In the Locators window that appears, click the Fast Menu, and then select Disable Locator Popup Always.

3. Close the Locators window.

TIMELINE FAST MENU SETTINGS: TRACK COLOR

The Track Color setting cannot be set until later in the chapter. In *To lay out the clips in the sequence*, Step 15, page 100, you will be instructed to return to this setting to modify your user profile.

■ **Track Color (selected)**—When this option is selected, you can specify colors for tracks (a track must be selected in the Timeline to see this option). When a sequence is displayed in the Timeline, the tracks have

Avid default colors; however, you can change track colors, and a good reason for doing so is to show relationships.

When choosing track colors, select the same color for a video track and its corresponding audio tracks. This coloring technique is helpful when multigrouping because you can immediately see the audio and video tracks that correspond to one another. The color palette in FIGURE 4-12 gives you an idea of the color choices available.

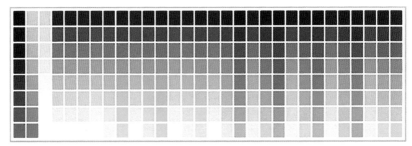

Figure 4-12. Color palette displaying the choices of Track Color available.

Once you have changed the track color, the track displays that color on those selected tracks, and it will apply to any sequences loaded in the Timeline window. When a sequence is displayed in the Timeline and the track colors have been changed, the tracks can look like those in FIGURE 4-13. Notice how easy it is to identify a video track and its corresponding audio tracks.

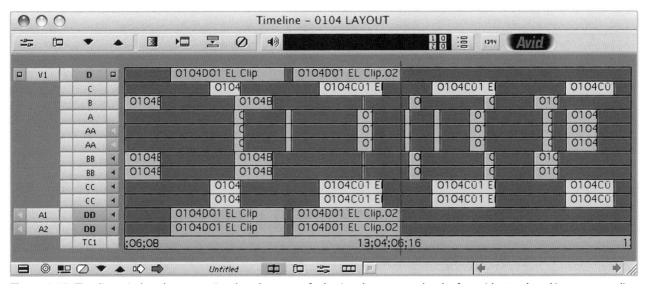

Figure 4-13. Timeline window demonstrating the advantage of selecting the same track color for a video track and its corresponding audio tracks through the use of four track colors for four video tracks each with two corresponding audio tracks.

To change a track color

1. Enable the track (or tracks) that you want to change.

2. Deselect the Timecode track (TC1). (TC1 can be colored too.)

3. Click the Timeline Fast menu.

4. Select Track Color.

5. Choose a color.

All-Camming the Day's Clips

Multigrouping is the first step in the pre-editing process where you can see how important it is to completely grasp the concepts of the previous chapters. Tapes/discs/cards incompletely captured or captured at the wrong resolution have frustrating and time-consuming effects when multigrouping.

Before you can begin the layout, all of the day's clips must be accumulated and placed into a bin. This process is known as *all-camming*.

To accumulate and place the day's clips in a bin (all-camming)

> **Note** | For details on creating user profiles and creating projects, see CHAPTER 1: *Getting Started in Avid* on pages 6 and 7, respectively.

1. Start Avid, and in the Select Project dialog box that appears, do the following, and then click OK.

    (a) In the User Profile menu, select an existing user profile.

    (b) In the Project list, select a project.

2. Create a bin (Mac: ⌘+N | PC: Ctrl+N).

3. Rename the new bin 0104 All Cameras, and then press Enter.

> **Note** | Not all clips, such as interviews or B-roll, need to be contained in a group. Clarify what your company includes in groups.

4. In the Bin window, click the Text tab.

5. On the Bin View menu, select Statistics.

6. Open the A camera bins.

> **Tip** | Holding down Option (Mac)|Alt (PC) copies the clips instead of moving them from one bin to another.

7. Select all of the clips in the first A camera bin (Mac: ⌘+A | PC: Ctrl+A), and copy them into the 0104 All Cameras bin (Mac: Option+Drag | PC: Alt+Drag).

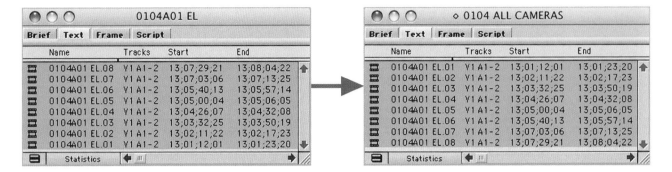

8. Make sure the original clips in the first A camera bin are no longer selected.

Note | Ensure that the clips in the original bins are not selected because clips that are already selected in the original bins will give the false impression that they were selected by the Select Media Relatives command in Step 12.

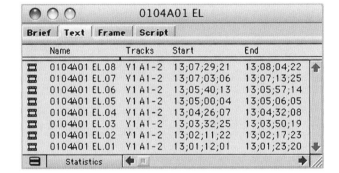

9. Repeat Steps 7–8 for the remaining A camera bins.

10. Select all of the clips in the 0104 All Cameras bin (Mac: ⌘+A | PC: Ctrl+A).

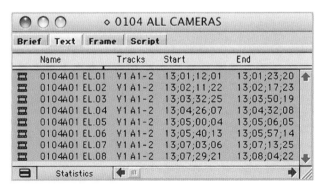

11. Click the 0104 All Cameras Bin Fast menu.

12. Choose Select Media Relatives.

13. Look at the clips in the original A camera bins and do one of the following:

(a) If all of the clips are selected, proceed to Step 14.

–or–

(b) If any of the clips are not selected, repeat Steps 7–12.

14. Repeat Steps 6–13 for B camera bins, C camera bins, etc., until all of the clips from all of the cameras have been copied into the 0104 All Cameras bin.

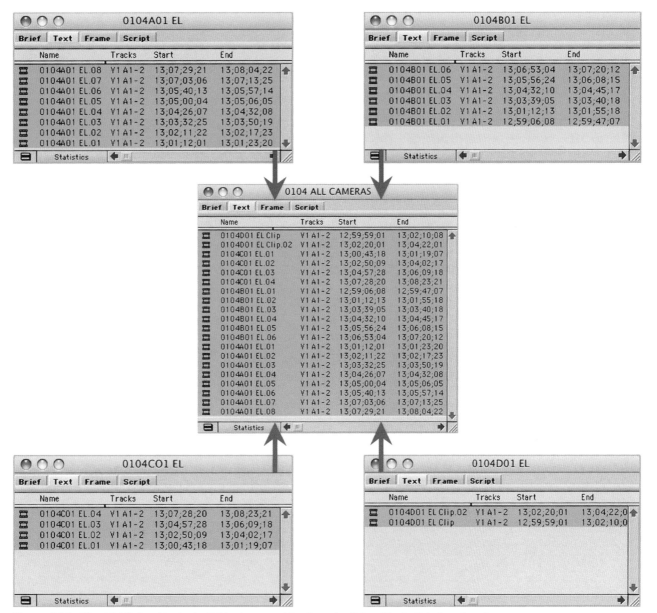

Figure 4-14. Clips highlighted in the individual camera bins from the Select Media Relatives function.

15. Close the camera bins.

16. Save the 0104 All Cameras bin (Mac: ⌘+S | PC: Ctrl+S).

Producing the Layout

Laying out all of the clips into a sequence involves time-consuming preparation, but taking the time to complete these steps correctly will save a lot of time and frustration on the back end. To make the process a little bit easier, subheadings have been inserted to break up the steps; however, all of the steps must be performed in the order presented.

Creating the Layout Sequence

To create the layout sequence

1. In the 0104 All Cameras bin, click the Start column heading to select the column as the sort criterion.

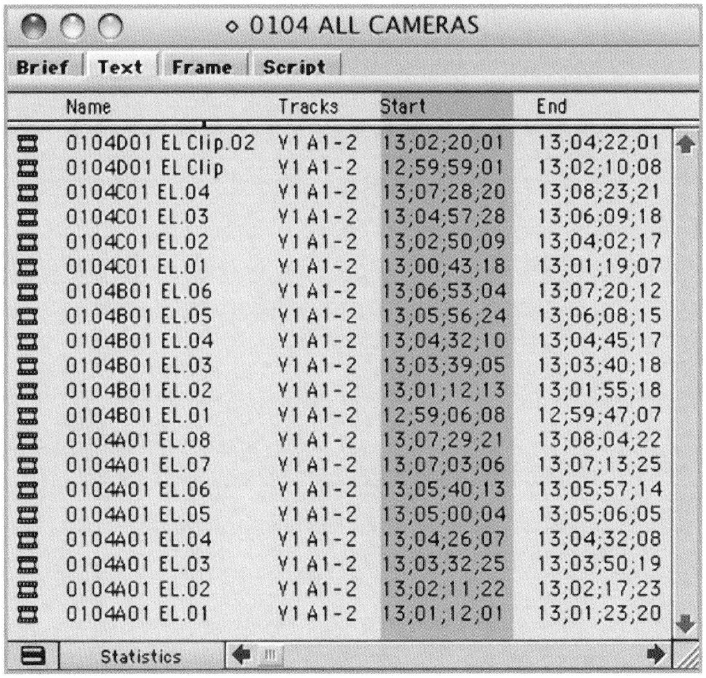

Figure 4-15. 0104 All Cameras bin with Start column selected as the sort criterion.

2. Sort the bin in ascending order based on the Start column (Mac: ⌘+E | PC: Ctrl+E).

3. Write down the Start timecode of the first clip of the day (see FIGURE 4-16). This information will be used in *To modify the layout sequence*, Step 2, page 92.

Tip |
◆ Sort in Ascending Order
  Press Mac: ⌘+E | PC: Ctrl+E

◆ Sort in Descending Order
  Press Mac: ⌘+Option+E |
  PC: Ctrl+Alt+E

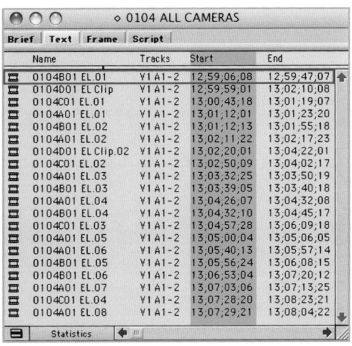

Figure 4-16. 0104 All Cameras bin after sorting the Start column with the first clip of the day highlighted.

The Start timecode of the first clip of the day is 12;59;06;08, and it is from Camera B.

DETERMINING THE TIMECODE OF THE FIRST CLIP OF THE DAY

Shoots That Cross Over Midnight

The timecode of the clip at the top of the Start column after sorting may or may not be the timecode of the first clip of the day. The first timecode in the Start column may be near midnight or soon after, and this may or may not be the first clip of the day. Shoots can begin at any time of the day, so the first timecode of the day could very well be the 1:00 a.m. timecode at the top of the Start column after sorting. But since shoots frequently cross over midnight, and a day's worth of tapes can begin, for example, at 9:00 a.m. on Wednesday and conclude at 4:00 a.m. on Thursday, then in this case, that 1:00 a.m. timecode at the top of the start column is not the first clip of the day; rather, the timecode of the first clip of the day is the 9:00 a.m. timecode further down the list. *Be vigilant and don't assume that the timecode of the first clip of the day is the one sorted to the top of the Start column.*

Shoots That Have DF and NDF Clips

Bins are sorted by DF and NDF clips and then by timecode in ascending order. As a result, the first clip of the day could be buried in the middle of the bin. After sorting, if the first and last clip in the bin are the same timecode type (both have semicolon separators within the timecode or both have colon separators), this is not an issue, and the first clip of the day is the first clip in the bin unless it is for a shoot that crosses over midnight. If after sorting the first and last clip in the bin are not the same timecode type (one has semicolon separators within the timecode and one has colon separators), then find the break between the two timecode types and determine which timecode is earlier. Remember, DF timecode uses semicolon separators and NDF timecode uses colon separators.

4. Click the End column heading to select the column as the sort criterion.

5. Sort the bin in ascending order based on the End column (Mac: ⌘+E | PC: Ctrl+E).

6. Write down the End timecode of the last clip of the day (see FIGURE 4-17). This information will be used in *To modify the layout sequence*, Step 13, page 96.

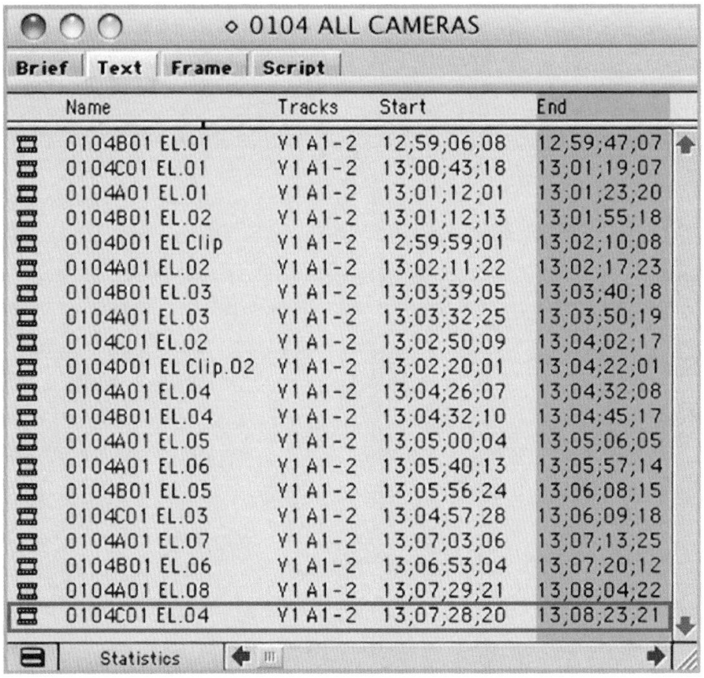

Name	Tracks	Start	End
0104B01 EL.01	V1 A1-2	12;59;06;08	12;59;47;07
0104C01 EL.01	V1 A1-2	13;00;43;18	13;01;19;07
0104A01 EL.01	V1 A1-2	13;01;12;01	13;01;23;20
0104B01 EL.02	V1 A1-2	13;01;12;13	13;01;55;18
0104D01 EL Clip	V1 A1-2	12;59;59;01	13;02;10;08
0104A01 EL.02	V1 A1-2	13;02;11;22	13;02;17;23
0104B01 EL.03	V1 A1-2	13;03;39;05	13;03;40;18
0104A01 EL.03	V1 A1-2	13;03;32;25	13;03;50;19
0104C01 EL.02	V1 A1-2	13;02;50;09	13;04;02;17
0104D01 EL Clip.02	V1 A1-2	13;02;20;01	13;04;22;01
0104A01 EL.04	V1 A1-2	13;04;26;07	13;04;32;08
0104B01 EL.04	V1 A1-2	13;04;32;10	13;04;45;17
0104A01 EL.05	V1 A1-2	13;05;00;04	13;05;06;05
0104A01 EL.06	V1 A1-2	13;05;40;13	13;05;57;14
0104B01 EL.05	V1 A1-2	13;05;56;24	13;06;08;15
0104C01 EL.03	V1 A1-2	13;04;57;28	13;06;09;18
0104A01 EL.07	V1 A1-2	13;07;03;06	13;07;13;25
0104B01 EL.06	V1 A1-2	13;06;53;04	13;07;20;12
0104A01 EL.08	V1 A1-2	13;07;29;21	13;08;04;22
0104C01 EL.04	V1 A1-2	13;07;28;20	13;08;23;21

Figure 4-17. 0104 All Cameras bin after sorting the End column with the last clip of the day highlighted.

The End timecode of the last clip of the day is 13;08;23;21, and it is from Camera C.

Determining the Timecode of the Last Clip of the Day

Shoots That Have DF and NDF Clips

Bins are sorted by DF and NDF clips and then by timecode in ascending order. As a result, the last clip of the day could be buried in the middle of the bin. After sorting, if the first and last clip in the bin are the same timecode type (both have semicolon separators within the timecode or both have colon separators), this is not an issue, and the last clip of the day is the last clip in the bin. If after sorting the first and last clip in the bin are not the same timecode type (one has semicolon separators within the timecode and one has colon separators), then find the break between the two timecode types and determine which timecode is later. Remember, DF timecode uses semicolon separators and NDF timecode uses colon separators.

> **Note** | When a sequence is created, its default name is Untitled Sequence.01.

7. Create a sequence (Mac: Shift+⌘+N | PC: Shift+Ctrl+N), and it automatically loads in the Timeline window.

8. Rename the sequence 0104 Layout.

9. Add video tracks to the sequence so that there is one video track for each camera in the 0104 All Cameras bin (Mac: ⌘+Y | PC: Ctrl+Y).

> **Note** | If there are four cameras, the sequence will have four video tracks and eight audio tracks.

10. Add audio tracks to the sequence so that there are two audio tracks for each camera in the 0104 All Cameras bin (Mac: ⌘+U | PC: Ctrl+U).

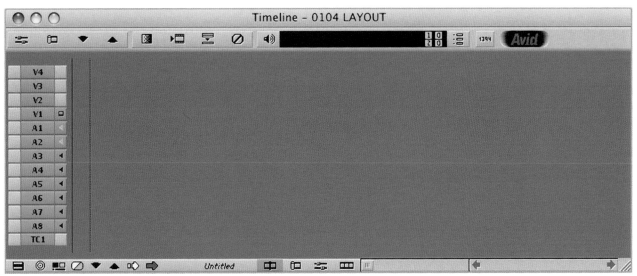

Figure 4-18. Timeline window displaying four video tracks and eight audio tracks with the default naming convention for each camera in the 0104 All Cameras bin.

11. Right-click the V1 track selector button to rename it, and then select Rename Track.

> **Note** | It is common to rename video track 1 as "A" and video track 2 as "B," and so on; and audio track 1 and audio track 2 each as "AA" and audio track 3 and audio track 4 each as "BB," and so on, to match the camera names.

12. In the Comments dialog box that appears, type a new track name, and then click OK.

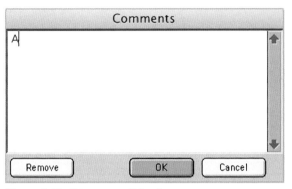

Figure 4-19. Comments dialog box.

13. Repeat Steps 11–12 for each of the remaining video and audio tracks.

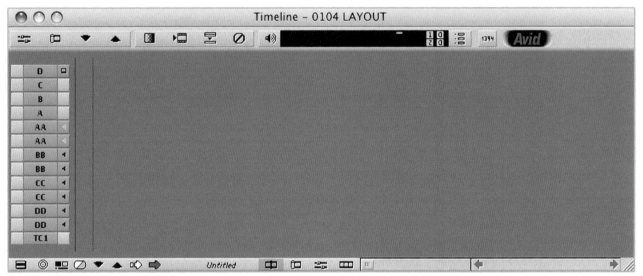

Figure 4-20. Timeline window displaying four video tracks and eight audio tracks with the suggested naming convention for each camera in the 0104 All Cameras bin.

Configuring the Timecode Window

The Timecode window is a valuable multigrouping resource because it displays the timecode of the clips in reference to their placement in the sequence.

To configure the Timecode window by adding one line for each camera

1. Select Tools≫Timecode Window, and the Timecode window appears. (The Timecode window may initially look like FIGURE 4-21.)

Note | Mas refers to the sequence's master timecode.

Figure 4-21. Timecode window on open.

2. In the Timecode window, click in the black area to display the Timecode menu. (This process will only work if there is a sequence loaded in the Timeline.)

3. In the Timecode menu, select Add Line.

4. Click the new line to display the Timecode menu, and then do the following:

    (a) Select Source.

    (b) Select V1.

    (c) Select TC1 (TC1 refers to the source timecode of the video clip that is present on video track 1).

5. Repeat Steps 2–4 to add a line for each camera in the 0104 All Cameras bin.

Tip | Select Size from the Timecode menu to resize the Timecode window to fit your workspace.

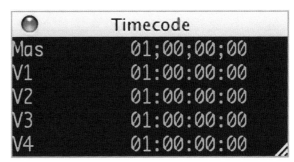

Figure 4-22. Timecode window after one line is added for each camera in the 0104 All Cameras bin.

In FIGURE 4-22, since there aren't any clips in the sequence, the tracks are displaying their default timecodes as non-drop-frame. Once clips are inserted into the sequence, the Timecode window will display colons or semicolons depending on the clip.

Modifying the Layout Sequence

Just as your workspace should be set up for easier navigation, so should your layout sequence. These steps prepare you for laying clips into the sequence in preparation for multigrouping.

To modify the layout sequence

1. Right-click in the Record monitor, and select Get Sequence Info (Mac: ⌘+I | PC: Ctrl+I).

2. In the Sequence Info dialog box that appears, in the Starting TC box, type the timecode of the first clip of the day (reference the information of from the task *To create the layout sequence*, Step 3, page 86), and then click OK.

Tip | Typing the desired timecode into the sequence's Start column in the bin can also change a sequence's Starting TC. (The Bin View menu must be set to Statistics to see the Start column heading.)

Note | Make sure you pay attention to whether the timecode of the first clip of the day is DF or NDF, and type semicolons or colons, respectively.

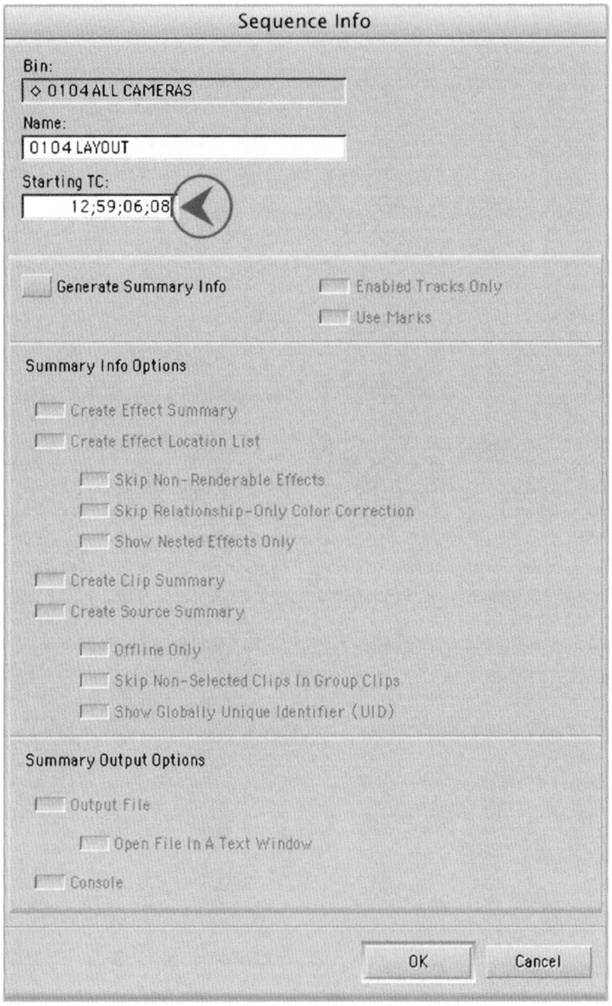

Figure 4-23. Sequence Info dialog box where you can enter the timecode of the first clip of the day in the Starting TC box.

3. In the 0104 All Cameras bin, double-click the first clip of the day, and then the clip appears in the Source monitor of the Composer window.

4. Mark Clip (press T).

Note | Only two audio tracks are used in the layout so that more cameras can be in the layout.

Since only 24 audio tracks can be placed in a sequence, if 2 audio tracks are used per camera, then you can lay out 12 cameras at a time; as opposed to using 4 audio tracks per camera and laying out only 6 cameras at a time.

Yes, there are shoots where 12 cameras are rolling at the same time!

5. Deselect audio tracks 3 and 4 (A3 and A4, respectively) if they are present. Only two audio tracks are needed for a layout.

6. Patch the source video and audio tracks to the desired record video and audio tracks. For example, if the first clip of the day was from camera B, patch the source tracks of the first clip to video track B (B) and audio tracks BB and BB (see FIGURE 4-24).

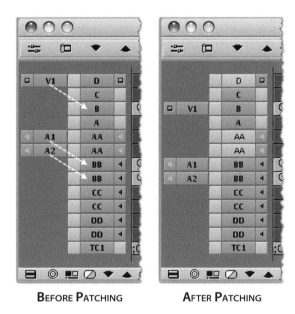

BEFORE PATCHING   **AFTER PATCHING**

Drag source track V1 to record track B.
Repeat for the other tracks.

Figure 4-24. Source video track 1 (V1) and source audio tracks 1 and 2 (A1 and A2, respectively) being patched to record video track B (B) and record audio tracks BB and BB.

When a clip is loaded into the Source monitor, it doesn't automatically patch to the desired record tracks. In FIGURE 4-24, source video track 1 (V1) is patched to record video track 4 (D) and source audio tracks A1 and A2 are patched to record audio tracks A1 and A2 (AA and AA), but the tracks should be patched to B, BB, and BB, respectively.

Tip | If you make a mistake, use the Undo command (Mac: ⌘+Z | PC: Ctrl+Z) and try again. You can undo up to 24 actions as long as the same sequence is loaded in the Timeline window.

7. Overwrite (press B) the clip to the sequence.

Figure 4-25. Timeline window displaying the first clip of the day from camera B overwritten to video track B (B) and audio tracks BB and BB.

8. Press Left Arrow to go backward one frame on this clip, and look in the Timecode window to see if the timecode of the clip matches the Mas timecode of the sequence, and then do one of the following:

   (a) If the timecode of the clip matches the Mas timecode of the sequence, proceed to Step 9.

   –or–

   (b) If the timecode of the clip does not match the Mas timecode of the sequence, undo the overwrite (Mac: ⌘+Z | PC: Ctrl+Z), and then repeat Steps 1–8.

> **Note |** When there are no other video clips in a sequence, all video tracks above a track with a clip in it will show that timecode.
>
> Conversely, any tracks below a track with a clip in it will not have timecode.
>
> This is an important concept to know because you could be looking at incorrect timecode if there isn't a clip on that particular video track.

Timecode	
Mas	12;59;47;06
V1	01:00:00:00
V2	12;59;47;06
V3	12;59;47;06
V4	12;59;47;06

Figure 4-26. Timecode window displaying the timecode *minus one frame* of the first clip overwritten to the sequence.

9. Click in the sequence, deselect all of the tracks in the sequence (Mac: Shift+⌘+A | PC: Shift+Ctrl+A), and then do one of the following:

   (a) If the topmost track of the sequence does not have a video clip in it, enable it.

–or–

(b) If the topmost track of the sequence has a video clip in it, enable the video track beneath it.

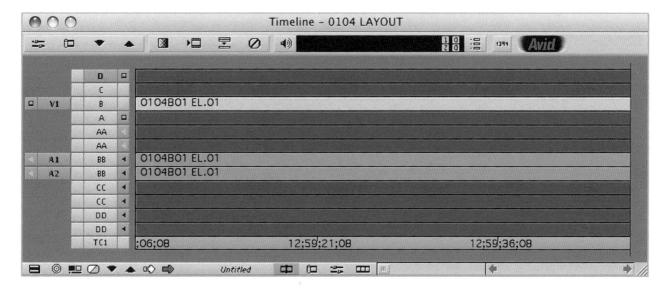

10. Press End to go to the end of the sequence.

11. Add Edit (press F8).

12. Trim Mode (press U), and a pink line (trim roller) appears.

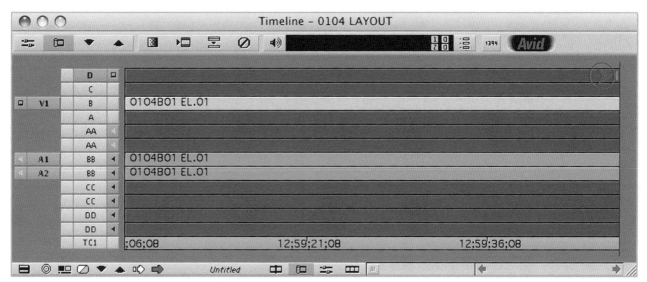

Figure 4-27. Timeline window in Trim mode displaying the pink trim roller.

The Source monitor and Record monitor will change to look like FIGURE 4-28 in Trim mode. Notice that the buttons beneath the monitors have changed and trim boxes have appeared.

Figure 4-28. The Composer window in Trim mode with the trim boxes highlighted.

> **Tip |** You will need to zoom out several times (Mac: ⌘+[| PC: Ctrl+[ ), so you have room to drag the pink line (trim roller) far enough to the right—that is, to trim the filler to the right.
>
> (Conversely, to zoom in press Mac: ⌘+] | PC: Ctrl+].)

13. Drag the pink line (trim roller) to the right until the timecode displayed in the Tracking Information menu (the timecode displayed next to Mas in the Record monitor) is later than the End timecode of the last clip of the day in the 0104 All Cameras bin (reference the information of *To create the layout sequence*, Step 6, page 88).

Adding filler (extra time) to the end of the sequence is necessary because a clip with a Start timecode of 13;07;29;21, for example, must be placed into a sequence at that exact timecode. It is impossible to lay this clip into the sequence at that point if that timecode doesn't exist in the sequence. Adding filler in this manner prevents you from having to place a clip on the sequence and manually move it down to a precise timecode.

Add filler to the end of the Timeline until there is enough filler on the sequence for all of the clips in the 0104 All Cameras bin to be placed on it. If the sequence is more than 24 hours, an error message may appear. In those instances, shorten the sequence until you no longer receive the error message.

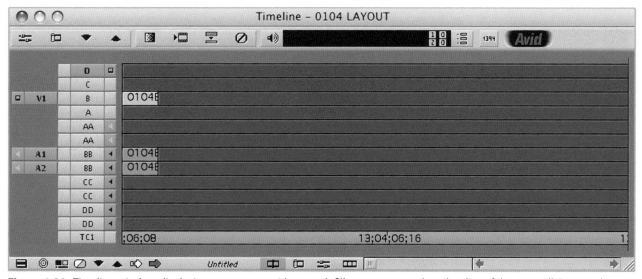

Figure 4-29. Timeline window displaying a sequence with enough filler to accommodate the clips of the 0104 All Cameras bin.

14. Trim Mode (press U) to exit the function.

15. Save the bin (Mac: ⌘+S | PC: Ctrl+S).

Laying Out the Clips

All of the day's clips have been accumulated into the 0104 All Cameras bin and a sequence with enough filler is ready for the clips to be placed into it.

Completing the layout is as simple as inserting each clip into the sequence at its Start timecode onto the correct tracks. For example, a clip that was shot on camera B from 13;04;32;10–13;04;45;17 would be cut into the layout beginning at 13;04;32;10 on video track B (B) and audio tracks BB.

To lay out the clips in the sequence

1. In the 0104 All Cameras bin, click the Name column heading to select the column as the sort criterion.

2. Sort the bin in ascending order based on the Name column (Mac: ⌘+E | PC: Ctrl+E).

   Sorting by Name rather than Start timecode is much more efficient for a layout. With the clips sorted by Name, all of the clips from the A cameras, B cameras, etc., will be sorted together, so the tracks will need to be patched only once for each camera.

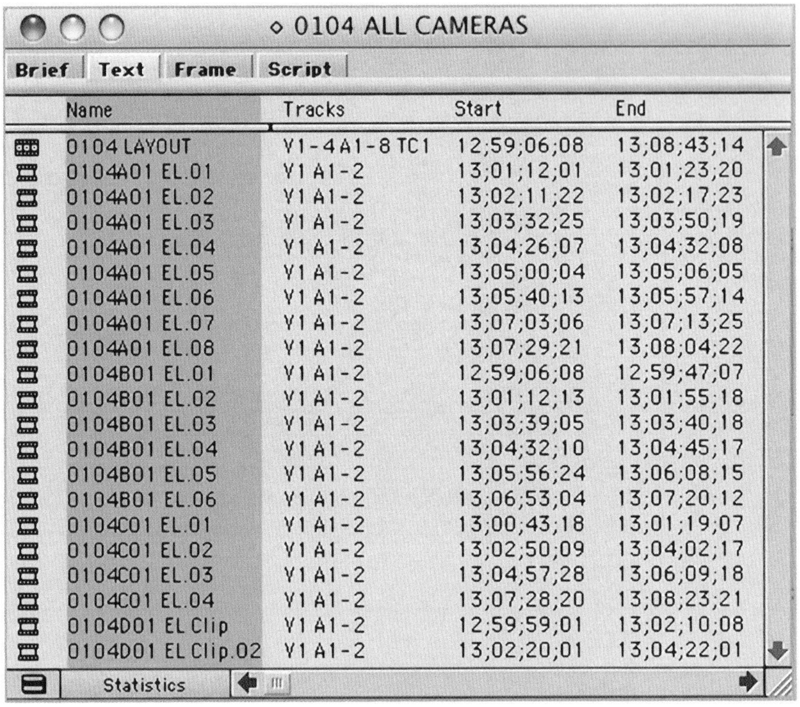
◇ 0104 ALL CAMERAS

Brief | Text | Frame | Script

Name	Tracks	Start	End
0104 LAYOUT	V1-4 A1-8 TC1	12;59;06;08	13;08;43;14
0104A01 EL.01	V1 A1-2	13;01;12;01	13;01;23;20
0104A01 EL.02	V1 A1-2	13;02;11;22	13;02;17;23
0104A01 EL.03	V1 A1-2	13;03;32;25	13;03;50;19
0104A01 EL.04	V1 A1-2	13;04;26;07	13;04;32;08
0104A01 EL.05	V1 A1-2	13;05;00;04	13;05;06;05
0104A01 EL.06	V1 A1-2	13;05;40;13	13;05;57;14
0104A01 EL.07	V1 A1-2	13;07;03;06	13;07;13;25
0104A01 EL.08	V1 A1-2	13;07;29;21	13;08;04;22
0104B01 EL.01	V1 A1-2	12;59;06;08	12;59;47;07
0104B01 EL.02	V1 A1-2	13;01;12;13	13;01;55;18
0104B01 EL.03	V1 A1-2	13;03;39;05	13;03;40;18
0104B01 EL.04	V1 A1-2	13;04;32;10	13;04;45;17
0104B01 EL.05	V1 A1-2	13;05;56;24	13;06;08;15
0104B01 EL.06	V1 A1-2	13;06;53;04	13;07;20;12
0104C01 EL.01	V1 A1-2	13;00;43;18	13;01;19;07
0104C01 EL.02	V1 A1-2	13;02;50;09	13;04;02;17
0104C01 EL.03	V1 A1-2	13;04;57;28	13;06;09;18
0104C01 EL.04	V1 A1-2	13;07;28;20	13;08;23;21
0104D01 EL Clip	V1 A1-2	12;59;59;01	13;02;10;08
0104D01 EL Clip.02	V1 A1-2	13;02;20;01	13;04;22;01

Statistics

Figure 4-30. 0104 All Cameras bin after sorting the Name column.

Note | See *To create the layout sequence*, Step 3, page 86.

3. Do one of the following:

   (a) If the first clip in the bin sorted by Name is also the first clip of the day, double-click the *second clip* in the bin.

   –or–

   (b) If the first clip in the bin sorted by Name is not the first clip of the day, double-click the *first clip* in the bin.

4. Mark Clip (press T).

5. Deselect source audio tracks 3 and 4 (A3 and A4, respectively) if they are present.

Tip | See *To modify the layout sequence*, Steps 6–7 and Figure 4-24, page 93, for patching instructions.

6. Patch the source video and audio tracks to the desired record video and audio tracks.

7. Click in the Record monitor, and then type the Start timecode of the clip (you do not need to type semicolons or colons).

   The Start timecode displays in the Start column of the clip in the bin. It is also present at the top of the Composer window if the First (lower) Row of Info check box or the Second Row of Info check box is selected. These two settings can be modified to display some of the information displayed in the Timecode window. It's limiting because it only displays two timecodes, but it's very helpful because you don't have to look in the Timecode window for often-used timecode information.

8. Press Enter to move the position indicator to that timecode.

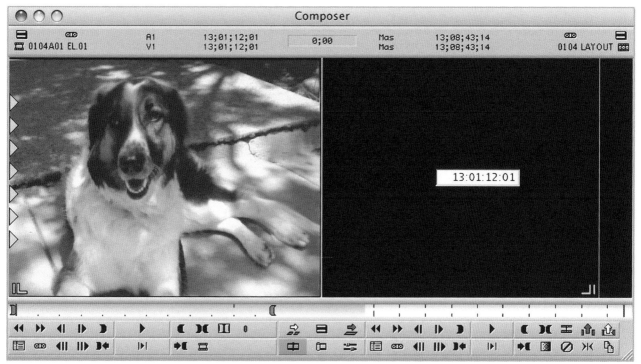

Figure 4-31. The Composer window displaying the typed-in timecode to move the position indicator (Record monitor) to overwrite the next clip from the 0104 All Cameras bin to the sequence (Source monitor).

9. Overwrite (press B) the clip into the sequence.

10. Press Left Arrow to go backward one frame on this clip, and look in the Timecode window to see if the timecode of the clip matches the Mas timecode of the sequence, and then do one of the following:

    (a) If the timecode of the clip matches the Mas timecode of the sequence, proceed to Step 11.

    –or–

    (b) If the clip's timecode does not match the Mas timecode of the sequence, do the following:

        (i) Undo the Overwrite in Step 9 (Mac: ⌘+Z | PC: Ctrl+Z).

        (ii) Repeat Steps 7–9.

11. Repeat Steps 3–10 for the remaining clips in the 0104 All Cameras bin while making sure that the correct clips are placed on the correct video and audio tracks.

12. Click the 0104 All Cameras bin and make sure that nothing is selected (Mac: Shift+⌘+A | PC: Shift+Ctrl+A).

13. Click the sequence in the bin.

14. Click the 0104 All Cameras Bin Fast menu and choose Select Media Relatives, and then do one of the following:

    (a) If all of the clips in the bin are selected, proceed to Step 15.

    –or–

    (b) If all of the clips in the bin are not selected, make note of the unselected clips, and then repeat Steps 3–10 until all clips are present in the sequence.

> **Note** | Track colors are visible when there are clips in the Timeline, and since there are clips in the sequence, this is the perfect time to modify the track colors.

15. Modify the track colors. See *Settings Needed: Timeline Fast Menu Settings: Track Color* on page 81 for instructions.

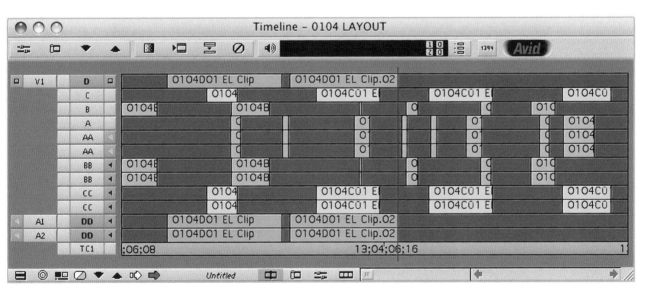

Figure 4-32. Timeline window displaying a finished layout with track colors modified to show relationships between video clips and their corresponding audio clips at a glance.

16. Save the bin (Mac: ⌘+S | PC: Ctrl+S).

Addressing Special Layout Circumstances

While doing a multigrouping layout, there will be clips that will not have time-of-day (TOD) timecode or the layout will include both DF and NDF clips. At first glance, it will seem impossible to find out where these clips are supposed to be placed. Fortunately, there are deductive steps that can be taken to discover where they truly belong.

CLIPS WITHOUT TOD TIMECODE

Clips that don't have TOD timecode can be very difficult to place into a sequence. You won't have a frame of reference as to where the clips are supposed to go. Was the tape shot during the day or night? Is that footage from a different location? Are there tape logs from the shoot? It all boils down to persistence and patience—and a considerable amount of time.

CLIPS IN DROP-FRAME/NON-DROP-FRAME TIMECODE

Clips that don't have the same timecode type are very easy to place in a sequence if you can assume that the timecode is correct other than the DF/NDF issue. Beware because although the timecode will be exact initially, later in the sequence it will start to drift. For now, place the clips into the sequence, and this issue will be addressed later in the multigrouping process in *Add Editing: Assigning Auxiliary Timecode to Clips* on page 121.

Eventing

It is possible to take an entire day's group and have one person finish the group entirely by themselves. This would take a considerable amount of time, and it is why most layouts are split into smaller, manageable portions—this process is known as *eventing*—so several people can work on a group simultaneously.

To split the layout into manageable portions (eventing)

1. In the bin, click the 0104 Layout sequence.

2. Duplicate the layout sequence (Mac: ⌘+D | PC: Ctrl+D), and then rename it 0104 Event.

3. Double-click the 0104 Event sequence.

4. Select all of the tracks in the sequence (Mac: ⌘+A | PC: Ctrl+A).

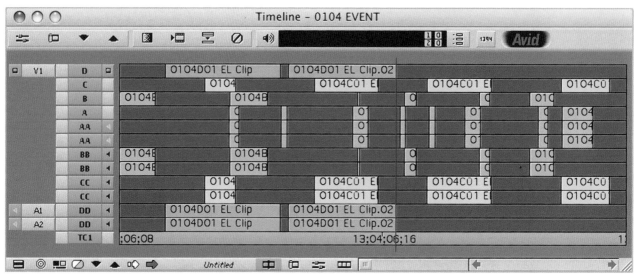

Figure 4-33. Timeline window displaying the 0104 Event sequence with all of the tracks selected.

5. Do one of the following:

   (a) If the layout does not cross midnight, proceed to Step 6.

   –or–

   (b) If the layout does cross midnight, type in the timecode "00;00;00;00" and Add Edit (press F8). (Since all of the tracks are selected, the add edit is placed through all of the tracks.)

   The first add edit must be placed at the midnight break (if the cameras for that day crossed over to the next day). Avid doesn't know if a camera shot at 00;01;20;33 was shot before or after 23;50;30;15, but based on the tape naming, you would know 00;01;20;33 was before 23;50;30;15. By placing an add edit point at midnight, those clips are automatically placed into their own multigrouping section and thus avoiding any timecode issues.

6. Look at the rest of the sequence and see if there are any natural camera breaks (that is, when all of the cameras are simultaneously not filming).

   It is customary to avoid placing an add edit in a multigrouping section that will have clips that cross over from one group to another. Clips that cross over from one section to another have to be dealt with very carefully, and it is wise to avoid this situation at all costs—although sometimes it is unavoidable.

7. Place the position indicator on a natural camera break.

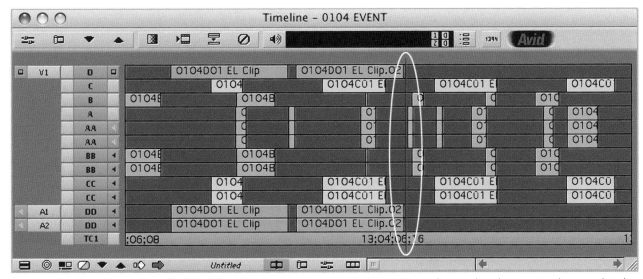

Figure 4-34. Timeline window displaying the 0104 Event sequence with the position indicator placed on a natural camera break.

8. Add Edit (press F8).

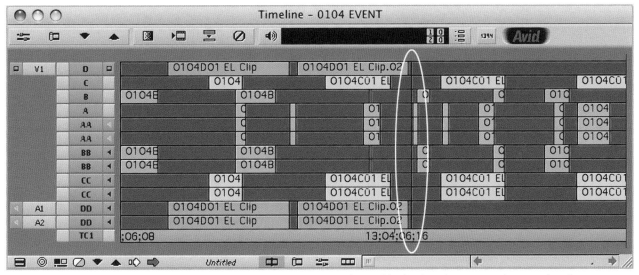

Figure 4-35. Timeline window displaying the 0104 Event sequence with an add edit placed on a natural camera break.

> **Note** | Three to four hour multigrouping sections are customary for a six-camera show.
>
> A show with more than six cameras should have shorter multigrouping sections; conversely, a show with less than six cameras should have longer multigrouping sections.

9. Continue placing add edits in the sequence until the sequence has been divided and each multigrouping section is about three to four hours long.

10. Move the position indicator to one of the evented sections.

11. Mark Clip (press T) in one of the multigrouping sections.

12. Confirm that all of the tracks are still selected.

Note | When a sequence is subclipped, it is referred to as a *subsequence.*

13. Subclip (press F7) that sequence into its own subsequence.

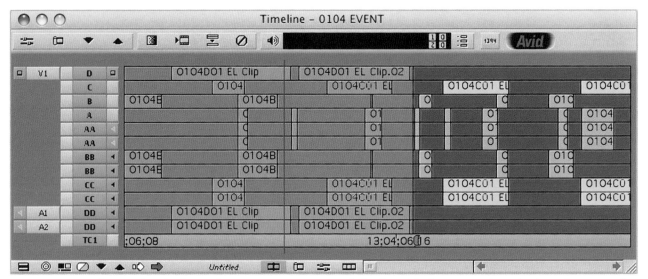

Figure 4-36. Timeline window displaying the 0104 Event sequence with the first add edit section selected—this is the section that will be its own subsequence.

Tip | Two other ways to subclip are as follows:

◆ To drag the sequence icon in the upper right corner of the Record monitor to the sequence in the bin.

◆ Mac: Option+Drag | PC: Alt+Drag from anywhere in the Record monitor to the bin.

Subclipping takes a section of a larger clip or sequence and makes it into its own separate smaller clip, or subclip, to save in a bin. These multigrouping sections must be separated from the larger sequence so multiple users can simultaneously group. When created, a subclip has ".sub.01" appended to the clip name.

14. Rename the subsequence according to the Start timecode of the first clip in the subsequence and the End timecode of the last clip in the subsequence (for example, 0104 Group 1 12;59 - 13;04).

When filming, the A camera may not be the first camera filming for the day. It could be D, G, or I camera, but the all-camming process is a lot more organized if you start from A and go in alphabetical order.

The examples show A camera starting at 13;01;12;01 because all-camming is completed in alphabetical order. The first group is labeled starting at 12;59 because that was the first clip of the day, not necessarily from A camera.

Tip | Putting the time range of the multigroup in the name makes it easier to find the needed group.

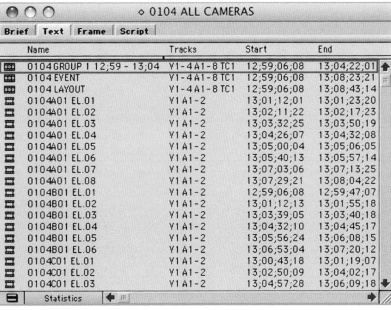

Figure 4-37. 0104 All Cameras bin displaying the subsequence 0104 Group 1 12;59 - 13;04.

Note | It is a good idea to create subsequences because the original layout sequence is preserved if you need to refer back to it.

15. Create a bin for the subsequence (Mac: ⌘+N | PC: Ctrl+N).

16. Rename the new bin exactly as the subsequence, and then press Enter.

17. Copy the subsequence into the new bin (Mac: Option+Drag | PC: Alt+Drag).

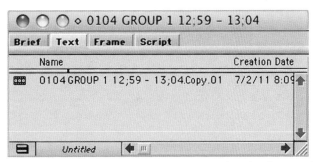

Figure 4-38. 0104 Group 1 12;59 - 13;04 bin displaying the 0104 Group 1 12;59 - 13;04 subsequence.

18. Remove ".Copy.01" from the end of the subsequence name.

19. Click the 0104 All Cameras bin.

20. Repeat Steps 10–19 (the subsequence and bin creation process) for the remaining events.

21. Click in the Project window to save all the bins (Mac: ⌘+S | PC: Ctrl+S).

Coloring Crossover Clips

With the subsequences in bins by themselves, it is possible for several people to work on a day's groups. This is an important reason why crossover clips should be avoided because it is difficult for two people to work on groups that contain crossover clips. However, if it can't be avoided, users must be alerted to their presence by coloring/identifying those clips.

Our example doesn't have crossover clips, but this section shows you the process if your sequence does.

To color crossover clips

1. Place the position indicator over one of the crossover clips.

2. Deselect all of the tracks except for the video track containing the crossover clip.

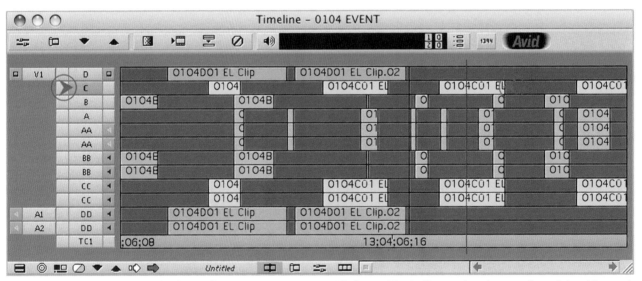

Figure 4-39. Timeline window displaying the 0104 Event sequence with the position indicator placed over a clip and the video track containing the clip selected.

3. Match Frame (press F4).

    Match Frame matches to the topmost selected track. To Match Frame the clip on video track C, for example, all tracks above video track C must be deselected.

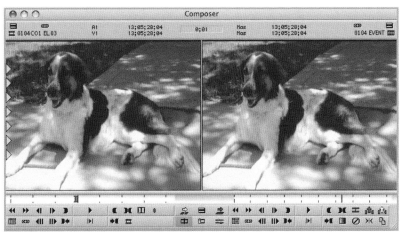

Figure 4-40. Composer window displaying the result of using the Match Frame command on the clip in the selected video track over which the position indicator is placed in the Timeline window of Figure 4-39, page 106. The Match Frame command loads the exact frame of that clip in the Source monitor.

Note | Click Find Bin to open the bin and highlight the clip that is loaded in the Source monitor or Record monitor.

There are two Find Bin buttons (one each for the Source monitor and the Record monitor) located in the Composer window, in the second row of the bottom toolbar.

(When using Match Frame, click Find Bin under the Source monitor to find the clip in the bin. To find a sequence's bin, click Find Bin under the Record monitor.)

4. Click Find Bin 🔳 and the clip is highlighted in the bin.

5. Select Edit≫Set Clip Color.

6. Select Cyan (for example).

7. Repeat Steps 1–6 until all crossover clips are colored.

The clip will be colored in the bin, event sequence, and event subsequence. If the color doesn't change in your sequence, make sure you have Source colors selected in the Timeline Fast menu. (See *Settings Needed: Timeline Fast Menu Settings—Clip Color (Source selected)* on page 80 for details.)

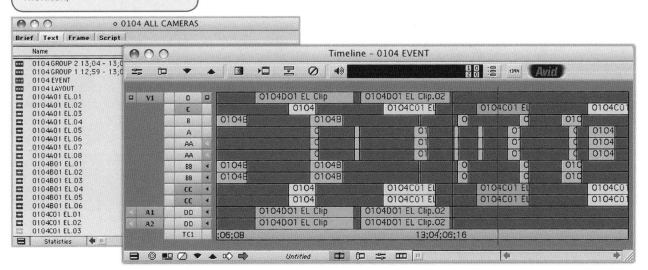

Figure 4-41. Timeline window displaying the same clip color as that of the corresponding clip in the project bin.

Syncing

While out on a shoot, all of the cameras are set up so that they record TOD timecode. If the time that the cameras start recording is 01:09 a.m., recording TOD timecode helps to ensure that all of the cameras will have timecodes of 01;09;00;00. Despite this plan, cameras can be as little as one frame and up to several hours off from one another. Assistant editors have to make up for this inaccuracy by nudging clips in the sequence until they all match up. The process of getting the clips in the sequence to all match up is called *syncing*.

Syncing is very tedious and complex, and it can take several hours. Fortunately, the secret to flawless multigrouping is focus. If you can stay focused during the entire syncing process, it is highly unlikely that there will be any mistakes.

To sync the clips

1. Open the bin containing the subsequence.

2. Click the event subsequence.

3. Duplicate the event subsequence (Mac: ⌘+D | PC: Ctrl+D).

4. Rename the sequence 0104 Group 1 12;59 - 13;04 Sync.

5. Double-click the 0104 Group 1 12;59 - 13;04 Sync sequence, and it loads in the Timeline.

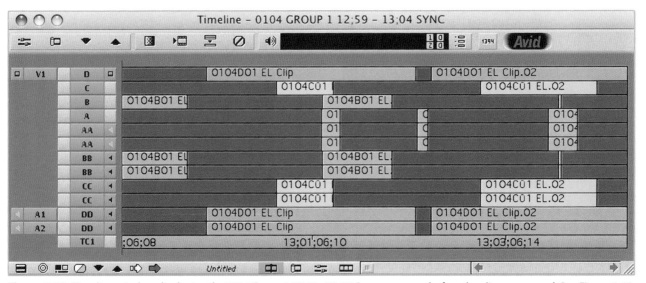

Figure 4-42. Timeline window displaying the 0104 Group 1 12;59 - 13; 04 Sync sequence before the clips are synced. See Figure 4-48, page 115, for the Timeline window of the sequence with all of the clips in sync.

6. Identify the first set of clips that need to be synced. This should be the first place where two or more clips overlap. In this example, there is a section where tracks A-D all overlap.

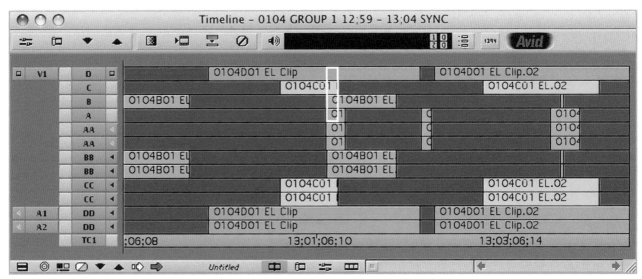

Figure 4-43. Timeline window displaying the 0104 Group 1 12;59 - 13; 04 Sync sequence identifying a section where tracks A-D all overlap.

7. Click the Timeline Fast menu.

8. Select Audio Data.

9. Select Sample Plot.

10. Mark IN (press I) and OUT (press O) points at the beginning of the out-of-sync clips and a little later in the sequence.

This draws the audio waveforms on each track. If your settings are correct, the waveforms only appear between the IN and OUT points. (If not, press Mac: ⌘+. [press period key] | PC: Ctrl+. [press period key] to stop the spinning wheel, and then see *Settings Needed: Timeline Settings Dialog Box: Display Tab: Show Marked Waveforms* on page 78.)

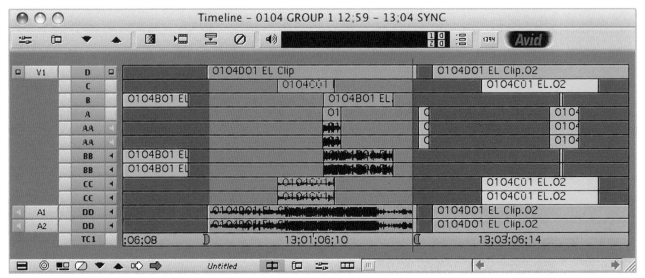

Figure 4-44. Timeline window displaying the 0104 Group 1 12;59 - 13;04 Sync sequence with the audio waveforms displayed between Mark IN and OUT points.

11. Locate similar looking waveforms (if there are any) on the audio tracks.

Cameras frequently film in the same location, and the audio in these situations will display identifiable patterns. It should be clear which cameras have matching audio, although many times it is necessary to use your ears. Play portions of clips to see if you hear the same words or sounds to help determine what clips to sync to one another.

Some shoots will help you sync because right before shooting a scene (but after cameras are filming) there will be a short but loud sound such as a clap, beep, or a door slam to make syncing easier. This distinct sound will have a very identifiable pattern in the audio waveforms and make syncing a lot faster. In the event this isn't the practice of your company, there are two actions that can help with finding audio points to sync to—soloing tracks and scrubbing.

Soloing Tracks—Sequences can contain numerous video and audio tracks and sometimes you will want to view or hear just one or two. It is possible to deselect all of the tracks and select the few that are needed, or you can solo out, or isolate, the tracks while leaving the rest selected. Press ⌘ (Mac) | Ctrl (PC) while clicking the speaker or video monitor of the track—it will turn green allowing you to hear or see only those soloed tracks.

Scrubbing—Scrubbing involves dragging the position indicator through the sequence to hear the audio at (usually) slower speeds than playing it. Make sure Caps Lock is enabled on your keyboard to hear the audio as you drag the position indicator through the sequence.

12. Place the position indicator at the moment of the similar audio pattern.

13. Solo one of the audio tracks of that clip (Mac: ⌘+Click | PC: Ctrl+Click).

14. Zoom in to that point (Mac: ⌘+] | PC: Ctrl+]).

15. Play the audio of that clip, and then stop playing at a distinct and memorable sound.

16. Deselect all of the tracks (Mac: Shift+⌘+A | PC: Shift+Ctrl+A).

17. Enable the video track that corresponds with the to-be-synced audio.

18. Add a Locator (press F10) at the moment of the possible sync point.

19. Deselect the first video track.

> **Note** | Be sure that the locators are placed exactly on the same sound on each track. Soloing and scrubbing frame by frame will help isolate the sound.
>
> Note that the locator will be added to the topmost selected track only, so pay attention to where you are adding the locators.
>
> It is customary to place locators on the video tracks only, as the audio tracks will eventually be deleted.

20. Zoom out from that point (Mac: ⌘+[| PC: Ctrl+[).

21. Unsolo the audio track (Mac: ⌘+Click | PC: Ctrl+Click).

22. Place the position indicator at the moment of the matching audio pattern.

23. Solo one of the audio tracks of that clip (Mac: ⌘+Click | PC: Ctrl+Click).

24. Zoom in to that point (Mac: ⌘+] | PC: Ctrl+]).

25. Play the audio of that clip and stop playing at a distinct and memorable sound.

   Multigrouping isn't always a neat process. Sometimes when you think you have found the matching audio for a clip, it isn't what you are looking for. Just remember to listen to other clips to see if they will sync to the first sound or moment that you are syncing to. Finding the correct clip to sync to is determined by how close the clips' timecodes match one another. The further off they are, the more you will have to search for the matching clips.

26. Deselect all of the tracks (Mac: Shift+⌘+A | PC: Shift+Ctrl+A).

27. Enable the video track that corresponds with the to-be-synced audio.

28. Add a Locator (press F10), at the moment of the possible sync point.

29. Zoom out from that point (Mac: ⌘+[| PC: Ctrl+[).

30. Click Lift/Overwrite Segment Mode ⟹ .

    Click Lift/Overwrite Segment Mode to click a clip in a sequence and move it around in the sequence. The Lift/Overwrite Segment Mode button is located in the Timeline window, on the bottom toolbar.

31. Shift+Click one of the video clips *and* its corresponding audio.

32. Move the clip until it is in sync with the clip being synced to. It may be necessary to move the position indicator and zoom in to the sequence to precisely match up the audio waveforms.

    If a clip only needs to be moved over a few frames, use the Trim Frame buttons on your keyboard—they are identified in FIGURE 4-45.

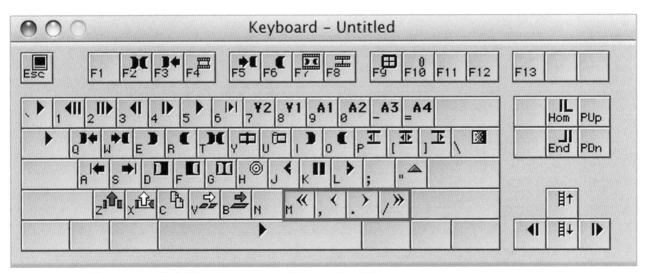

Figure 4-45. Avid Keyboard with the Trim Frame command buttons identified.

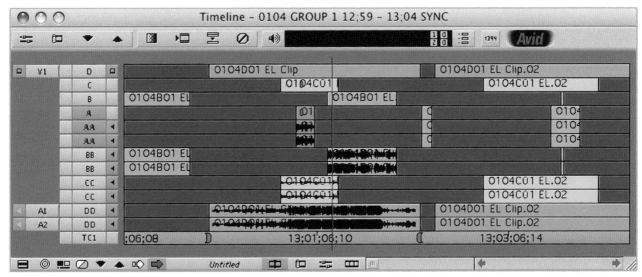

Figure 4-46. Timeline window displaying the 0104 Group 1 12;59 - 13; 04 Sync sequence showing clips being synced with locators, audio waveforms, and soloed audio track as syncing tools.

> **Tip** | Another way to exit the Lift/Overwrite Segment Mode function and other tools is to click in the Timecode bar in the Timeline window.

33. Click Lift/Overwrite Segment Mode to exit the function.

34. Place the position indicator before the synced point.

35. Solo the audio tracks of the clips that have been synced.

36. Play (press L) and listen. The clips should be perfectly in sync (if they are not, see *To fix sync as you go* below).

37. Look for the next clip without a locator.

38. Repeat Steps 10–37 until all clips are in sync and have locators.

To fix sync as you go

The clips should be in sync, but if you hear some strange echoes, something is out of sync. Fortunately, this is an easy fix. Remember that sometimes you won't be able to hear both tracks at once if one track is significantly louder than the other.

1. Place the position indicator at the synced point.

2. Zoom in to that point (Mac: ⌘+] | PC: Ctrl+]).

3. Look at the waveforms to see what is out of sync.

4. Click Lift/Overwrite Segment Mode.

5. Shift+Click one of the video clips and its corresponding audio tracks.

6. Press the Trim Frame buttons (see FIGURE 4-45 on page 112) until the clip is in sync with the other video clips.

7. Click Lift/Overwrite Segment Mode to exit the function.

This fine-tuning should leave the two clips in perfect sync with one another; however, there is another check you can do while syncing just to make sure that the clips are in sync: playing the video of one camera while listening to the audio of another. (This will only work if you can see the lips of a person talking.)

8. Solo one of the synced video tracks (Mac: ⌘+Click | PC: Ctrl+Click).

9. Solo the audio tracks of the other synced clip (Mac: ⌘+Click | PC: Ctrl+Click).

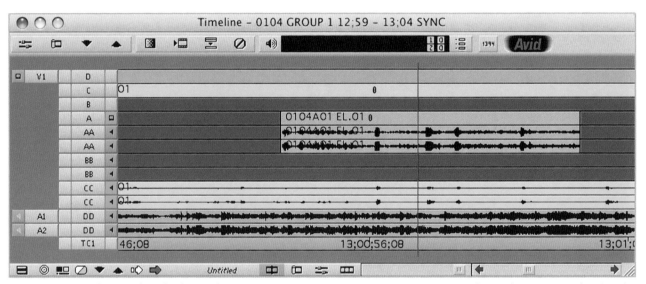

Figure 4-47. Timeline window displaying the 0104 Group 1 12;59 - 13;03 Sync sequence zoomed in to the sequence showing the audio waveforms in sync with one another. Note that the locators are not perfectly aligned because locators put you in the ballpark. Waveforms always supersede locators!

10. Play (press L) to view the video of a clip while listening to the audio of another clip.

For example, play back the video of camera A while listening to the audio of camera C.

Remember, all of these checks don't need to be performed but at least one should be to make sure the clips are synced correctly. It cannot be stressed enough that fixing incorrectly synced clips is a very time-consuming process that sometimes necessitates syncing an entire sequence from the very beginning.

11. Unsolo the video and audio clips (Mac: ⌘+Click | PC: Ctrl+Click).

Tip | This is a good time to take a look at Appendix 4: *Multigrouping Helpful Hints* on page 327.

12. Zoom out from that point (Mac: ⌘+[| PC: Ctrl+[).

Figure 4-48. Timeline window displaying the 0104 Group 1 12;59 - 13; 04 Sync sequence *after* the clips are synced. See Figure 4-42 for the Timeline window that displays the sequence before the clips are synced. (Figure 4-42 is repeated below for easy comparison.)

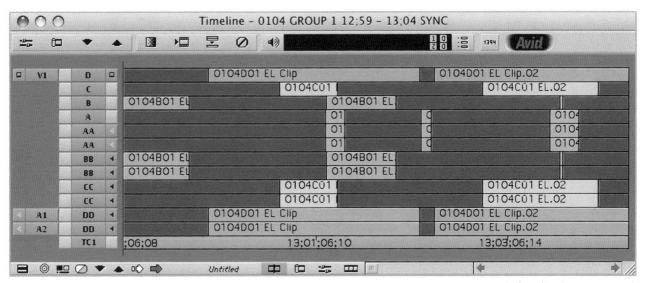

Figure 4-42. (Repeated) Timeline window displaying the 0104 Group 1 12;59 - 13; 04 Sync sequence *before* the clips are synced. See Figure 4-48 (above) for the Timeline window of the sequence after the clips are synced.

13. Click the Timeline Fast menu.

14. Select Audio Data.

15. Select None.

16. Save the bin (Mac: ⌘+S | PC: Ctrl+S).

Special Syncing Circumstances

This method of laying all of the clips from all of the bins into a group comes with minor issues. There are certain clips that shouldn't stay within a group because they don't belong there. These clips are junk, interview, and surveillance clips.

JUNK CLIPS

Junk clips are clips that would never be usable as video. This includes color bars and tone, video shots where the camera is drastically moving around (make sure there isn't usable audio on that clip), or the clip is very short. When these clips are encountered in a group, they should be removed from the sequence.

To remove junk clips from the sequence

1. Deselect all of the tracks (Mac: Shift+⌘+A | PC: Shift+Ctrl+A).

2. Enable the video and audio tracks where the clip is.

3. Place the position indicator directly over the clip.

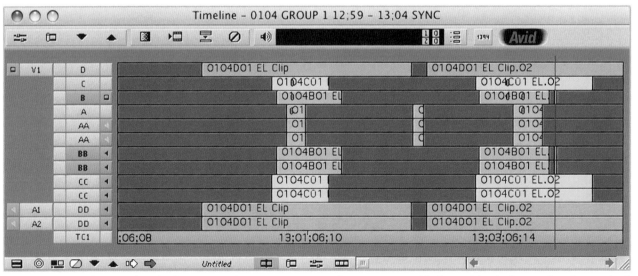

Figure 4-49. Timeline window displaying 0104 Group 1 12;59 - 13;04 Sync sequence with the position indicator placed over a junk clip and its video and audio tracks enabled.

4. Mark Clip (press T).

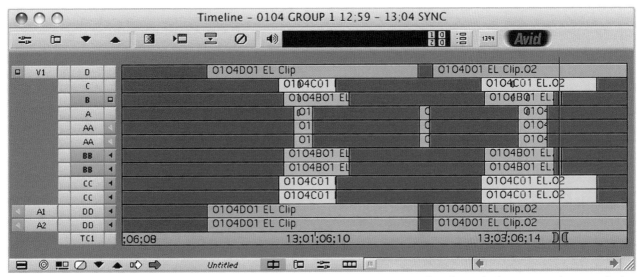

Figure 4-50. Timeline window displaying 0104 Group 1 12;59 - 13;04 Sync sequence after the Mark Clip command was applied to the junk clip.

> **Note** | Lift (press Z) removes a clip from a sequence and leaves space where the clip previously was. Extract (press X) removes a clip from a sequence and shifts all the enabled tracks down.

5. Lift (press Z) the clip out of the sequence.

6. Clear Both Marks (press G).

Figure 4-51. Timeline window displaying 0104 Group 1 12;59 - 13;04 Sync sequence with the junk clip removed using the Lift command. The Lift command removes a marked clip and leaves a space where the clip previously was.

INTERVIEW CLIPS

The number of interviews filmed depends on the type of show you are working on. If your show has interviews of 2 people, it wouldn't be a problem to include the 2 interviews in the groups; however, a show that has interviews of 16 people would be a bit too big for inclusion in the groups and should be removed before the multigroup is created. Check with your company's guidelines to see if interviews are included in their groups.

SURVEILLANCE CLIPS

Surveillance clips come in various forms—home, phone, and car surveillance are the three most common. These cameras are used to get those portions of action that are difficult to film with a traditional camera crew. These cameras may or may not be wired for sound and may not have TOD timecode, and that can make multigrouping very difficult.

Any of these types of surveillance may have moments when there is nothing being filmed other than a wall or something that probably won't be used in the show. The camera may have been left filming on something insignificant, but audio may be going to this camera. In the event the camera is left running and there isn't any audio, it is okay to leave a small portion of the clip and lift the unwanted portion.

PROS AND CONS

There is a school of thought that all clips should be sorted before multigrouping so that junk, interview, and surveillance clips can be discovered, sorted, and removed before they appear in a group layout. However, the number of these clips in proportion to the amount of groupable footage is minute. It isn't uncommon for companies to have their assistant editors label (above and beyond tape naming) all of the clips associated with a show. This takes a considerable amount of time that takes away from multigrouping, which can be a very important component of editing. Whatever route your company chooses to take, you are now aware of both.

Add Editing

Add edits break the sequence into the individual groups that will make up the multigroup. They need to be placed throughout the sequence.

To place add edits throughout the sequence

1. Click the sync subsequence in the bin.

2. Duplicate the sync sequence (Mac: ⌘+D | PC: Ctrl+D).

3. Rename the sequence by replacing "Sync" with "Add Edit": 0104 Group 1 12;59 - 13;04 Add Edit.

4. Double-click the add edit sequence.

5. Deselect all tracks (Mac: Shift+⌘+A | PC: Shift+Ctrl+A).

6. Select all of the audio tracks.

Tip | If you click a track while pressing Shift, you can drag up or down to select multiple tracks.

7. Press Delete, and in the Delete Track dialog box that appears, click OK, and the sequence should only have video tracks now.

Figure 4-52. Delete Track dialog box.

8. Select all of the tracks of the sequence (Mac: ⌘+A | PC: Ctrl+A).

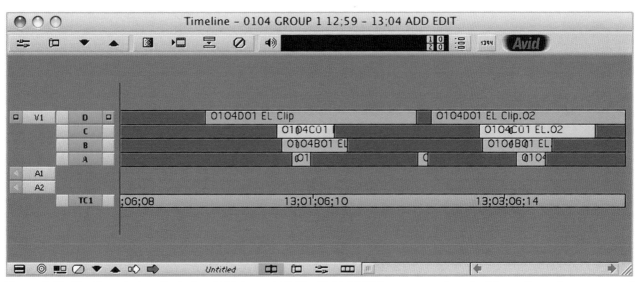

Figure 4-53. Timeline window displaying 0104 Group 1 12;59 - 13;04 Add Edit sequence after all of the audio tracks are removed and all of the remaining tracks selected.

9. Snap to the head of the clip closest to the beginning of the sequence (Mac: ⌘+Click | PC: Ctrl+Click).

10. Focus (press H) to zoom in.

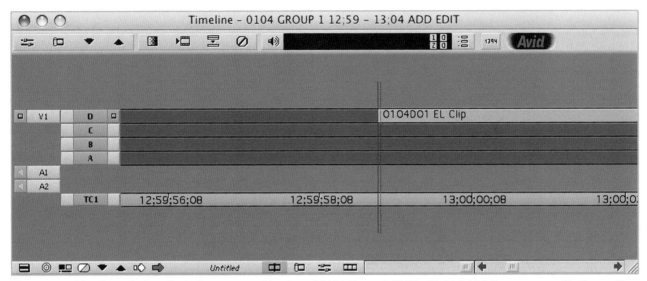

Figure 4-54. Timeline window displaying a zoomed-in view of 0104 Group 1 12;59 - 13;04 Add Edit sequence with the position indicator snapped to the head of the clip closest to the beginning of the sequence.

11. Place an Add Edit (press F8) through all of the tracks.

12. Focus (press H) to zoom out.

13. Scrub to the head of the next clip (Mac: ⌘+Drag | PC: Ctrl+Drag). (Make sure Caps Lock is enabled on your keyboard to hear the audio during scrubbing.)

14. Repeat Steps 9–13 until the entire sequence has all of the necessary add edits.

> **Note** | Make sure the position indicator is at the head of the clip. It is a common mistake to think a location is the head of a clip, if you are zoomed out too far.
>
> Zooming in each time will make sure add edits are placed in the correct place, especially if two clips start close to one another.

Figure 4-55. Timeline window displaying 0104 Group 1 12;59 - 13;04 Add Edit sequence with add edits through all of the tracks placed at the head of each clip.

Assigning Auxiliary Timecode to Clips

During the syncing process, some of the clips on the video and audio tracks may have been moved, and it is necessary to assign new timecode to the clips. This new timecode is called *auxiliary timecode*.

To assign auxiliary timecode to clips

1. Click the group bin.

2. Click the Bin Fast menu.

3. Select Set Bin Display.

> **Note** | When Show reference clips is selected, all of the clips that are contained in a sequence are displayed in the bin.

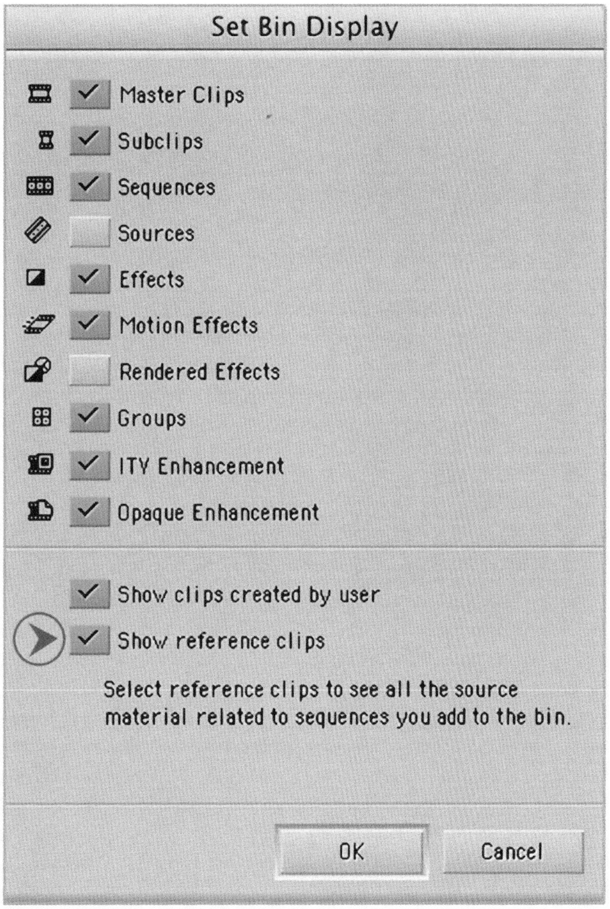

4. In the Set Bin Display dialog box that appears, select the Show reference clips check box, and then click OK.

Figure 4-56. Set Bin Display dialog box.

5. Click the Bin Fast menu.

6. Select Headings.

7. Click All/None *twice*.

8. Select only Auxiliary TC1, Mark In, and Start.

9. Click OK.

10. Drag the Resize box, if necessary, to scale the size of the bin so that all three column headings are visible.

11. Go to the sequence and enable the track with the clip closest to the start of the sequence.

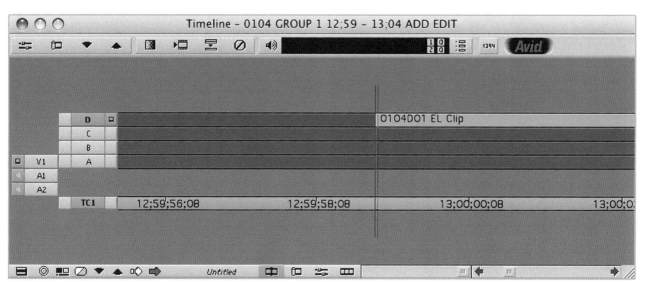

Figure 4-57. Timeline window displaying 0104 Group 1 12;59 - 13;04 Add Edit sequence with the track of the clip closest to the start of the sequence enabled.

12. Snap to go the first add edit point (Mac: ⌘+Click | PC: Ctrl+Click).

13. Focus (press H) to make sure the position indicator is at the very beginning of the clip.

14. Match Frame (press F4), and the exact frame of that clip loads in the Source monitor.

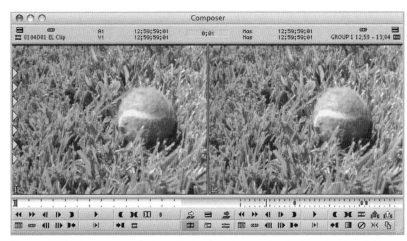

Figure 4-58. Composer window displaying the result of using the Match Frame command on the clip in the selected video track over which the position indicator is placed in the Timeline window of Figure 4-57 on page 122. The Match Frame command loads the exact frame of that clip in the Source monitor.

15. Click Find Bin and that clip is highlighted in the group bin.

    If this step is done correctly, you will know for certain that you are at the head of a clip because the clip Mark IN time in the bin will be exactly the same time as the Start time of the clip. If there is any discrepancy, you are not at the head of the clip.

    It is imperative that you are at the head of the clip when placing auxiliary timecode on the clips in the bin.

16. Click the Timeline window to load the Mas timecode in the Timecode window.

17. Look at the Mas timecode in the Timecode window.

> **Note |** The Mas timecode is the same as the clip's timecode because this clip wasn't moved in the sequence.

Timecode	
Mas	12;59;59;01
V1	01:00:00:00
V2	01:00:00:00
V3	01:00:00:00
V4	12;59;59;01

Figure 4-59. Timecode window displaying the Mas timecode.

18. Type that Mas timecode in the Auxiliary TC1 column of that clip (the clip highlighted by the Find Bin function).

    If there are DF and NDF clips, this is the time to account for those differences. Depending on whether the multigroup is DF or NDF, type semicolons or colons, respectively, for the clips that need to be switched. They should be switched to whatever format the sequence is.

19. Press Enter.

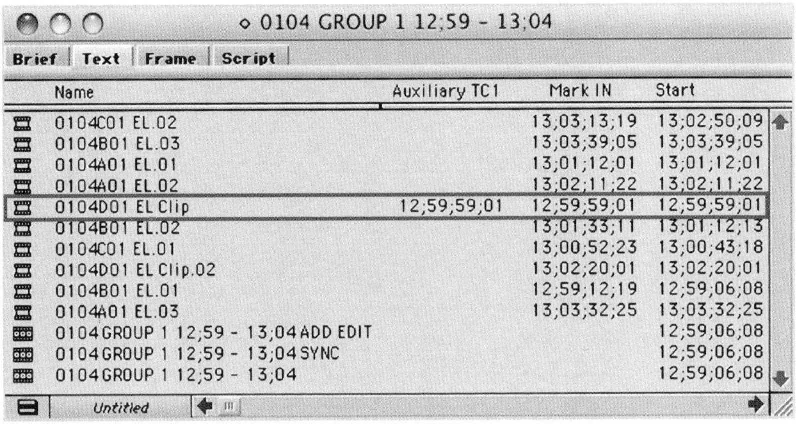

Figure 4-60. The 0104 Group 1 12;59 - 13;04 bin displaying the clip with auxiliary timecode assigned to it. Since this clip wasn't moved during the syncing process, its auxiliary timecode and start timecode are the same.

20. Go back to the sequence and snap to the head of the next clip in the current track (Mac: ⌘+Click | PC: Ctrl+Click).

21. Repeat Steps 13–20 until all of the clips for that track have auxiliary timecode assigned to them.

22. When one track is complete, disable one track, enable the next track, and repeat Steps 11–21 until all of the clips have auxiliary timecode assigned to them.

23. Save the bin (Mac: ⌘+S | PC: Ctrl+S).

> **Tip** | Make sure you are at the very beginning of the clip before assigning the timecode!
>
> And don't miss any small clips because you are zoomed out too far!

Subclipping

After placing the add edits and assigning the auxiliary timecode, it is time to create subclips. This process is pretty straightforward, although it is possible to make a mistake if you aren't careful.

To create a subclip

1. Click the group bin.

2. Click the Bin Fast menu.

3. Select Set Bin Display.

4. In the Set Bin Display dialog box that appears, do the following:

(a) Clear the Show reference clips check box.

(b) Clear the Sequences check box.

(c) Click OK, and then the bin appears to be empty.

Despite not being visible in the bin, the sequences are still present. To access sequences previously loaded in the Timeline window, click the Clip Name Menu (where the name of the sequence appears in the Record monitor) and a list appears of any sequences loaded in the Timeline window.

5. Click in the Timeline window.

6. Deselect all of the tracks (Mac: Shift+⌘+A) | PC: Shift+Ctrl+A).

7. Enable the track with a video clip on it closest to the start of the sequence. This track may not be video track 1 (V1).

8. Place the position indicator on the first clip (it can be anywhere within the clip; it doesn't have to be on the first frame).

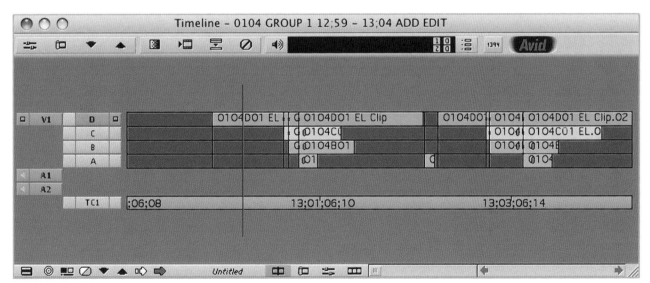

Figure 4-61. Timeline window displaying 0104 Group 1 12;59 - 13;04 Add Edit sequence with the position indicator on the first clip in the sequence.

9. Press F2, F3, F4, F5, F6, and F7, and a subclip appears in the bin.

Figure 4-62. The 0104 Group 1 12;59 - 13;04 bin displaying the created subclip.

As you create the subclips, pay close attention to the Auxiliary TC1 heading in the bin. As each subclip is made, it inherits auxiliary timecode from the master clip (which was typed during the auxiliary timecode process in *To assign auxiliary timecode to clips*, Step 18, page 123).

If there are three clips in a subclip section, there should be three subclips in the bin with the exact same auxiliary timecode. If one of the clips has different auxiliary timecode, something is wrong.

10. Deselect that track and select the next track in that add edit section. If there isn't another clip in that group, move to the bottom clip (the clip on the lowest track) of the next group.

> **Note |** If a subclip is created in error, click that subclip in the bin and press Delete, and then continue with subclipping.

11. Repeat Steps 8–10 until all of the clips have been subclipped. (Make sure you don't miss any clips by being zoomed too far out of the sequence.)

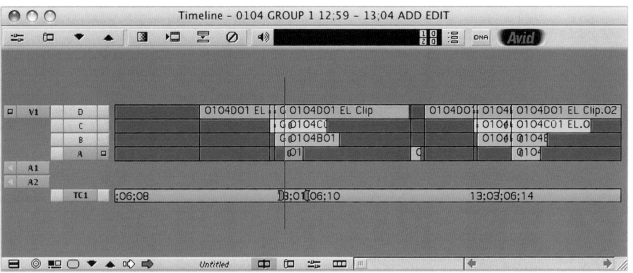

Figure 4-63. Timeline window displaying 0104 Group 1 12;59 - 13;04 Add Edit sequence with a clip in another add edit section selected from the subclip process.

This is the general process. If there is an A, B, and C camera in an add edit section, you will press F2–F7 while on the A camera, then do the same for camera B and camera C. Keep in mind that it will only work if only one track is selected, so each time you press F2–F7, you have to deselect a track and select the next one before pressing F2–F7 again.

To create flawless groups, check the bin for matching auxiliary timecodes after you subclip every add edit section. *Four clips in an add edit section equal four subclips with matching auxiliary timecode.* There is never an exception.

If you encounter a group where the auxiliary timecodes do not match after subclipping, it is most likely that the auxiliary timecode was typed in incorrectly during the auxiliary timecode process. The main reason auxiliary timecode is typed on the master clips is to prevent typing a new auxiliary timecode on every single subclip. As a result, if one of the subclips is different than the others in that group, simply change the auxiliary timecode for that subclip.

This is especially helpful when it comes to crossover clips. Remember that crossover clips are present in two separate groups. Depending on when the auxiliary timecode is assigned to a crossover clip, determines what auxiliary timecode the subclip will have. In the event the crossover's subclip doesn't have the correct timecode, change the auxiliary timecode in the subclip.

Creating Multigroups

With all subclips created, it is time to create the multigroup.

To create a multigroup

1. In the 0104 Group 1 12;59 - 13;04 bin, click the Name column heading, and then Shift+Click the Auxiliary TC1 column heading to select both columns.

2. Sort these columns in ascending order (Mac: ⌘+E | PC: Ctrl+E).

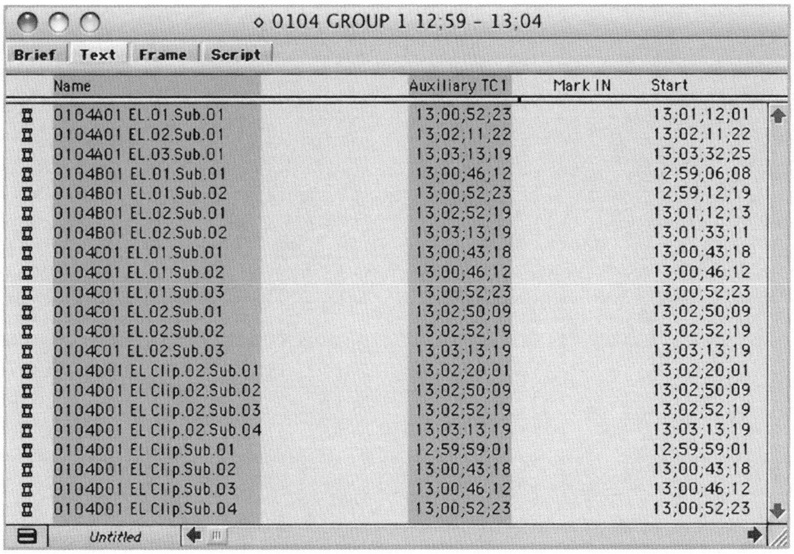

Note | Sorting by name and auxiliary timecode allows a group within a multigroup to appear in alphabetical order—from left to right—in the split-screen view.

Figure 4-64. 0104 Group 1 12;59 - 13;04 bin sorted by Name column and Auxiliary TC1 column in ascending order.

3. Select all the items in the bin (Mac: ⌘+A | PC: Ctrl+A).

4. Select Bin≫MultiGroup.

5. In the Sync Selection dialog box that appears, select Auxiliary TC1, and then click OK.

In the Sync Selection dialog box, there are different options for multigrouping clips. Each option requires a commonality among the clips for the multigrouping process to finish. In this situation, since new timecode is assigned to these clips Auxiliary TC1 is chosen.

Figure 4-65. Sync Selection dialog box.

Now the bin has a bunch of new items in it—these new items are groups. And at the very top should be one of these groups with a plus sign (+) next to it. This is the *multigroup*. The multigroup is a sequence containing all of the groups in the bin.

> **Note** | Multigroups only open in the Source monitor.

Name	Auxiliary TC1	Mark IN	Start
MultiGroup.01			12;59;59;01
0104A01 EL.03.Sub.01.Grp.01			13;03;32;25
0104B01 EL.02.Sub.01.Grp.01			13;01;12;13
0104C01 EL.02.Sub.01.Grp.01			13;02;50;09
0104A01 EL.01.Sub.01.Grp.01			13;01;12;01
0104B01 EL.01.Sub.01.Grp.01			12;59;06;08
0104C01 EL.01.Sub.01.Grp.01			13;00;43;18
0104A01 EL.01.Sub.01	13;00;52;23		13;01;12;01
0104A01 EL.02.Sub.01	13;02;11;22		13;02;11;22
0104A01 EL.03.Sub.01	13;03;13;19		13;03;32;25
0104B01 EL.01.Sub.01	13;00;46;12		12;59;06;08
0104B01 EL.01.Sub.02	13;00;52;23		12;59;12;19
0104B01 EL.02.Sub.01	13;02;52;19		13;01;12;13
0104B01 EL.02.Sub.02	13;03;13;19		13;01;33;11
0104C01 EL.01.Sub.01	13;00;43;18		13;00;43;18
0104C01 EL.01.Sub.02	13;00;46;12		13;00;46;12
0104C01 EL.01.Sub.03	13;00;52;23		13;00;52;23
0104C01 EL.02.Sub.01	13;02;50;09		13;02;50;09
0104C01 EL.02.Sub.02	13;02;52;19		13;02;52;19
0104C01 EL.02.Sub.03	13;03;13;19		13;03;13;19
0104D01 EL.Clip.02.Sub.01	13;02;20;01		13;02;20;01

Window title: ◇ 0104 GROUP 1 12;59 – 13;04
Tabs: Brief | Text | Frame | Script
Bottom: Untitled

Figure 4-66. 0104 Group 1 12;59 - 13;04 bin containing a multigroup.

6. Rename the multigroup exactly as the bin.

Multigroups for one day are usually kept in a group bin specifically for that day. Sometimes multigroups are kept in a bin for a series of days. However your company keeps the multigroups, make sure the bins are labeled correctly and the multigroups are in the correct locations.

Checking and Fixing Multigroups

After a group has been completed, the work should be checked. A different person should always check another person's groups. The person who made the group may not find syncing errors, and it is much easier for a fresh set of eyes to find a mistake. When checking a group, there are several things you should look out for, but first, let's get familiar with the multigroup.

■ Double-click the completed multigroup, and it loads in the Source monitor.

■ Click Toggle Source/Record in Timeline 🖥 to see the multigroup.

Clicking Toggle Source/Record in Timeline switches the Timeline display of clips and sequences between those loaded in the Source monitor (the button and the position indicator are green) and the Record monitor (this is the default state—the button is black and the position indicator is blue). The Toggle/Source Record in Timeline button is located in the Timeline window, on the bottom toolbar.

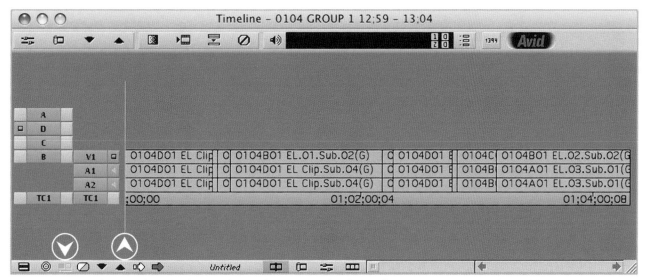

Figure 4-67. Timeline window displaying clips and sequences loaded in the Source monitor evidenced by the green Toggle Source/Record in Timeline button and green position indicator. When the Toggle Source/Record in Timeline button is black and the position indicator is blue (the default state), the Timeline window is displaying sequences loaded in the Record monitor.

Facts about a multigroup:

- A multigroup is comprised of groups.

- Each group represents the individual video clips within a single add edit section.

- A multigroup will not display in split-screen view by default. It is necessary to press F9 on your modified keyboard.

- Even when a multigroup is in split-screen view, if only one camera is in that group, it will appear full screen.

- Hold down Ctrl to see the names of the cameras in the multigroup.

- Layout sequence clips only have two audio tracks. Multigroups have four audio tracks because subclips are created by accessing the master clips, not the clip that was present in the layout sequence.

Checking and fixing multigroups involves the following tasks:

- Checking for missed add edits/fixing add edits.

- Checking for duplicates/fixing duplicates.

- Checking for irregular duplicates/fixing irregular duplicates.

- Checking for missed subclips/fixing missed subclips.

- Checking for sync/fixing sync.

Settings Needed for Checking and Fixing Multigroups

MULTICAMERA MODE

- Press F9 to put the multigroup in MultiCamera mode.

  When looking at a group in the Source monitor, the video should be displayed in MultiCamera mode. While in MultiCamera mode, all of the cameras are displayed in a split-screen view, and you merely have to click on a frame of video in the Source monitor to select that camera. (If it doesn't, that group may only have one image.)

SOURCE MONITOR GROUP MENU SETTING:

Audio Follow Video

Navigation: Composer window | Second Row of Information above Source monitor | Group Menu button

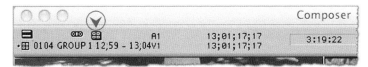

Figure 4-68. Group Menu button in the Second Row of Information above the Source monitor in the Composer window.

- **Audio Follow Video (selected)**—When this option is selected from the Group menu, you can listen to the audio associated with each specific camera.

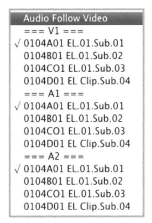

Figure 4-69. Group menu with Audio Follow Video option selected.

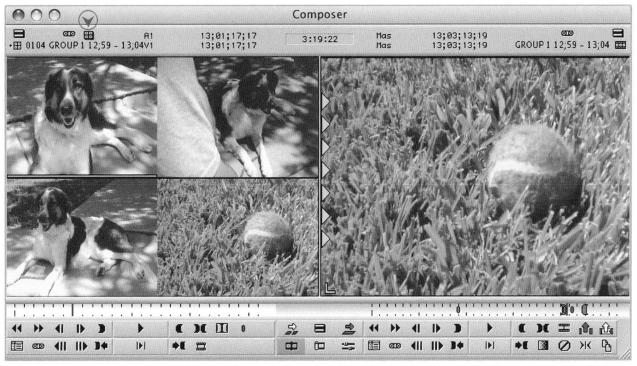

Figure 4-70. Group Menu button in the Second Row of Information above the Source monitor in the Composer window displayed in green indicating that the Audio Follow Video option is selected.

There will be occasions when a multigroup is in the Source monitor, but the Group Menu button is not displayed. In those cases, click throughout the multigroup and make sure you are on a group that has multiple cameras in it.

Checking for Missed Add Edits

Checking for missed add edits involves checking the add edit sequence and making sure that the head of every clip has an add edit through all of the tracks. A missed add edit affects the other checks you will perform on the completed multigroup and needs to be completed first.

To check for missed add edits

1. Click the Bin Fast menu.

2. Select Set Bin Display.

3. In the Set Bin Display dialog box that appears, do the following, and then click OK.

    (a) Select the Sequences check box.

    (b) Clear the Subclips check box.

4. Double-click the add edit sequence, and it loads in the Timeline window. If necessary, click Toggle Source/Record in Timeline to view the sequence.

5. Press Home to place the position indicator at the beginning of the sequence.

6. Select all of the tracks of the sequence (Mac: ⌘+A | PC: Ctrl+A).

7. Snap to the head of the first clip in the sequence (Mac: ⌘+Click | PC: Ctrl+Click) and confirm that there is an add edit.

8. Zoom in to the sequence (Mac: ⌘+] | PC: Ctrl+]).

9. Do one of the following:

    (a) If there is an add edit at the head of the clip, snap to the head of the next clip (Mac: ⌘+Click | PC: Ctrl+Click).

    –or–

    (b) If there isn't an add edit at the head of the clip, confirm that all of the tracks are selected and add an add edit (press F8).

10. Zoom out of the sequence (Mac: ⌘+[| PC: Ctrl+[).

11. Repeat Steps 7–10 until the entire add edit sequence has been checked for add edits.

Fixing Missed Add Edits

To fix missed add edits

1. Click the Bin Fast menu.

2. Select Set Bin Display.

3. In the Select Bin Display dialog box that appears, do the following, and then click OK.

   (a) Clear the Sequences check box.

   (b) Select the Subclips check box.

4. Select all of the groups and subclips in the bin (Mac: ⌘+A | PC: Ctrl+A).

5. Press Delete.

6. Click OK.

7. Click in the Timeline window.

8. Deselect all of the tracks (Mac: Shift+⌘+A | PC: Shift+Ctrl+A).

9. Enable the track with a video clip on it closest to the start of the sequence. This track may not be video track 1 (V1).

10. Place the position indicator on the first clip (it can be anywhere within the clip; it doesn't have to be on the first frame).

11. Press F2, F3, F4, F5, F6, and F7, and a subclip appears in the bin.

12. Deselect that track and select the next track in that add edit section.

13. If there isn't another clip in that group, move to the bottom clip (the clip on the lowest track) of the next group.

14. Repeat Steps 11–13 until all of the clips have been subclipped. (Make sure you don't miss any clips by being zoomed too far out of the sequence.)

15. In the bin, click the Name column heading, and then Shift+Click the Auxiliary TC1 column heading to select both columns.

16. Sort these columns in ascending order (Mac: ⌘+E | PC: Ctrl+E).

17. Select all the items in the bin (Mac: ⌘+A | PC: Ctrl+A).

18. Select Bin≫MultiGroup.

19. In the Sync Selection dialog box that appears, select Auxiliary TC1, and then click OK.

20. Rename the multigroup exactly as the bin.

21. Double-click the new multigroup, and it loads in the Source monitor.

22. Repeat *Checking for Missed Add Edits* on page 132 and *Fixing Missed Add Edits* on page 133 from the beginning until you are certain that all of the required add edits are in the sequence.

Checking for Duplicates

A duplicate, or *dupe*, indicates that there are duplicate camera angles within a group. This happens when you accidentally press F2–F7 on the same video track twice.

To check for duplicates

1. Click the Bin Fast menu.

2. Select Set Bin Display.

3. In the Set Bin Display dialog box that appears, do the following, and then click OK.

    (a) Select the Sequences check box.

    (b) Clear the Subclips check box.

4. Click in the Timecode window.

5. Click the V1 line.

6. Select Source.

7. Select V1.

8. Select Aux1. (Aux1 refers to the auxiliary timecode assigned to the video clip. It is necessary to view the auxiliary timecode, since it is probably different from the source timecode and the multigroup was created using auxiliary timecode.)

9. Double-click the multigroup, and it loads in the Source monitor.

10. Double-click the add edit sequence, and it loads in the Timeline window.

11. Place the position indicator over the subclip section of the add edit sequence that has the most cameras. (For example, if the sequence has cameras A–D, find a subclip section that has video on all four tracks.)

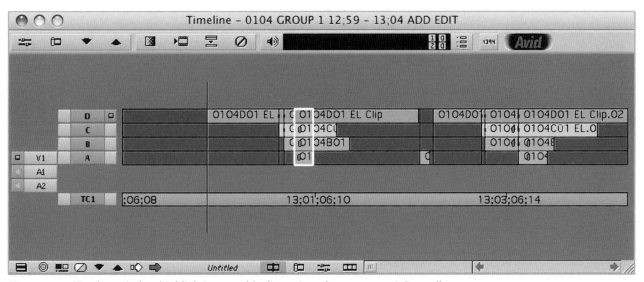

Figure 4-71. Timeline window highlighting an add edit section where cameras A-D are all present.

12. Note the timecode of that add edit section and find it in the multigroup.

13. Click Toggle Source/Record in Timeline to view the multigroup.

14. Press F9 to put the multigroup in MultiCamera mode.

Note | Click on all of the camera angles in a multigroup because dupe detection lines only appear on selected cameras that are duplicated.

15. Click each of the camera angles in the Source monitor while looking at the multigroup in the Timeline window, and look for dupe detection lines.

False dupe detection lines can occur at the end of a group section and the beginning of the next section. These are usually only a frame in duration and don't actually signal duplicates.

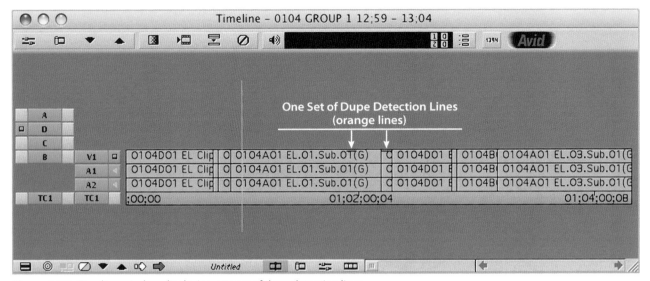

Figure 4-72. Timeline window displaying one set of dupe detection lines.

16. Snap to the head of any group that has dupe detection lines (Mac: ⌘+Click | PC: Ctrl+Click).

17. Write down the auxiliary timecode of all of the groups that have dupe detection lines.

Fixing Duplicates

If there is a mistake, delete the groups, make changes to the subclips, and multigroup again.

To fix duplicates

1. Select all of the items in the bin (Mac: ⌘+A | PC: Ctrl+A).

2. Press Delete.

3. Select the groups only—don't delete the subclips or the sequence, or else the subclipping process will have to be redone.

4. Click OK.

5. Click the Bin Fast menu.

6. Select Set Bin Display.

7. In the Set Bin Display dialog box that appears, do the following, and then click OK.

    (a) Clear the Sequences check box.

    (b) Select the Subclips check box.

8. Click the Auxiliary TC1 column heading.

9. Sort the Auxiliary TC1 column in ascending order (Mac: ⌘+E | PC: Ctrl+E).

10. Locate the timecode of the dupe.

11. Click the duplicate subclip. (For example, two A cameras with the same auxiliary timecode.)

12. Press Delete and *delete the duplicate subclip only*—leaving one subclip.

13. Click OK.

14. Repeat Steps 10–13 until all duplicate subclips are deleted.

15. Click the Name column heading.

16. Shift+Click the Auxiliary TC1 column. Both columns should be selected.

17. Sort these columns in ascending order (Mac: ⌘+E | PC: Ctrl+E).

18. Select all of the items in the bin (Mac: ⌘+A | PC: Ctrl+A).

19. Select Bin≫MultiGroup.

20. Select Auxiliary TC1.

21. Click OK.

22. Rename the multigroup exactly as the bin.

23. Double-click the new multigroup, and it loads in the Source monitor.

24. Repeat *Checking for Duplicates* on page 134 and *Fixing Duplicates* on page 136 from the beginning until you are certain there aren't any duplicates present.

Checking for Irregular Duplicates

Irregular dupes are indicated when ///// (hashmarks) appear over the top of a group.

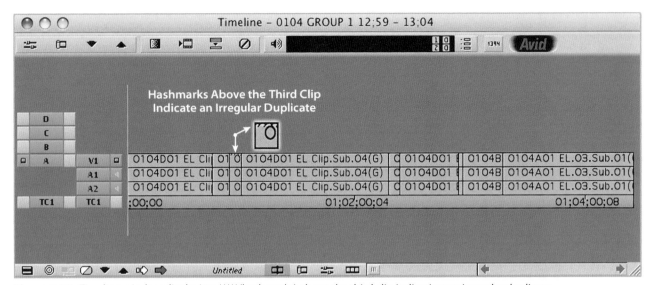

Figure 4-73. Timeline window displaying ////// (hashmarks) above the third clip indicating an irregular duplicate.

Irregular dupes usually are an indication that an auxiliary timecode was placed incorrectly on a clip. It is possible to look for irregular dupes just by looking at the auxiliary timecodes in a bin. Any add edit section of subclips should all have the same auxiliary timecode; if they don't, investigate to determine why. At the same time, it is possible to find an irregular dupe without looking at all of the auxiliary timecodes in a bin.

To check for irregular duplicates

1. Double-click the multigroup, and it loads in the Source monitor.

2. Press F9 to put the multigroup in MultiCamera mode.

3. Click Toggle Source/Record in Timeline.

4. Place the position indicator over the group with the most camera angles.

5. Click each of the camera angles in the Source monitor while looking at the multigroup in the Timeline window.

6. Look and see if any irregular dupe lines appear.

7. Snap to the head of any group that has irregular dupe lines (Mac: ⌘+Click | PC: Ctrl+Click).

8. Write down the timecode of all of the groups that have irregular dupe lines.

Fixing Irregular Duplicates

To fix irregular duplicates

1. Select all of the items in the bin (Mac: ⌘+A | PC: Ctrl+A).

2. Press Delete.

3. Select the groups only—don't delete the subclips or the subclipping process will have to be redone.

4. Click OK.

5. Click the Auxiliary TC1 column heading.

6. Sort the Auxiliary TC1 column in ascending order (Mac: ⌘+E | PC: Ctrl+E).

7. Locate the timecode of the irregular dupe subclip. (The auxiliary timecode of one or more of the subclips will be different than the Mas timecode of the sequence.)

8. Click in the Auxiliary TC1 section for that clip.

9. Change the auxiliary timecode to the correct timecode.

10. Repeat Steps 7–9 for all of the irregular dupe subclips.

11. Click the Name column heading.

12. Shift+Click the Auxiliary TC1 column. Both columns should be selected.

13. Sort these columns in ascending order (Mac: ⌘+E | PC: Ctrl+E).

14. Select all of the items in the bin (Mac: ⌘+A | PC: Ctrl+A).

15. Select Bin≫MultiGroup.

16. Select Auxiliary TC1.

17. Click OK.

18. Rename the multigroup exactly as the bin.

19. Double-click the new multigroup, and it loads in the Source monitor.

20. Repeat *Checking for Irregular Duplicates* on page 137 and *Fixing Irregular Duplicates* on page 139 from the beginning until there aren't any irregular dupes present.

Checking for Missed Subclips

As demonstrated in *Checking for Duplicates* on page 134, an error involves checking, fixing, rechecking, and possibly fixing to make sure the multigroup is error free. It is necessary to recheck after a fix has been made because sometimes a fix can highlight hidden errors. As mentioned before, that is why focusing on all aspects of the multigrouping process is crucial.

Checking for Missed Subclips involves a similar checking process to that of *Checking for Duplicates* on page 134. A missed subclip occurs when you forget to press F2–F7 on a video track, and it is easily discovered by going through the multigroup from add edit to add edit.

To check for missed subclips

1. Double-click the multigroup, and it loads in the Source monitor.

2. Press Home to place the position indicator at the beginning of the multigroup.

3. Press F9 to put the multigroup in MultiCamera mode.

4. Select all of the tracks of the multigroup (Mac: ⌘+A | PC: Ctrl+A).

5. Click the Bin Fast menu.

6. Select Set Bin Display.

7. In the Set Bin Display dialog box that appears, do the following, and then click OK.

    (a) Select the Sequences check box.

    (b) Clear the Subclips check box.

8. Double-click the add edit sequence, and it loads in the Timeline.

9. Press Home to place the position indicator at the beginning of the add edit sequence.

10. Select all of the tracks of the sequence (Mac: ⌘+A | PC: Ctrl+A).

11. Click Toggle Source/Record in Timeline (if necessary) to view the sequence.

12. Open the Command palette (Mac: ⌘+3 | PC: Ctrl+3).

13. Click the Move tab.

14. Select Active Palette.

Figure 4-74. Command palette with Active Palette selected. Note the Fast Forward button in the third column.

15. Click the Timeline window.

16. Click Fast Forward (in the Command palette on the Move tab) to go to the first add edit of the sequence.

17. Click in the Source monitor, and then click Fast Forward.

    The number of camera angles in the Source monitor should equal the number of clips in the add edit section of the sequence. If they don't, a subclip was missed.

Note | The Rewind and Fast Forward buttons can be mapped to your keyboard.

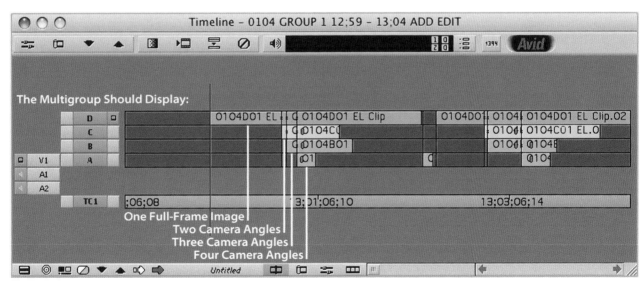

Figure 4-75. Timeline window displaying an add edit sequence where individual sections are segmented and each section's corresponding number of camera angles that should be displayed in the Source monitor is noted.

18. Press Ctrl to see camera names to determine what camera angle/subclip was missed.

    The multigroup in FIGURE 4-76 on page 142 would have four clips in the corresponding add edit section of the sequence.

Figure 4-76. Composer window with a multigroup displayed in the Source monitor. The clip names are displayed as a result of clicking in the Source monitor and pressing Ctrl.

19. Write down the timecode of any missed subclips. (You will need this information in *To fix missed subclips*, Step 8, page 143.)

20. Repeat Steps 15–19 until the multigroup has been checked against the add edit sequence.

    Make sure you move from one add edit point at a time looking back and forth between the multigroup and the sequence.

21. Close the Command palette.

Fixing Missed Subclips

To fix missed subclips

1. Select all of the items in the bin (Mac: ⌘+A | PC: Ctrl+A).

2. Press Delete.

3. Select the groups only—don't delete the subclips or the sequence or the subclipping process will have to be redone.

4. Click OK.

5. Double-click the add edit sequence.

6. Click the Bin Fast menu.

7. Select Set Bin Display.

   (a) Clear the Sequences check box.

   (b) Select the Subclips check box.

   (c) Click OK.

8. Enable the track that has the missing subclip (reference the timecode written down in *To check for missed subclips*, Step 19, page 142).

9. Place the position indicator over the clip.

10. Press F2–F7 to create the subclip, and it appears in the bin. Make sure the correct auxiliary timecode is displayed.

11. Click the Name column heading.

12. Shift+Click the Auxiliary TC1 column. Both columns should be selected.

13. Sort these columns in ascending order (Mac: ⌘+E | PC: Ctrl+E).

14. Select all of the items in the bin (Mac: ⌘+A | PC: Ctrl+A).

15. Select Bin≫MultiGroup.

16. Select Auxiliary TC1.

17. Click OK.

18. Rename the multigroup exactly as the bin.

19. Double-click new multigroup, and it loads in the Source monitor.

20. Repeat *Checking for Missed Subclips* on page 140 and *Fixing Missed Subclips* on page 142 from the beginning until all subclips are in the multigroup.

Checking for Sync

If you didn't complete a group, every single group in a multigroup must be checked for sync. Checking for sync, although most important, should be the last item checked because a mistyped auxiliary timecode or a missed subclip can fix sync issues.

To check for sync

1. Double-click the multigroup, and it loads in the Source monitor.

2. Press Home to go to the beginning of the multigroup.

3. Press F9 to put the multigroup in MultiCamera mode.

4. Ensure that Audio Follow Video is selected.

5. Click camera A.

6. Play (press L).

7. While listening to camera A's audio, look at the other frames of video that sync with that audio. They should be in sync.

8. Continue checking for sync until the multigroup has been checked. Be mindful that checking for sync is a long process, despite the brief number of steps presented.

> **Note** | Listening to the audio of one camera while looking at the video of another camera is a sure way to check sync.
>
> However, don't forget to check the sync of all of the cameras because in that particular group frame, cameras A and C may be in sync with one another while cameras B and D are in sync with each other. Check all of the cameras!
>
> It is possible to check for video sync by looking for an obvious motion and seeing if they are in sync with one another.

Fixing Sync

Focus is the secret to multigrouping and especially syncing. If you or the person who completed the multigroup weren't focused during syncing, it can be very time consuming to fix.

To fix sync

1. Click the Bin Fast menu.

2. Select Set Bin Display.

3. In the Select Bin Display dialog box that appears, do the following, and then click OK.

   (a) Select the Sequences check box.

   (b) Select the Subclips check box.

   (c) Select the Groups check box.

4. Select all of the groups, subclips, and only the add edit sequence in the bin. (Do not select the original event sequence and sync sequence.)

5. Press Delete.

6. Make sure sequences, subclips, and groups are selected.

7. Click OK.

8. Double-click the Sync sequence.

9. Click Toggle Source/Record in Timeline (if necessary) to view the sequence.

Multigrouping At-A-Glance

This section is a duplication of the multigrouping instructions without the supplemental information; figures; and tips, notes, and cautions. The tasks included in this section are listed in TABLE 4-1 with the original page numbers cross-referenced to this section's page numbers.

TABLE 4-1. MULTIGROUPING AT-A-GLANCE TASK LIST		
Task	**Original Page Number**	**This Section's Page Number**
To sync the clips	109	145
To fix sync as you go	113	147
To place add edits throughout the sequence	118	147
To assign auxiliary timecode to clips	121	148
To create a subclip	124	149
To create a multigroup	127	150

All of the tasks in this section—except for *To sync the clips*—start at Step 1 and correspond to the step numbers in the original tasks. *To sync the clips* starts at Step 7 and corresponds to the step numbers in the original task.

To sync the clips

7. Click the Timeline Fast menu.

8. Select Audio Data.

9. Select Sample Plot.

10. Mark IN (press I) and OUT (press O) points at the beginning of the out-of-sync clips and a little later in the Timeline.

11. Locate similar looking waveforms (if there are any) on the audio tracks.

12. Place the position indicator at the moment of the similar audio pattern.

13. Solo one of the audio tracks of that clip (Mac: ⌘+Click | PC: Ctrl+Click).

14. Zoom in to that point (Mac: ⌘+] | PC: Ctrl+]).

15. Play the audio of that clip, and then stop playing at a distinct and memorable sound.

16. Deselect all of the tracks (Mac: Shift+⌘+A | PC: Shift+Ctrl+A).

17. Enable the video track that corresponds with the to-be-synced audio.

18. Add a Locator (press F10) at the moment of the possible sync point.

19. Deselect the first video track.

20. Zoom out from that point (Mac: ⌘+[| PC: Ctrl+[).

21. Unsolo the audio track (Mac: ⌘+Click | PC: Ctrl+Click).

22. Place the position indicator at the moment of the matching audio pattern.

23. Solo one of the audio tracks of that clip (Mac: ⌘+Click | PC: Ctrl+Click).

24. Zoom in to that point (Mac: ⌘+] | PC: Ctrl+]).

25. Play the audio of that clip and stop playing at a distinct and memorable sound.

26. Deselect all of the tracks (Mac: Shift+⌘+A | PC: Shift+Ctrl+A).

27. Enable the video track that corresponds with the to-be-synced audio.

28. Add a Locator (press F10), at the moment of the possible sync point.

29. Zoom out from that point (Mac: ⌘+[| PC: Ctrl+[).

30. Click Lift/Overwrite Segment Mode.

31. Shift+Click one of the video clips *and* its corresponding audio.

32. Move the clip until it is in sync with the clip being synced to. It may be necessary to move the position indicator and zoom in to the sequence to precisely match up the audio waveforms.

33. Click Lift/Overwrite Segment Mode to exit the function.

34. Place the position indicator before the synced point.

35. Solo the audio tracks of the clips that have been synced.

36. Play (press L) and listen. The clips should be perfectly in sync (if they are not, see *To fix sync as you go* on page 147).

37. Look for the next clip without a locator.

38. Repeat Steps 10–37 until all clips are in sync and have locators.

To fix sync as you go

1. Place the position indicator at the synced point.

2. Zoom in to that point (Mac: ⌘+] | PC: Ctrl+]).

3. Look at the waveforms to see what is out of sync.

4. Click Lift/Overwrite Segment Mode.

5. Shift+Click one of the video clips and its corresponding audio tracks.

6. Press the Trim Frame buttons (see FIGURE 4-45 on page 112) until the clip is in sync with the other video clips.

7. Click Lift/Overwrite Segment Mode to exit the function.

8. Solo one of the synced video tracks (Mac: ⌘+Click | PC: Ctrl+Click).

9. Solo the audio tracks of the other synced clip (Mac: ⌘+Click | PC: Ctrl+Click).

10. Play (press L) to view the video of a clip while listening to the audio of another clip.

11. Unsolo the video and audio clips (Mac: ⌘+Click | PC: Ctrl+Click).

12. Zoom out from that point (Mac: ⌘+[| PC: Ctrl+[).

13. Click the Timeline Fast menu.

14. Select Audio Data.

15. Select None.

16. Save the bin (Mac: ⌘+S | PC: Ctrl+S).

To place add edits throughout the sequence

1. Click the sync subsequence in the bin.

2. Duplicate the sync sequence (Mac: ⌘+D | PC: Ctrl+D).

3. Rename the sequence by replacing "Sync" with "Add Edit."

4. Double-click the add edit sequence.

5. Deselect all tracks (Mac: Shift+⌘+A | PC: Shift+Ctrl+A).

6. Select all of the audio tracks.

7. Press Delete, and in the Delete Track dialog box that appears, click OK, and the sequence should only have video tracks now.

8. Select all of the tracks of the sequence (Mac: ⌘+A | PC: Ctrl+A).

9. Snap to the head of the clip closest to the beginning of the sequence (Mac: ⌘+Click | PC: Ctrl+Click).

10. Focus (press H) to zoom in.

11. Place an Add Edit (press F8) through all of the tracks.

12. Focus (press H) to zoom out.

13. Scrub to the head of the next clip (Mac: ⌘+Drag | PC: Ctrl+Drag). (Make sure Caps Lock is enabled on your keyboard to hear the audio during scrubbing.)

14. Repeat Steps 9–13 until the entire sequence has all of the necessary add edits.

To assign auxiliary timecode to clips

1. Click the group bin.

2. Click the Bin Fast menu.

3. Select Set Bin Display.

4. In the Set Bin Display dialog box that appears, select the Show reference clips check box, and then click OK.

5. Click the Bin Fast menu.

6. Select Headings.

7. Click All/None twice.

8. Select only Auxiliary TC1, Mark In, and Start.

9. Click OK.

10. Drag the Resize box, if necessary, to scale the size of the bin so that all three column headings are visible.

11. Go to the sequence and enable the track with the clip closest to the start of the sequence.

12. Snap to go the first add edit point (Mac: ⌘+Click | PC: Ctrl+Click).

13. Focus (press H) to make sure the position indicator is at the very beginning of the clip.

14. Match Frame (press F4), and the exact frame of that clip loads in the Source monitor.

15. Click Find Bin and that clip is highlighted in the group bin.

16. Click the Timeline window to load the Mas timecode in the Timecode window.

17. Look at the Mas timecode in the Timecode window.

18. Type that Mas timecode in the Auxiliary TC1 column of that clip (the clip highlighted by the Find Bin function).

19. Press Enter.

20. Go back to the sequence and snap to the head of the next clip in the current track (Mac: ⌘+Click | PC: Ctrl+Click).

21. Repeat Steps 13–20 until all of the clips for that track have auxiliary timecode assigned to them.

22. When one track is complete, disable one track, enable the next track, and repeat Steps 11–21 until all of the clips have auxiliary timecode assigned to them.

23. Save the bin (Mac: ⌘+S | PC: Ctrl+S).

To create a subclip

1. Click the group bin.

2. Click the Bin Fast menu.

3. Select Set Bin Display.

4. In the Set Bin Display dialog box that appears, do the following:

   (a) Clear the Show reference clips check box.

   (b) Clear the Sequences check box.

   (c) Click OK, and then the bin appears to be empty.

5. Click in the Timeline window.

6. Deselect all of the tracks (Mac: Shift+⌘+A) | PC: Shift+Ctrl+A).

7. Enable the track with a video clip on it closest to the start of the sequence. This track may not be video track 1 (V1).

8. Place the position indicator on the first clip (it can be anywhere within the clip; it doesn't have to be on the first frame).

9. Press F2, F3, F4, F5, F6, and F7, and a subclip appears in the bin.

10. Deselect that track and select the next track in that add edit section. If there isn't another clip in that group, move to the bottom clip (the clip on the lowest track) of the next group.

11. Repeat Steps 8–10 until all of the clips have been subclipped. (Make sure you don't miss any clips by being zoomed too far out of the sequence.)

To create a multigroup

1. In the bin, click the Name column heading, and then Shift+Click the Auxiliary TC1 column heading to select both columns.

2. Sort these columns in ascending order (Mac: ⌘+E | PC: Ctrl+E).

3. Select all the items in the bin (Mac: ⌘+A | PC: Ctrl+A).

4. Select Bin≫MultiGroup.

5. In the Sync Selection dialog box that appears, select Auxiliary TC1, and then click OK.

6. Rename the multigroup exactly as the bin.

During the checking and fixing sync process, it is evident that not correctly syncing the first time around can take a lot of time to fix. You essentially have to redo all of the steps involved with multigrouping.

It is possible to fix a sync error in a group without going through all of these steps. However, a word to the wise, it takes a very experienced grouper to figure out what steps are and are not crucial to the syncing process.

The best way to guard against having to go through this fixing process is to group, and especially sync, properly the first time. If you are checking a group for someone else, it may be your responsibility to fix the errors. Although it seems undesirable, fixing another person's errors can help you become a better grouper because you won't make the mistakes that lead to the errors you are fixing. At the same time, it would also be good practice for the person who created the group to correct their own errors because they should also learn from their mistakes. Who corrects groups is largely determined by time.

Multigrouping Checklist

Given the intense nature of multigrouping, we are going to break away from *Did I Do This Correctly?* and make a checklist available. All of the answers to this checklist should be yes, and if there is a no, there should be an acceptable explanation or you will need to reexamine the multigrouping process.

☐ Were all of the necessary clips copied into an All Camera bin?

☐ Were all of the clips placed into a sequence at the correct timecode?

☐ Was the layout sequence properly broken into manageable sections?

☐ Were crossover clips colored?

☐ Were separate bins and subsequences created for the event sections?

☐ Do all of the clips have locators in the sequence?

☐ Were all junk, interview, and surveillance clips removed? (If required by your company.)

☐ Were all of the interview clips sorted into their respective bins?

☐ Do all of the clips have the correct auxiliary timecode assigned to them?

☐ Do all of the clips have add edits correctly placed?

☐ Are all of the subclips present for each add edit section of the sequence?

☐ Were the multigroups created using auxiliary timecode?

☐ Were the multigroups renamed?

☐ Were the multigroups checked for missed add edits, dupes, irregular dupes, missed subclips, and sync?

☐ If any errors were discovered, were those errors fixed and rechecked?

CHAPTER 5:
Rough Cuts

Tasks in This Chapter

THE ÆDVENTURES OF KARS & GRETIG

ROUGH CUTS ARE A preliminary string out of clips. Depending on the type of show you are working on, rough cuts can contain clips, interviews, or a combination of the two. Rough cuts are given to assistant editors to edit together to facilitate the editing process.

Rough cuts are usually separated into acts and constructed from scripts provided by producers. The producers are responsible for their episode and can be on set making notes about occurrences or special events that may occur while they are there.

Rough cuts can have several different formats, but they all are basically the same because they will provide timecode and a short transcript for the desired clips.

When you receive a rough cuts script, edit the sequence in Avid to mirror the script on paper from top to bottom. When you use a rough cuts script for the first time, you will probably overwrite clips to the sequence and add new material at the end of the Timeline. While you are doing this, there are two issues to factor in: (1) Audio Follow Video and (2) lifting and extracting clips from the Timeline (if you make a mistake). Inserting editing occurs when you receive the same script with revisions and need to add those changes in the middle of the sequence instead of at the end.

Settings Needed

USING SYNC LOCKS

Use sync locks to keep clips in sync while adding material to a sequence.

Clicking the Sync Lock All button in the Track Selector Panel turns on all of the sync locks so everything in a sequence will stay in sync because the tracks are locked to one another.

Figure 5-1. Track Selector Panel with Sync Lock All button highlighted.

As shown in FIGURE 5-2, since all sync locks are enabled, when filler is insert edited into the sequence, the video and audio of the clip are shifted at the same time.

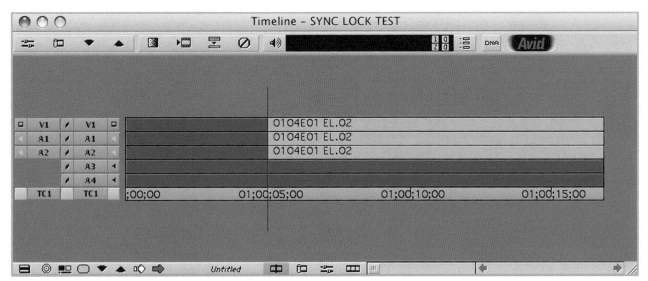

Figure 5-2. Timeline window displaying the effect on video and audio clips of filler insert edited into the sequence when all sync locks are enabled.

As shown in FIGURE 5-3, since none of the sync locks are enabled and filler is inserted only on video track 1 (V1), the clip is now out of sync. The video track shifted down, but the audio on audio tracks A1 and A2 remain in their original positions.

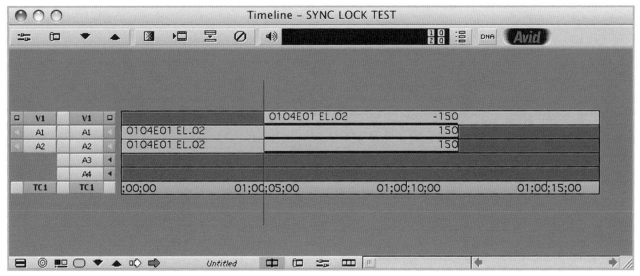

Figure 5-3. Timeline window displaying the effect on video and audio clips of filler insert edited into the sequence when sync locks are not enabled.

Overwriting Clips into a Sequence

Rough cuts scripts, such as that in FIGURE 5-4 on page 156, list the interviews and reality moments in two columns. This is a common format, but it is not the only one that you will encounter. Once you start editing the elements into your sequence, the style of the script should become clear. If it doesn't, ask the person who gave you the script or another assistant editor.

Reality	Interview
	0104E01 EL 10;04;05;22 Ruff! Ruff! Ruff!
0104A01 EL 13;01;16;28 You are so lazy! All you do is just lie around!	
0104A01 EL 13;04;30;00 CU of Elvis looking at Ellie.	**0104E01 EL 10;07;00;00** (Quizzical look on Elvis' face.)
0104A01 EL 13;02;25;19 CU of Elvis' ball.	
0104B01 EL 13;03;15;11 Elvis whines at Ellie.	**0104E01 EL 10;01;25;00** He loves that ball! I don't know why he isn't playing with it.

Figure 5-4. Rough cuts script.

To overwrite clips into a sequence

1. Create a bin (Mac: ⌘+N | PC: Ctrl+N).

2. Rename the new bin.

3. In the Bin window, click the Text tab.

4. On the Bin View menu, select Statistics.

5. Create a sequence (Mac: Shift+⌘+N | PC: Shift+Ctrl+N).

6. Rename the sequence (for example, 0226 EL 101 Act 1), and then press Enter.

7. Add audio tracks until there are at least four (Mac: ⌘+U | PC: Ctrl+U).

8. Start at the upper right of the rough cuts script page and determine if it contains a reality bite or an interview clip.

9. Double-click the interview bin specified in the rough cuts script.

10. In the Bin window, click the Text tab.

11. On the Bin View menu, select Statistics.

Tip | A common naming system is show, episode, and act (for example, EL 101 Act 1).

Tip | When creating sequences, you can either keep the default setting and simply add/subtract video and audio tracks as needed each time, or you can define the number of tracks that are automatically created.

The default setting is the master timecode track (TC1), at least one video track (V1), and at least two audio tracks (A1 and A2).

To change the default setting and define the number of tracks that are automatically created when a sequence is created, do the following:

◆ In the Project window, on the Settings tab, select Timeline.

◆ In the Timeline Settings dialog box that appears, on the Edit tab, select the number of video and audio tracks for new sequences, and then click OK.

Figure 5-5. Interview bin displaying Statistics view.

12. In the interview bin, locate the correct clip by looking at the tape names and corresponding timecodes found in the Start and End column headings.

13. Double-click the correct interview, and it loads in the Source monitor.

Figure 5-6. Source monitor displaying the interview clip.

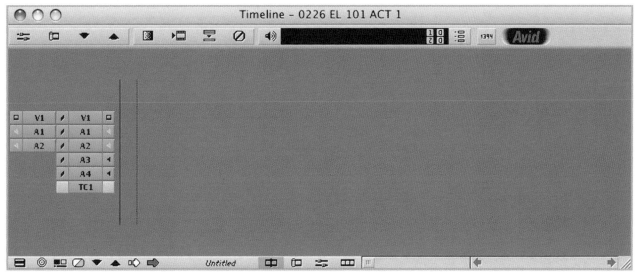

Figure 5-7. Timeline window displaying the 0226 EL 101 Act 1 sequence at this point.

14. Play (press L). (The Spacebar plays a clip too.)

   Press Play (press L) and a clip plays in real time, and you will hear
   every word distinctly and clearly. However, this can take a considerable
   amount of time if the section you need is at the end of the clip.

   Press Play (press L) multiple times to accelerate the speed of the clip
   being played; however, the more times you press Play, the less you
   may be able to understand what is being said.

15. Find the first word of the interview.

16. Mark IN (press I) at the beginning of that word.

   You can Mark IN and OUT points while a clip is being played. The
   Mark IN and OUT points will appear in the Source monitor position
   bar once the clip has stopped. If the Mark IN and OUT points aren't
   exactly where they are supposed to be, place the position indicator at
   the correct moment, and Mark IN or OUT at that location.

> **Tip** | If you are close to the first word and need to move backward or forward one frame at a time, press Left Arrow or Right Arrow, respectively. Make sure Caps Lock is enabled to hear the audio scrubbing while moving forward or backward one frame at a time.

17. Play (press L).

   In addition to pressing Play multiple times, you can also move the
   position indicator within the Source monitor position bar. When
   Caps Lock is selected, you will be able to hear the audio as the position
   indicator is being moved.

   Additionally, you can use the numeric keypad to type in the desired
   timecode. However, typing in the timecode isn't always the best option
   because script timecodes aren't always accurate.

18. Mark OUT (press O) at the end of the interview section.

   For additional ways to use Mark IN and OUT see APPENDIX 5: *Mark
   IN and OUT* on page 337.

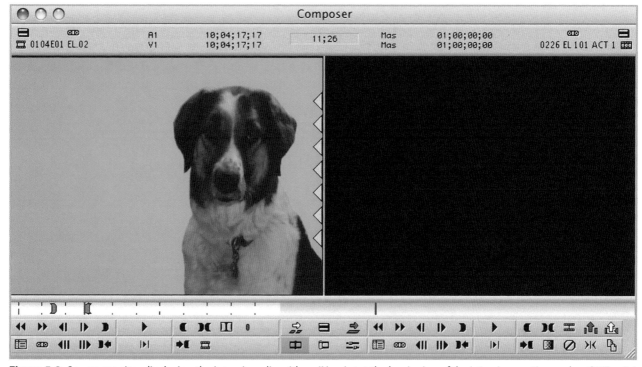

Figure 5-8. Source monitor displaying the interview clip with an IN point at the beginning of the interview section and an OUT point at the end.

> **Note** | Each company is different, so make sure you know your company's specifications. For our purposes, interview audio will go on audio tracks 1 and 2, and reality audio will go on tracks 3 and 4.

19. Patch the source video and audio tracks to the desired record video and audio tracks.

When capturing, all audio tracks on a tape are selected even though only one or two may be used. When those tracks are chosen for a rough cuts script, they should be the audio tracks with the best audio. The best audio is usually from the lavalier mic because it is typically attached to the speaker; however, this isn't always the case, so you need to check to make sure. The lavalier microphone's channels are usually channel 1 and channel 2. To know which track is the best, solo each audio track to listen to each channel individually.

To solo an audio track, ⌘+Click (Mac) or Ctrl+Click (PC) the stereo icon of the source track on the Track Selector Panel, and it turns green.

Figure 5-9. Track Selector Panel with source audio track (A1) soloed.

Additionally, when soloing the audio tracks, you may only have one audio track that is usable. As such, it wouldn't make sense to lay down two audio tracks when only one is needed. In those instances, you should lay down that usable audio track twice: for example, once onto audio track 1 (A1), and then patch it and overwrite to audio track 2 (A2).

20. Overwrite (press B) the video and audio to the sequence.

   In this example, the source video clip only had two tracks of audio, as a result, you would only need to select the source video and audio tracks to overwrite to the sequence—that is, you would not have to deselect the unwanted audio tracks (audio tracks A3 and A4).

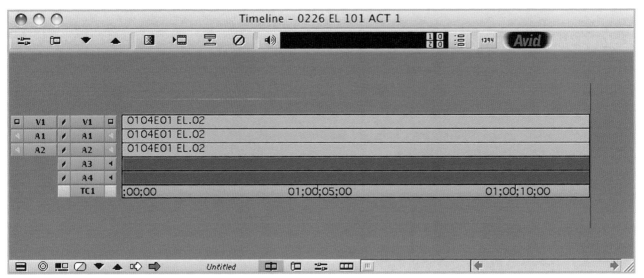

Figure 5-10. Timeline window displaying 0226 EL 101 Act 1 sequence with interview clip video and audio tracks overwritten to the sequence.

However, if the source video and audio tracks are the same as the record video and audio tracks, you would have to deselect the unwanted tracks, patch the selected source tracks to the desired record tracks, and then overwrite the remaining tracks to the sequence (as shown in FIGURE 5-11—notice audio tracks 3 and 4 are not selected; A3 and A4, respectively). Otherwise, all of the source audio tracks will be overwritten to the sequence (that is, four tracks will be overwritten instead of just the two needed).

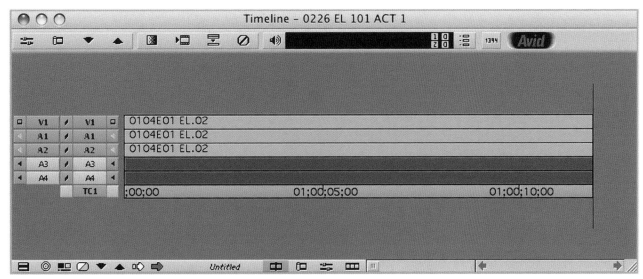

Figure 5-11. Timeline window displaying source and record audio tracks 3 and 4 (A3 and A4, respectively) deselected to prevent four audio tracks from being overwritten to the sequence.

After overwriting the interview on the track, go back to the rough cuts script to see what the next element is. The next element for this rough cuts script is a reality moment.

In our example, the next clip is 0104A01 EL 13;01;16;28 located in 0104 Group 1 12;59 - 13;04.

Figure 5-12. 0104 Groups bin containing the next clip in our example located in 0104 Group 1 12;59 - 13;04.

21. Open the bin that contains the groups or clips specified in the rough cuts script.

22. In the Bin window, click the Text tab.

23. On the Bin View menu, select Statistics.

24. Within that bin, locate the correct clip by looking at the names and corresponding timecodes found in the Start and End column headings of the bin.

Note | Bins can contain one type of clip such as interviews of a specific person, B-roll shots of a particular house, or music from a certain composer. This helps to keep the project organized so material is easily found.

25. Double-click the correct multigroup or clip, and it loads in the Source monitor.

Some postproduction companies don't work in a multicamera environment, but the overall steps outlined here still apply in those instances with the exception of two processes: (1) choosing different camera angles (Step 26), and (2) the Audio Follow Video function (Step 27).

> **Tip** | Holding Ctrl when the Source monitor has a multigroup loaded displays the name of each clip in that multigroup.

26. Press F9 to place the multigroup in Multicamera mode. (Multigroups only.)

27. Enable Audio Follow Video. (Multigroups only.)

Figure 5-13. Source monitor displaying the multigroup in Multicamera mode. Notice the clip names as a result of holding Ctrl when the Source monitor has a multigroup loaded. Also notice the Group Menu button in the Second Row of Information above the Source monitor is green indicating that the Audio Follow Video function is enabled.

28. Find the first word of the reality moment.

In our example, it is "You" from 0104A01 EL 13;01;16;28—You are so lazy! All you do is just lie around!

Figure 5-14. Source monitor displaying the position indicator at the first word of the reality moment.

Note | The script will sometimes list the desired camera angle that the producer wants, but sometimes it is up to you to choose the camera angles. This gives you a chance to edit, and the editors will appreciate your effort. This is all mainly dependent on the script and the workload for your shift.

29. Mark IN (press I) at the beginning of that word.

30. Listen for the last word of the reality moment.

In our example, it is "around" from 0104A01 EL 13;01;16;28—You are so lazy! All you do is just lie around!

31. Mark OUT (press O) at the end of the word.

32. Click the camera specified in the rough cuts. (Multigroups only.)

In our example, it is camera A01, which is the upper left clip in the Source monitor—see FIGURE 5-13 on page 162.

33. Patch the source video and audio tracks to the desired record video and audio tracks.

In our example, since reality audio is on tracks 3 and 4 (A3 and A4, respectively), then source reality audio tracks 1 and 2 (A1 and A2, respectively) are patched to record A3 and A4.

34. Make sure the position indicator is at the end of the sequence.

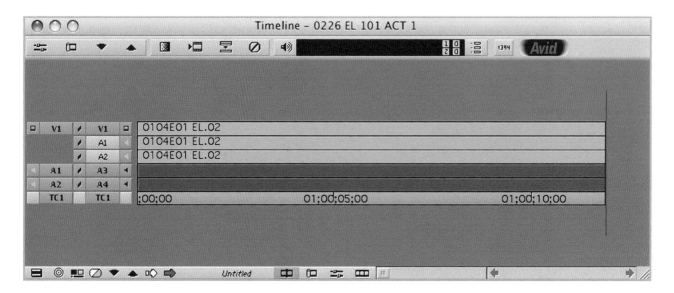

35. Overwrite (press B) the video and audio to the sequence.

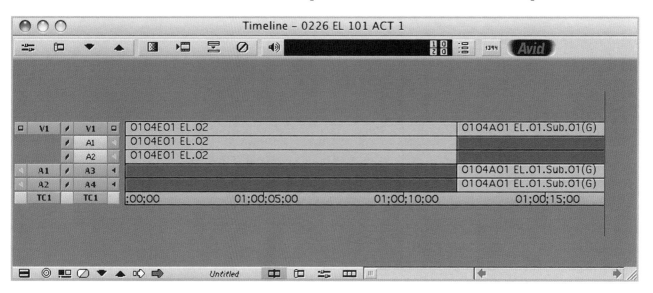

Tip | If you make a mistake, undo that action (Mac: ⌘+Z | PC: Ctrl+Z). You can undo up to 24 actions as long as the same sequence is loaded in the Timeline window.

36. Save the bin (Mac: ⌘+S | PC: Ctrl+S).

The process of following the script and finding the correct elements in the bins is repeated until the rough cuts is completed.

In our example, since the interview section to the right of 0104A01 EL 13;01;16;28 in the script is blank, you would proceed to 0104A01 EL 13;04;30;00 (that is, the order to follow in the rough cuts script is left to right from top to bottom).

Make sure you review the rough cuts from beginning to end before giving it to an editor. It is sloppy and embarrassing to have interview or reality moments with missing or clipped words, unsuitable audio, and poorly chosen camera shots because the rough cuts wasn't reviewed.

Enabling Audio Follow Video

As discussed in multigrouping, the Audio Follow Video function is used to keep a multicamera angle with its native audio. There are times when the audio from a camera is paired with video from another camera. In these instances, it is best to overwrite the better audio tracks with the undesired video track into the sequence—because it is more time-consuming to change two audio channels than it is to change one video channel.

To switch a multigroup's audio or video tracks

1. Overwrite (press B) A camera's video and audio to the sequence.

2. Place the position indicator over that clip.

3. Enable the video track in the sequence that needs to be changed.

> **Tip** | You can also right-click the video track that needs to be changed, and select the desired camera angle (that is, the desired clip).

4. Press Up Arrow/Down Arrow to select the desired camera angle (that is, the clip).

√ 0104A01 EL.01.Sub.01
0104B01 EL.01.Sub.02
0104C01 EL.01.Sub.03
0104D01 EL Clip.Sub.04

Figure 5-15. The Multi-angle View menu displays the other camera angles available for selection.

Figure 5-16. The Record monitor displays the changed camera angle. The 0104A01 EL camera angle was initially overwritten to the sequence and changing the camera angle to 0104C01 changes the image and clip name in the sequence.

Insert Editing Clips into a Sequence

There are occasions when you receive a revised rough cuts script that has clips that need to be added to an existing sequence. Sometimes the clips will be added to the end of the sequence, and sometimes those clips will be added somewhere in the middle. Instead of re-editing the sequence from beginning to end, insert edit those clips into the existing sequence.

Rough cuts scripts can contain material to add to a sequence, but they can also instruct you to remove existing material while adding new material. It is wise to go clip to clip in the sequence and check against the rough cuts script. If you are lucky, a producer has highlighted the changes in the rough cuts script, but if not, check the sequence clip by clip to ensure the resulting sequence mirrors the rough cuts script.

To insert edit clips into a sequence

1. Open the bin containing the sequence that needs insert edits, and then double-click the correct sequence.

2. Place the position indicator at the location in the sequence that needs the additional clip.

3. Mark IN (press I).

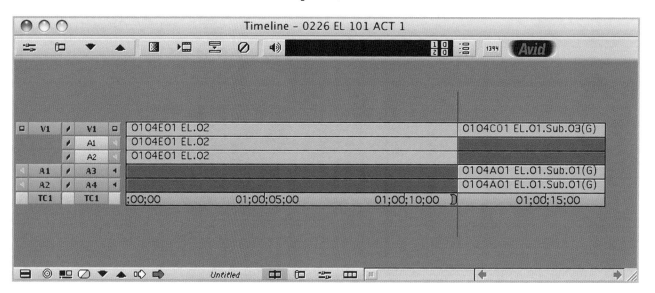

4. Open the bin that contains the additional clip.

5. In the Bin window, click the Text tab.

6. On the Bin View menu, select Statistics.

7. Locate the additional clip by looking at the tape names and the corresponding timecodes found in the Start and End column headings of the bin, and then double-click the correct clip.

8. Play (press L).

9. Mark IN (press I) at the beginning of that word.

10. Mark OUT (press O) at the end of the last word.

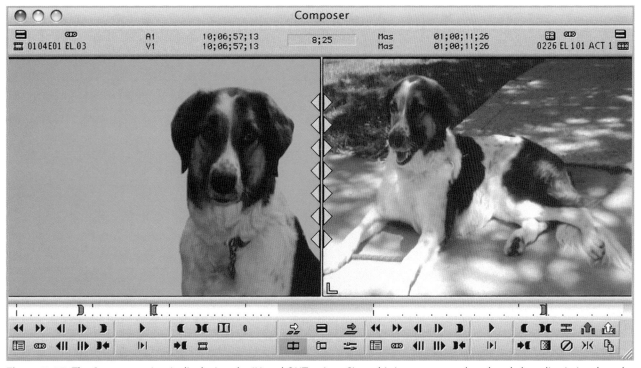

Figure 5-17. The Source monitor is displaying the IN and OUT points. Since this is a sequence that already has clips in it, when the position indicator is in the middle of the sequence, the Record monitor shows the first frame of the clip it will be inserted before.

11. Patch the source video and audio tracks to the desired record video and audio tracks.

12. Click Sync Lock All on the Track Selector Panel.

Note | Remember, Sync Lock All keeps clips in the Timeline in sync while adding material to a sequence or removing material from a sequence.

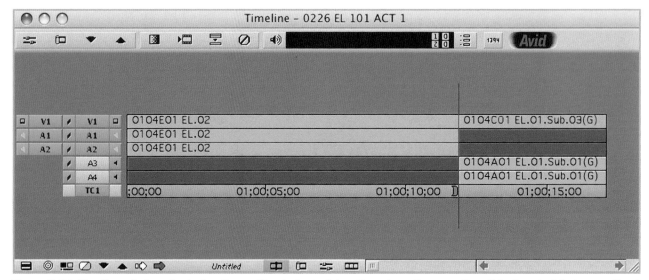

Figure 5-18. Timeline window displaying the position indicator's location where the new clip will be inserted (between clips 1 and 2).

13. Insert (press V) the video and audio to the sequence.

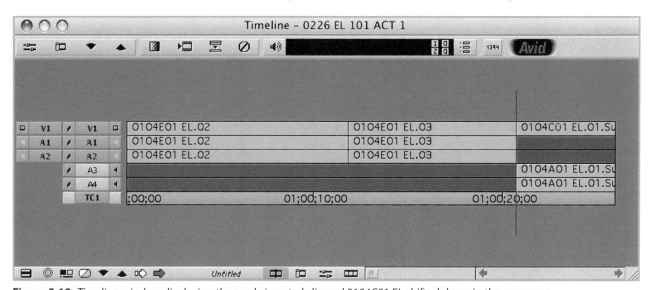

Figure 5-19. Timeline window displaying the newly inserted clip and 0104C01 EL shifted down in the sequence.

14. Save the bin (Mac: ⌘+S | PC: Ctrl+S).

Lifting and Extracting

When a rough cuts script instructs you to remove material from a sequence, there are two functions to choose from: Lift and Extract. Both functions require an IN and an OUT point placed in a sequence.

Lift (press Z)—Use Lift when you need to remove material and leave a hole in its place. The hole consists of black filler and silence. The duration of the sequence remains the same. Lift would be used to remove a portion of a clip to replace with another clip of the same duration. For example, when you want to put another clip in that location but don't immediately know what to overwrite there. When playing the sequence, you would see black until you overwrite a new clip to that location.

Extract (press X)—Use Extract when you need to remove material and close the gap. The duration of the sequence is shortened accordingly. Extract would be used when you want to permanently remove a portion of a clip. For example, if an interview subject coughs at the end of a sound bite, the cough should be removed permanently from the sequence, and it won't be replaced by anything else.

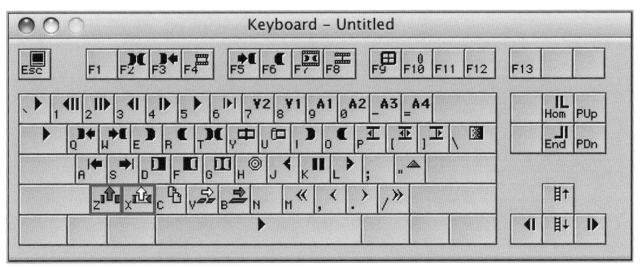

Figure 5-20. Avid Keyboard with the Lift (press Z) key and Extract (press X) key highlighted.

Play around using the Lift and Extract functions with different combinations of IN and OUT points, sync locks, and enabled tracks. The results you receive may not be what you expect! Let's practice.

To lift and extract clips

1. Open a bin containing a sequence that has at least one video track and four audio tracks.

2. Duplicate the sequence (Mac: ⌘+D | PC: Ctrl+D).

3. Rename the sequence Lift/Extract Test, and then press Enter. (It's a good idea to move this sequence to a new bin, but it isn't necessary.)

4. Double-click the Lift/Extract Test sequence.

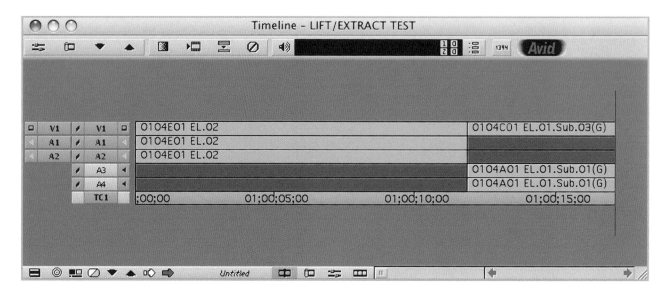

5. Mark IN (press I) in the sequence.

6. Place the position indicator a few seconds past the IN point.

7. Mark OUT (press O) in the sequence.

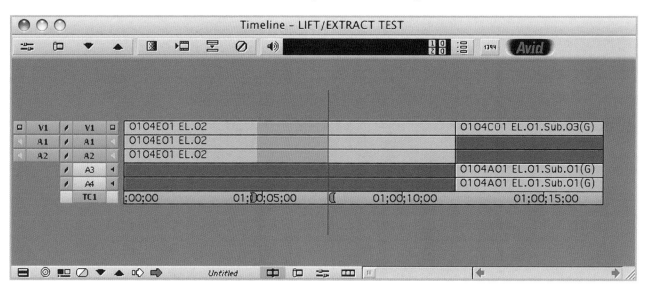

8. Enable the tracks that should be removed.

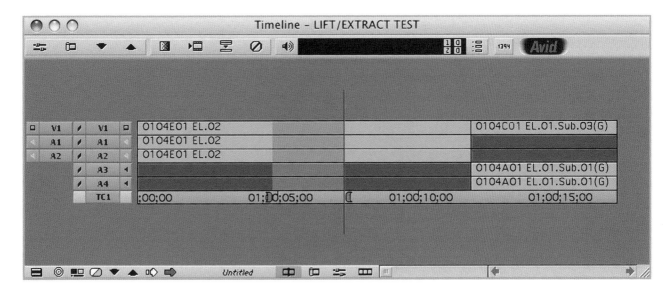

9. Lift (press Z).

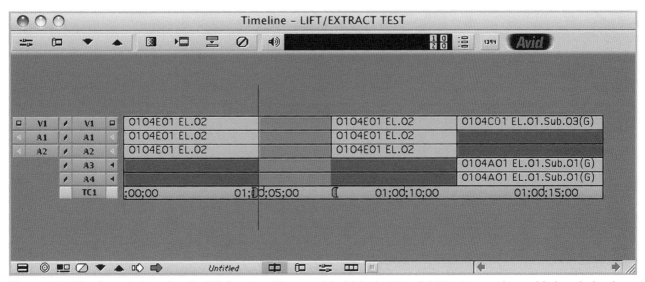

Figure 5-21. Timeline window after the Lift function. The material within the IN and OUT points on the enabled tracks has been removed from the sequence, there is a hole in its place, and the duration of the sequence remains the same.

10. Undo to restore the footage (Mac: ⌘+Z | PC: Ctrl+Z).

11. Extract (press X).

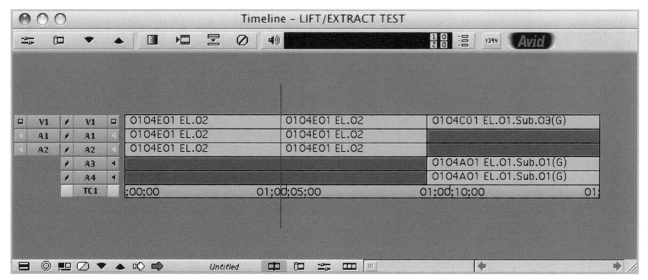

Figure 5-22. Timeline window after the Extract function. The material within the IN and OUT points on the enabled tracks has been removed from the sequence, all of the footage after the OUT point has shifted and is now adjacent to the material before the IN point, and the duration of the sequence is shortened.

12. Click the Lift/Extract Test sequence, and then press Delete.

13. Click OK.

Did I Do This Correctly?

■ **Are all of the reality moments and interview sound bites from the script present in the rough cuts?**

Watching the rough cuts while referencing the paper rough cuts will ensure all elements are present.

■ **Was the best audio chosen for reality moments and interview sound bites?**

While listening to the rough cuts, the audio should be clear.

■ **Is the bin labeled correctly?**

Verify that the bin name is in accordance with your company's naming convention, and if it is not, rename the bin.

■ **Is the sequence labeled correctly?**

Verify that the sequence name is in accordance with your company's naming convention, and if it is not, rename the sequence.

■ **Is the reality and interview audio on the correct audio tracks?**

Verify that the reality and interview audio are on the correct audio tracks according to your company's requirements. Use the Lift/Overwrite Segment Mode tool to move the audio channels to the correct tracks.

■ **Were the camera angles chosen in the rough cuts?**

It is best to choose the angle with the person talking or the one with the most action. You even cut back and forth during a conversation to give an editor a starting point.

CHAPTER 6:
Audio Passes

Tasks in This Chapter

IF EDITORS SIMPLY CUT down the rough cut to make an episode cut, audio passes would not be necessary, but that is not the case. Instead of cutting down the rough cut, editors add new reality, interviews, music, and sound effects to a sequence to make it as entertaining as possible. Since time is of the essence when editing, and since editors don't always choose the best audio or lay in sound effects and music at the correct levels, it is your responsibility as the assistant editor to do an audio pass on an episode before it goes to the executives. When the executives view the episode, they should be able to make notes without being distracted by music that is too loud or interviews and reality that can barely be heard.

Therefore, when completing a rough cut for an editor, choose the best audio for all of the interview and reality clips. Use your best judgment. If you ever think to yourself, "What did they say?" the audio needs to be fixed. Any audio that detracts from the main focus of the scene—such as inaudible dialogue, loud music, distracting ambient sounds, and network unacceptable profanity—should be raised, lowered, or bleeped, as appropriate.

When completing an audio pass, there are three things to consider:

- Has the best audio been chosen for the interviews and reality?

- Has the volume level of anything too soft or too loud been adjusted?

- Have all curse words been bleeped?

Choosing the Best Audio

To choose the best audio

1. In the Project window, on the Bins tab, open the bin containing the sequence that needs an audio pass, and then double-click the sequence.

2. Open the Audio tool (Mac: ⌘+1 | PC: Ctrl+1).

3. In the Timeline window, place the position indicator at the beginning of the sequence.

4. Play (press L) and listen to the interviews and reality to determine if the best audio has been chosen, and do one of the following:

   (a) If the best audio has been chosen, close the bin.

   –or–

   (b) If the best audio has not been chosen, proceed to Step 5.

5. Place the position indicator over that clip.

6. Enable only the audio tracks of that clip.

7. Mark Clip (press T).

8. Go to In (press Q).

9. Match Frame (press F4).

10. Solo one of the source audio speaker tracks (Mac: ⌘+Click | PC: Ctrl+Click).

11. Play (press L) and listen.

12. Solo another source audio speaker track to compare to that of Step 10 (Mac: ⌘+Click | PC: Ctrl+Click).

13. Select the channel with the best audio.

14. Patch the source audio tracks to the record audio tracks.

15. Deselect the source video track.

16. Overwrite (press B) the best audio to the sequence.

17. Continue watching the sequence while listening for bad audio, and repeat Steps 5–16 as necessary.

18. Save the bin (Mac: ⌘+S | PC: Ctrl+S).

> **Note** | In the sequence, there may be two audio tracks, but there may only be one good audio track from the source clip. Therefore, once you choose the best track, overwrite that same track onto the second track in the sequence so that there is a left and right channel heard through the speakers.

Adjusting the Volume Level

While listening to the interviews and reality, pay attention to the music and sound effects. Music and sound effects should complement the scene not overpower the drama. At times, editors will intentionally make something softer or louder to make an editorial point. If you have questions, ask someone; otherwise, make the music and sound effects as complementary as possible.

To adjust the volume level of one audio track

1. In the Project window, on the Bins tab, open the bin containing the sequence that needs an audio pass, and then double-click the sequence.

2. In the Timeline window, place the position indicator at the beginning of the sequence.

3. Play (press L) the sequence and listen for audio that is too soft or too loud, and then Stop when you encounter it.

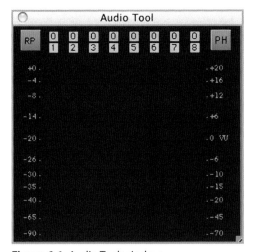

Figure 6-1. Audio Tool window.

4. Place the position indicator over that clip.

5. Enable the audio tracks for that clip.

6. Select Tools≫Audio Mixer.

7. On the Audio Mixer tool that appears, raise or lower the audio level of a clip by moving the Volume Level slider of the corresponding audio tracks in the sequence up or down.

Note | It is a good practice to have the Audio tool open while doing audio passes, so you can easily see where the levels are.

The type of work you are doing, where the final product will be viewed, and the requirements from the network will determine what the audio levels should be for your sequence.

Determine your company's specifications, but remember that you are doing a rough pass. Once the episode is completely finished, an audio engineer will finesse the audio levels to perfection.

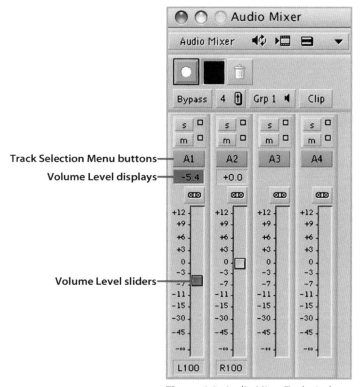

Track Selection Menu buttons ─

Volume Level displays ─

Volume Level sliders ─

Figure 6-2. Audio Mixer Tool window.

8. Continue watching the sequence while listening for bad audio and repeat Steps 3–7 as necessary (skip Step 6 because the Audio Mixer tool will already be open).

9. Save the bin (Mac: ⌘+S | PC: Ctrl+S).

Ganging Audio

Audio tracks are usually placed in the sequence in pairs. Frequently, one action performed on one audio track should be performed on the other as well. In the instance of raising and lowering audio, it can be time consuming to, for example, lower audio track 1 (A1) and then lower audio track 2 (A2). Fortunately, with *ganging* it is possible to group adjustments across tracks and adjust two or more Volume Level sliders simultaneously.

To adjust the volume level of two or more audio tracks simultaneously using ganging

1. In the Project window, on the Bins tab, open the bin containing the sequence that needs an audio pass, and then double-click the sequence.

2. In the Timeline window, place the position indicator over the clip.

3. Enable the audio tracks for that clip.

4. Select Tools≫Audio Mixer.

5. On the Audio Mixer tool that appears, click Gang for each track that needs to be adjusted.

6. Raise or lower the audio level for all ganged tracks simultaneously by moving the Volume Level slider of one of the ganged tracks up or down.

7. Save the bin (Mac: ⌘+S | PC: Ctrl+S).

> **Tip** | Audio levels can also be adjusted by typing a number into the Volume Level display of the Audio Mixer tool.

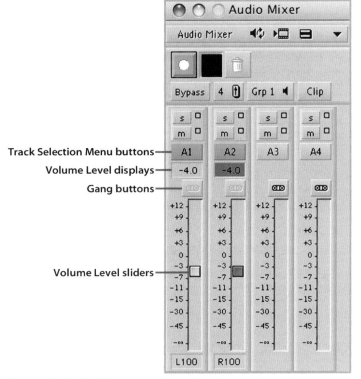

Figure 6-3. Audio Mixer tool with the Gang buttons labeled.

Bleeping Curse Words

Lowering the volume of curse word audio and replacing it with tone media is known as *bleeping*. *Tone media* is a constant 1000 Hz audio signal. There are some situations where a horn, bell, or funny sound effect is used in place of tone or where no sound at all is called for. Whatever your company's preference, this chapter will prepare you to handle it.

There isn't an industry-standard list of curse words to bleep because the list is situational—that is, it is company- and show-specific. However, you can be assured that s***, a**hole, and f*** (or any derivative of this word) probably will have to be bleeped. B**** is sometimes bleeped. It is best to ask an informed person what can stay and what needs to be bleeped.

To bleep curse words and replace them with tone media or a sound effect

1. In the Project window, on the Bins tab, open the bin containing the sequence that needs an audio pass, and then double-click the sequence.

2. In the Timeline window, place the position indicator at the beginning of the sequence.

3. Play (press L) the sequence, and listen for an unacceptable curse word, and then Stop when you encounter one.

4. Deselect all tracks (Mac: Shift+⌘+A | PC: Shift+Ctrl+A).

5. Enable the audio track (or tracks) with the curse word.

6. Place the position indicator at the beginning of the curse word.

7. Add Edit (press F8) at that point.

8. Play or scrub through the sequence to the end of the curse word. (Make sure Caps Lock is enabled on your keyboard to hear the audio during scrubbing.)

9. Place the position indicator at the end of the curse word.

10. Add Edit (press F8) at that point.

> **Tip** | Do not remove the portion of the audio clip that contains the curse word from the sequence because uncensored versions of an episode may be delivered to different markets or used for DVD material, and it is time-consuming to bring the removed audio back.
>
> Instead, lower the portion of the audio clip that contains the curse word to – ∞ (minus infinity), so it is silent.

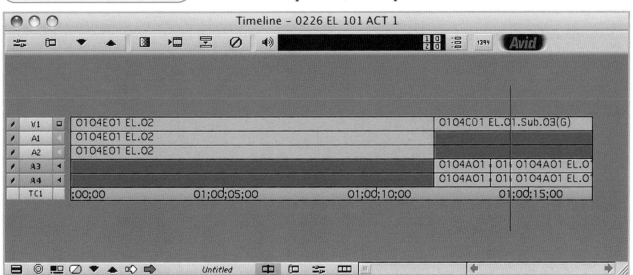

Figure 6-4. Timeline window of 0226 EL 101 Act 1 displaying add edits around the curse word on audio tracks 3 and 4 (A3 and A4, respectively).

11. Place the position indicator over the add edit section.

12. Select Tools≫Audio Mixer, and click Gang for each of the tracks of the add edit section.

13. Lower the audio level for each of the tracks of the add edit section simultaneously by moving the Volume Level slider for one of the ganged tracks down to − ∞ (minus infinity).

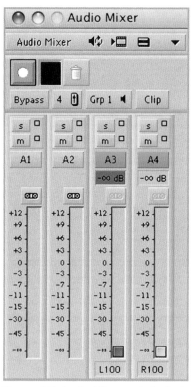

Figure 6-5. Audio Mixer tool displaying the audio levels for audio tracks 3 and 4 (A3 and A4, respectively) lowered to − ∞ (minus infinity).

14. Create a bin (Mac: ⌘+N | PC: Ctrl+N).

15. Rename the new bin. (For example, Mica Work Bin. This bin is used for supplemental materials you will frequently use.)

16. Open the Audio tool (Mac: ⌘+1 | PC: Ctrl+1), click PH (peak hold), and then select Create Tone Media.

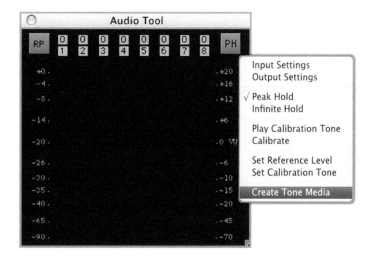

17. In the Create Tone Media dialog box that appears, do the following, and then click OK.

    (a) In the Number of Tracks menu, select 2.

    (b) In the Target Bin menu, select the bin for the tone.

    (c) In the Target Drive menu, select the drive to save the media to.

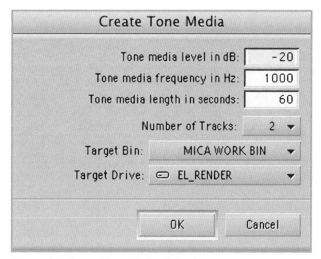

Figure 6-6. Create Tone Media dialog box.

18. In the Timeline window, confirm that the position indicator is over the add edit section, and then Mark Clip (press T).

19. Double-click the tone (created in Step 17) in the bin (or whatever sound is being used to cover the bleep) to load it into the Source monitor.

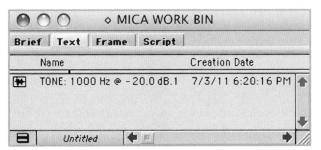

Figure 6-7. Mica Work bin displaying the newly created tone media.

20. Patch the source audio tracks to unused record audio tracks (this can be above or below the add edit section).

21. Overwrite (press B) the tone into the sequence.

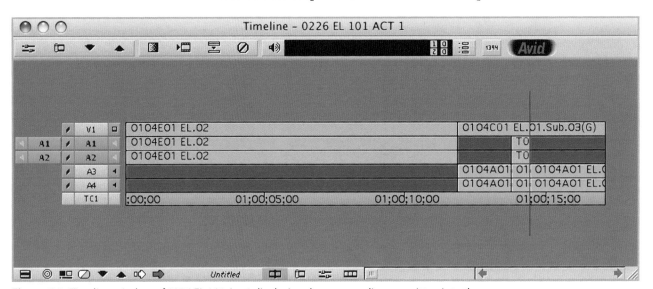

Figure 6-8. Timeline window of 0226 EL 101 Act 1 displaying the tone media overwritten into the sequence.

22. Play back the bleeped section to determine if the curse word is completely bleeped, and then do one of the following:

(a) If the curse word is completely bleeped, proceed to Step 23.

–or–

(b) If the curse word is not completely bleeped, press undo until the curse word section is restored to its original state (that is, when the add edits are no longer in the sequence, which is at Step 6), and then repeat Steps 7–22(a). It isn't necessary to repeat the steps for creating tone media (that is, Steps 14–17) because undo will not undo the creation of the tone media.

23. Repeat Steps 3–22 until all curse words are completely bleeped.

24. Save the bin (Mac: ⌘+S | PC: Ctrl+S).

Did I Do This Correctly?

■ **Was the best audio chosen for the episode?**

Make sure the audio is clear.

■ **Has the volume level of anything too soft or too loud been adjusted?**

Any audio that is too soft or too loud distracts the viewers. While watching a show, a viewer shouldn't have to cover their ears or get closer to the speakers to understand what is being heard.

■ **Was a curse word accidentally deleted?**

The curse word should not be deleted. Instead it will be silent because the audio has been lowered to $-\infty$ (minus infinity). This is done because there could be uncensored versions of an episode delivered to different markets or for DVD material.

■ **Have all sounds regarding the curse word been silenced?**

If a curse word has not been entirely silenced, it will be possible to hear "f" or "sh" sounds, for example, that indicate what a person might be saying beneath the bleep. This is due to incorrectly placed add edits.

■ **Was tone added?**

There should be tone beneath the lowered audio curse word unless given specific instructions by your company to use something else. Sometimes a horn, bell, or funny sound effect is used in place of tone.

CHAPTER 7:
Backgrounds and Effects

Tasks in This Chapter

THE ÆDVENTURES OF KARS & GRETIG

M ANY INTERVIEWS AND OTHER graphical elements for a show are filmed against a green screen that is easily removed from the shot (keyed out) and replaced by a video or graphic background. This practice efficiently accommodates postproduction companies' need for flexibility regarding background elements.

Overwriting a Background into a Sequence

To overwrite a background into a sequence

1. In the Project window, on the Bins tab, open the bin containing the sequence that needs backgrounds, and then double-click the sequence.

2. Scroll through the sequence and locate the first interview clip (for example) that needs a background.

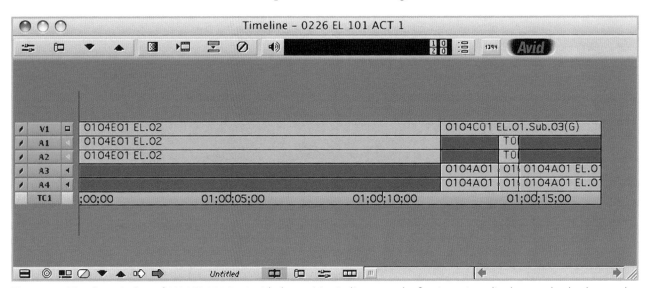

Figure 7-1. Timeline window of 0226 EL 101 Act 1 with the position indicator on the first interview clip that needs a background.

3. Create a video track, if needed (Mac: ⌘+Y | PC: Ctrl+Y).

In our example, a video track is needed because the interview clip and the background need to be on separate tracks.

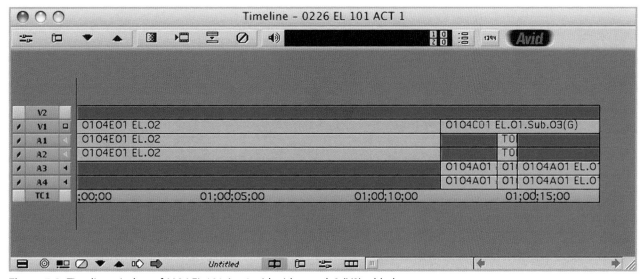

Figure 7-2. Timeline window of 0226 EL 101 Act 1 with video track 2 (V2) added.

4. Click Lift/Overwrite Segment Mode ![icon] .

5. Hold down Ctrl and then click the interview clip on video track 1 (V1) and drag it to video track 2 (V2).

> **Note** | Holding Ctrl prevents the selected clip from being moved horizontally (that is, the clip is restricted to vertical movement only).

6. Click Lift/Overwrite Segment Mode to exit the function.

7. Deselect all tracks (Mac: Shift+⌘+A | PC: Shift+Ctrl+A).

> **Tip** | Another way to exit the Lift/Overwrite Segment Mode function and other tools is to click in the Timecode bar in the Timeline window.

8. Click V2.

9. Place the position indicator on the interview clip.

10. Mark Clip (press T).

See APPENDIX 5: *Mark IN and OUT* on page 337 for more information about Mark Clip.

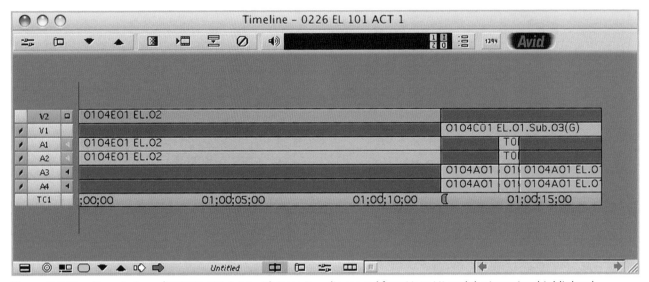

Figure 7-3. Timeline window of 0226 EL 101 Act 1 with interview clip moved from V1 to V2 and the interview highlighted.

11. Click V1.

> **Note** | After deselecting all of the video tracks, you could click V1 and use Mark Clip (press T) to achieve the same result.

12. Deselect V2, but make sure the V2 Record Track Monitor button is active.

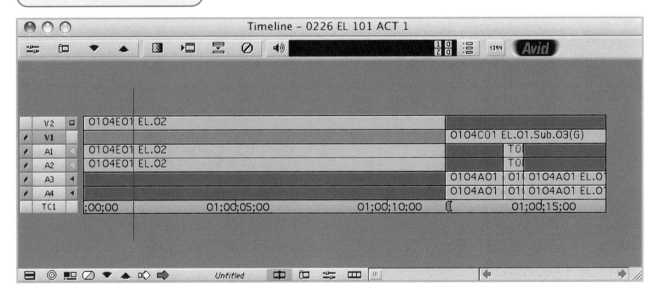

13. Open the bin containing the backgrounds.

14. Double-click the correct background.

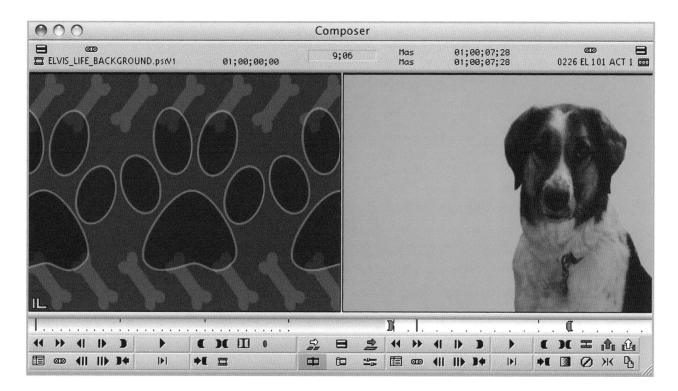

15. Make sure the source video track is patched to record video track 1.

16. Overwrite (press B) the background into the sequence.

> **Note** | Mark IN and Mark OUT points weren't placed in the background clip because this is a static graphic. If your background isn't static, make sure you Mark IN at the appropriate start point.

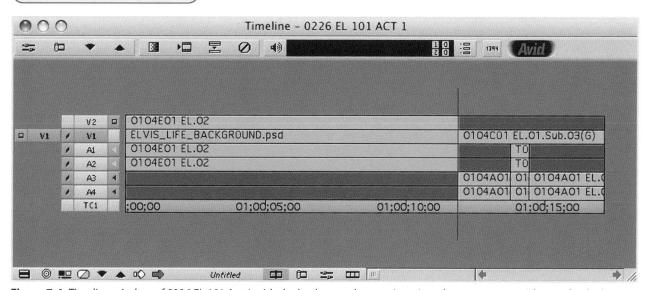

Figure 7-4. Timeline window of 0226 EL 101 Act 1 with the background overwritten into the sequence on video track 1 (V1).

17. Save the bin (Mac: ⌘+S | PC: Ctrl+S).

Keying Out a Background

The sequence now has the interview on V2 (with the green screen background) and the graphic/video background on V1. However, although the interview and the graphic/video background are on the correct tracks (that is, interview track V2 is above graphic/video background track V1), you cannot see through the green screen background on V2 to see the graphic/video background on V1. To make the graphic/video background on V1 visible, remove (key out) the green screen background on V2.

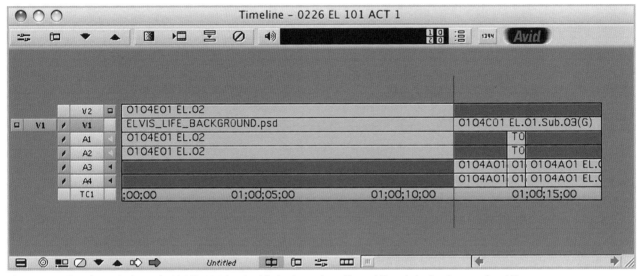

Figure 7-5. Timeline window of 0226 EL 101 Act 1 with the interview clip on V2 and the background on V1.

To key out a background

> **Tip |** You can also access the Effect palette by clicking the Effects tab on the Project window.

1. Open the Effect palette (Mac: ⌘+8 | PC: Ctrl+8).

2. On the left pane of the Effect palette, click Key in the Effect Category list.

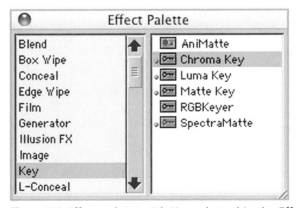

Figure 7-6. Effect palette with Key selected in the Effect Category list and Chroma Key selected in the right pane.

3. In the right pane, drag the Chroma Key icon onto the clip on V2, and the Chroma Key effect appears on the interview clip (V2).

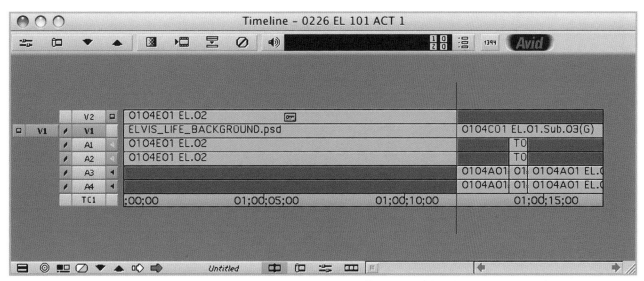

Figure 7-7. Timeline window of 0226 EL 101 Act 1 with the Chroma Key effect icon displayed on the interview clip (V2).

Although the Chroma Key effect is on the interview clip (V2) in the Timeline window, it may not have any visible effect on the video clip in the Effect Preview monitor if the Chroma Key parameters are not configured properly.

The Chroma Key defaults to remove blue backgrounds. If the background of your video clip is green (as in our example), the keyed color must be changed from blue to green.

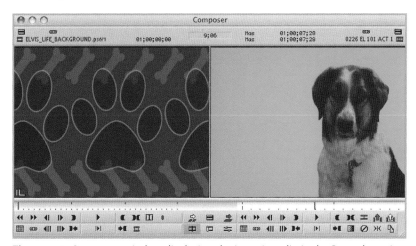

Figure 7-8. Composer window displaying the interview clip in the Record monitor and the Chroma Key effect not having an effect on the clip.

4. Click V2.

Note | To change the parameters of an effect, click Effect Mode. Entering the Effect mode opens the Effect Editor and transforms the Record monitor into the Effect Preview monitor.

5. In the Timeline window, with the position indicator on the interview clip, click Effect Mode ⚏ .

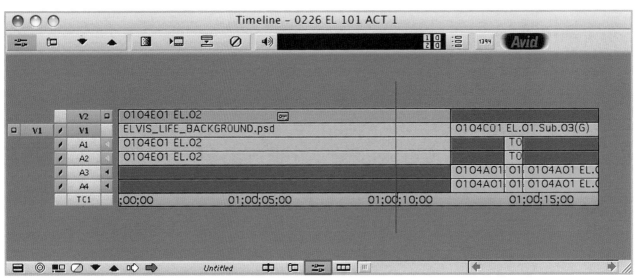

Figure 7-9. Timeline window of 0226 EL 101 Act 1 with the position indicator on the interview clip and the Effect Mode button highlighted.

6. In the Effect Editor that appears, in the Key area, position the cursor over the Color Preview box (underneath the Chroma Key effect icon on the upper right) until the cursor changes to an eyedropper.

7. Click and drag the eyedropper to the green screen background in the Effect Preview monitor and click on the green color, and the green screen background is removed (keyed out).

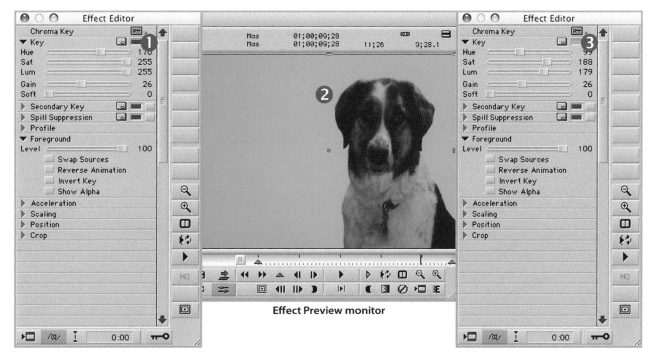

Effect Preview monitor

❶ Position the cursor over the Color Preview box until the cursor changes to an eyedropper.
❷ Drag the eyedropper to the green screen background in the Effect Preview monitor.
❸ The new chroma key color is reflected in the Color Preview box.

Figure 7-10. Color Preview of the Effect Editor being changed from the default blue to the green present in the interview clip.

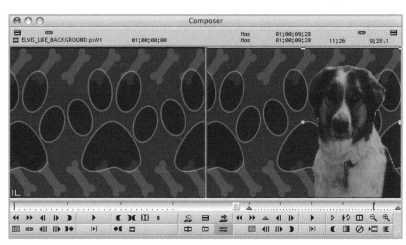

Figure 7-11. Composer window displaying the green color removed from the interview clip revealing the graphic as the background.

FIGURE 7-11 is the result of Steps 6–7. Don't worry about any remnants of green around the interview subject—executives are aware that it is removed later in the editing process.

Do play around with the Chroma Key parameters to make the video look as good as possible at this point, but be aware that you might not have the time to do this. So practice on your own time!

8.   Close the Effect Editor.

9.   Save the bin (Mac: ⌘+S | PC: Ctrl+S).

Nesting Effects

There are occasions when a video clip requires more than one effect. For example, application of a Chroma Key effect to remove a video background and then application of a 16:9 Letterbox effect (Effect palette | Reformat category) to display a video clip in a different aspect ratio.

When more than one effect is placed on a video clip, it is called *nesting*. Nested effects must be placed on video clips in a certain order to ensure that they don't override one another. Furthermore, the order of the effects determines how the nested effects play in the sequence. Press Option (Mac) | Alt (PC) and drag the effect onto the video clip to place effects on top of one another.

An easy way to see if a clip has nested effects on it is to Step In on that clip.

Play with nesting effects on your own time to see how the nested effects play in a sequence, and Step In and Step Out of those clips to see them in the Timeline window.

To determine if a clip has nested effects on it

1.   Click the video track with the suspected multiple effects on it.

2.   Place the position indicator on that video clip.

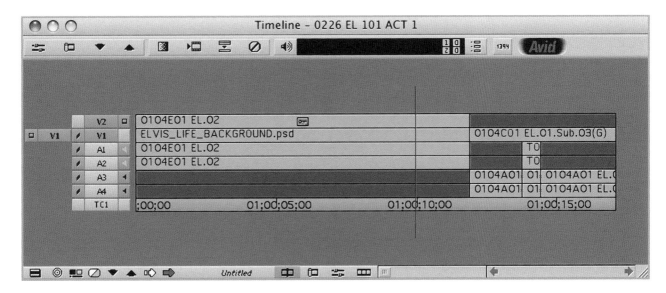

3. Click Step In ![Step In] .

When Step In is clicked, the sequence disappears from view and only that specific video clip is visible in the Timeline window. If an additional effect is present, it appears on the video clip. (There isn't one in this example.)

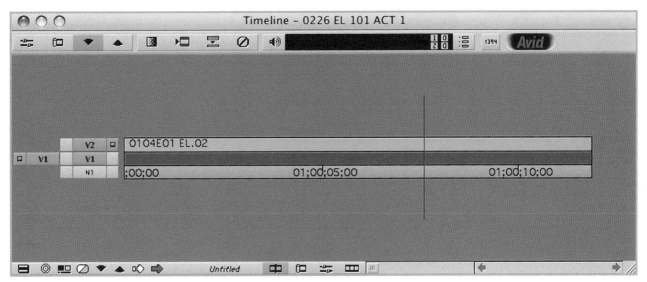

Figure 7-12. Timeline window of 0226 EL 101 Act 1 stepped in to the clip on V2.

4. Click Step Out ![Step Out] to return to the normal view of the Timeline window.

You can also click Lift/Overwrite Segment Mode and double-click the video clip to see if a video clip has multiple effects. Double-clicking the effect on V2 shows that there was a Resize effect on this clip in addition to the Chroma Key effect.

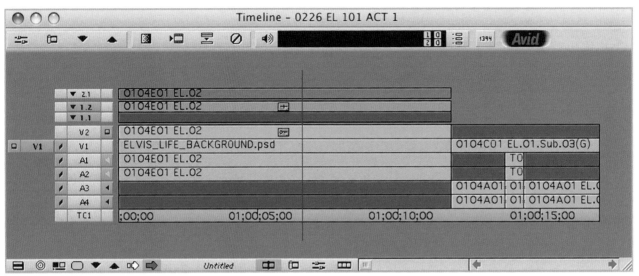

Figure 7-13. Timeline window of 0226 EL 101 Act 1 displaying a nested Resize effect on the clip in V2 (see 1.2) in addition to the Chroma Key effect. You use Lift/Overwrite Segment Mode to double-click on a video clip to see if a video clip has multiple effects.

Saving Effects

Effects that will be used repeatedly should be configured once and saved to a bin. The Chroma Key effect created for the interview will be used repeatedly, so it makes sense to save it.

To save an effect

Tip | You can save any effect to a bin using this method.

1. With the Effect Editor open, drag the Chroma Key effect icon from the Effect Editor to a bin.

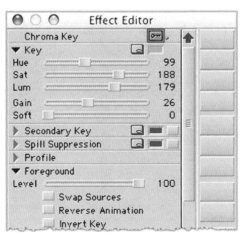

Figure 7-14. Effect Editor window with the Chroma Key effect icon highlighted.

2. Close the Effect Editor.

3. Rename the Chroma Key effect in the bin.

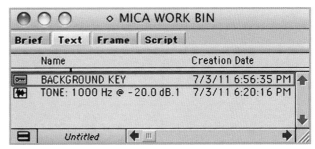

Figure 7-15. Mica Work bin showing the saved and renamed Chroma Key effect.

4. Save the bin (Mac: ⌘+S | PC: Ctrl+S).

To apply a saved effect

1. Drag the saved Chroma Key effect (Background Key) from the bin onto the video clip in the sequence.

2. Confirm there is a background behind the video clip.

3. Save the bin (Mac: ⌘+S | PC: Ctrl+S).

Placing the Same Effect on Multiple Clips

For situations where it is necessary to place the same effect on multiple clips, click Lift/Overwrite Segment Mode in the Timeline window. A good example of this is adding a Reformat effect to multiple interview clips.

To place the same effect on multiple clips

1. Click Lift/Overwrite Segment Mode.

2. Press Shift+Click on each clip that needs the effect.

3. In the Effect palette, select the category in the left pane, and double-click the desired effect in the right pane, and then the effect appears on all selected clips.

4. Click Lift/Overwrite Segment Mode to exit the function.

Deleting a Single Effect from a Clip

To delete a single effect from a clip

1. Place the position indicator over the clip with the effect.

2. Click the track button of the video and/or audio tracks with the effect.

3. Do one of the following to delete the effect:

   (a) If in Effect mode, press Delete.

   –or–

   (b) If in Source/Record mode, on the Record monitor (bottom toolbar; row 2), click Remove Effect ⊘ .

Figure 7-16. Record monitor bottom toolbar with Remove Effect button highlighted.

Did I Do This Correctly?

■ **Do all video clips that require backgrounds have them?**

Scrub through the act completely to make sure you haven't missed keying out the interview backgrounds and replacing them with their correct backgrounds.

■ **Are all backgrounds the exact length of the interview thereby eliminating flash frames?**

It isn't uncommon to cut in a background that is one frame longer or shorter than the interview. In these instances, when this interview section is played, a *flash frame* appears that is distracting to viewers. This is why the background must be the exact length of the interview. Avoid this problem by using Mark Clip.

■ **Are all green screens keyed out?**

All interviews should have the green screen removed from the interview frame so that the background beneath it is visible.

CHAPTER 8:
Titles

Tasks in This Chapter

THE ÆDVENTURES OF KARS & GRETIG

202   THE AVID ASSISTANT EDITOR'S HANDBOOK

T ITLES ARE MAINLY USED for identification purposes: to identify an interview subject, clarify what someone is saying, identify a location, or give credit to the people who worked on a show.

The Title tool is the instrument to create titles. Review APPENDIX 6: *Title Tool* on page 353 before beginning this chapter so that you are familiar with the Title tool and its functions.

Settings Needed

Configure the following setting before beginning the tasks in this chapter.

GRID BUTTON

Navigation: Command palette | FX tab | Grid button

Shortcut: Command palette: Mac: ⌘+3 | PC: Ctrl+3

You should map the Grid button to your keyboard or workspace. The Grid button is located on the FX tab of the Command palette (Mac: ⌘+3 | PC: Ctrl+3).

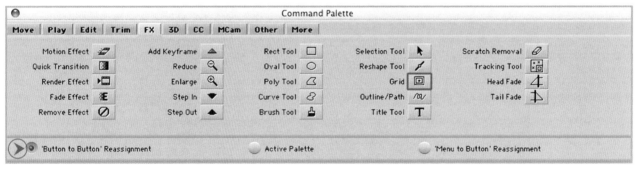

Figure 8-1. Command palette with 'Button to Button' Reassignment selected and the Grid button highlighted.

Clicking the Grid button displays the *safe title area* (also called the *title safe area*) and the *safe action area* in the Record monitor to verify that titles are within the appropriate boundary.

Reviewing the Major Types

Lower Thirds

Lower thirds are mainly used to identify the characters of an episode and typically are a two-part element: a graphic background and a title on top of the background.

Figure 8-2. Lower thirds.

Subtitles

Subtitles are used to clarify unintelligible speech due to a person speaking softly, mumbling their words, or speaking in a different language.

Figure 8-3. Subtitles.

Executive Credits

Executive credits appear at the beginning of a show and list the executives of the show.

Figure 8-4. Executive Credits.

End Credits

End credits appear at the end of a show and list everyone who worked on the show.

STORY PRODUCER
Flora McCarthy

ASSOCIATE STORY PRODUCER
Dan Otto

PRODUCTION ASSISTANT
Chip Hart

Figure 8-5. End credits.

Creating Titles

Creating titles is a pretty standard procedure. In a nutshell, creating titles is as simple as typing or copying/pasting text into the Title Tool window, modifying the look and location of the text within the Title Tool window, and saving the title.

To create a title

1. Open the bin containing the sequence that needs titles, and then double-click the correct sequence.

2. Locate the first video clip that needs a title, and then place the position indicator over that clip.

> **Tip** | By placing the position indicator over the video clip that needs the title prior to opening the Title Tool window, the Title Tool window appears displaying the video clip as the title background.

3. Select Tools≫Title Tool.

    The Menu toolbar changes when the Title Tool window is open: Script, Object, and Alignment are added as menu options. These options can be used in conjunction with the Title Tool toolbar.

 Avid Media Composer   File   Edit   Bin   Clip   Output   Special   Tools   Toolset   Windows   Script   Object   Alignment   Help

Figure 8-6. The Menu toolbar highlighting the three options that are added when the Title Tool window is open: Script, Object, and Alignment.

4. In the New Title dialog box that appears, click Title Tool, and the Title Tool window appears.

Note | The Marquee tool is an advanced version of the Title tool. For our purposes, it isn't necessary to use the Marquee tool, but you should explore the Marquee tool when you have time.

Figure 8-7. New Title dialog box.

Note | The Title Tool window opens displaying the same aspect ratio as that of the Source/Record monitors.

If the Source/Record monitors are 4:3, that is how the Title Tool window will appear. (As shown in Figure 8-8.)

If the aspect ratio of your project is 16:9, you can change the aspect ratio of the Source/Record monitors (and by consequence the Title Tool window) by doing the following:

◆ In the Project window, on the Settings tab, select Composer from the Settings list.

◆ In the Composer Settings dialog box that appears, on the Window tab, select 16:9 monitors.

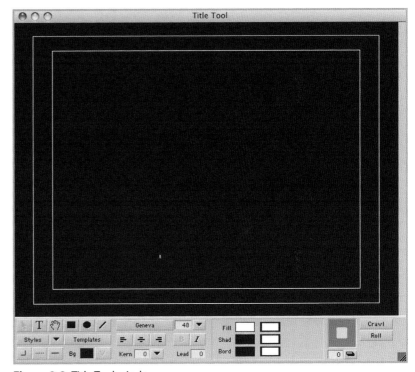

Figure 8-8. Title Tool window.

5. Click the Text tool.

6. Click in the Title Tool window and type the title text.

7. Select the text.

Tip | Copy (Mac: ⌘+C|PC: Ctrl+C) and paste (Mac: ⌘+V|PC: Ctrl+V) title text from an electronic text file (this file must exist on the Avid computer) to prevent typing errors and to speed up the title creation process.

8. Modify the text using the Text Formatting tools and the Color and Transparency Blend tools.

The Title Tool Text Formatting tools operate in a manner similar to those in most document creation software.

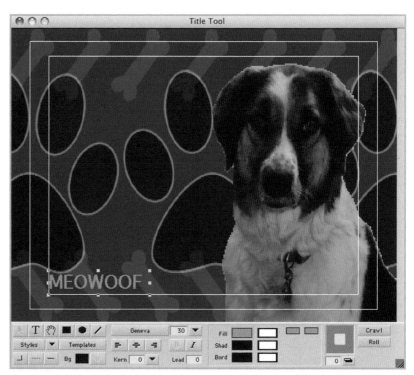

Figure 8-9. Title Tool window showing text created over a video background.

Note | Position the title text within safe title area (also called the title safe area) and in accordance with "no-fly-zone" parameters.

The no-fly-zone is an area of the television screen reserved for network graphics. This area differs from network to network.

9. Click the Selection tool and position the title text.

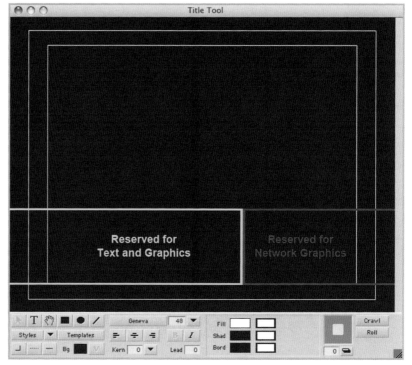

Reserved for Text and Graphics

Reserved for Network Graphics

Figure 8-10. Title Tool window highlighting the area of the "no-fly-zone" where text can and cannot be placed.

Tip | Right-clicking in the Title Tool window also brings up a save option.

10. Save the title (Mac: Shift+⌘+S | PC: Shift+Ctrl+S), and then in the Save Title dialog box that appears, click Save. (Remember, save it to the correct bin, on the correct drive, and in the correct resolution.)

Figure 8-11. Save Title dialog box.

11. Close the Title tool.

Note | After closing the Title Tool window, the newly created title automatically loads in the Source monitor.

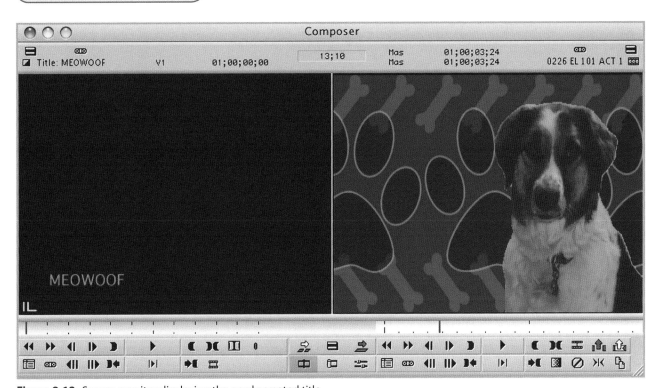

Figure 8-12. Source monitor displaying the newly created title.

12. Save the bin (Mac: ⌘+S | PC: Ctrl+S).

Overwriting a Title into a Sequence

Once a title is created, you can overwrite the title into a sequence.

To overwrite a title into a sequence

1. Open the bin containing the titles.

2. Double-click the correct title, and the Composer window displays the title in the Source monitor.

3. Open the bin containing the sequence that needs titles.

4. Double-click the correct sequence, and the Timeline window displays the sequence.

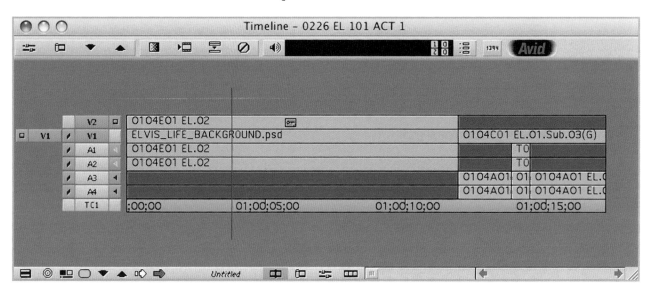

5. Do one of the following:

    (a) If there is only one video track in the sequence, and if the title is to appear without a video background, proceed to Step 6.

    –or–

    (b) If there is only one video track in the sequence, and if the title is to appear with a video background, create a video track (Mac: ⌘+Y | PC: Ctrl+Y), and then proceed to Step 6.

6. Deselect all of the audio tracks.

7. Patch the source video track to the desired record video track.

> **Note** | To overwrite a title on top of a video clip, two video tracks are necessary: one for the title and one for the video clip.

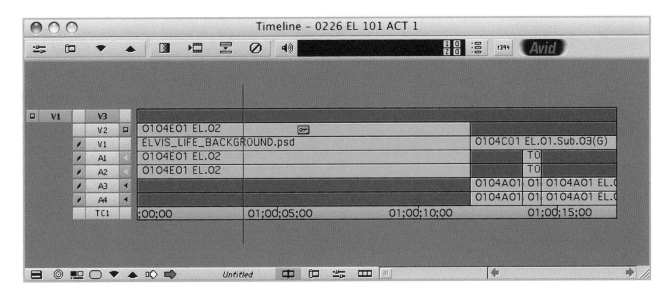

8. Mark IN (press I) in the sequence at the first point for the title.

9. Mark OUT (press O) in the sequence at the last point for the title.

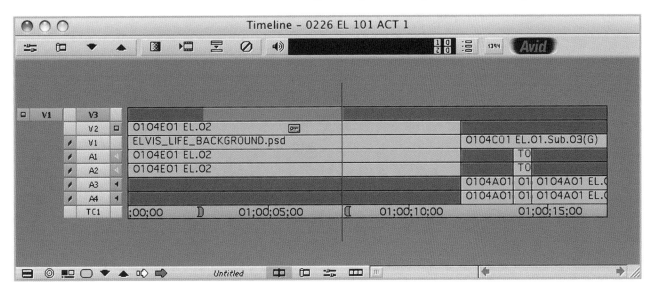

10. Overwrite (press B) the title into the sequence.

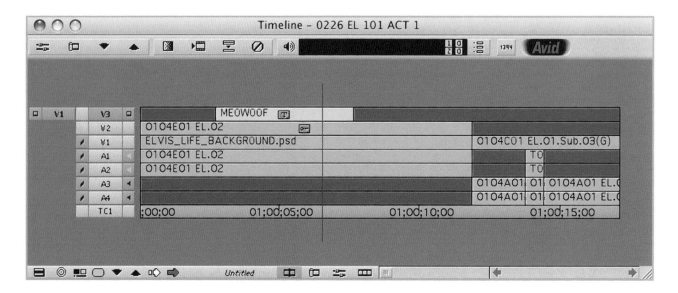

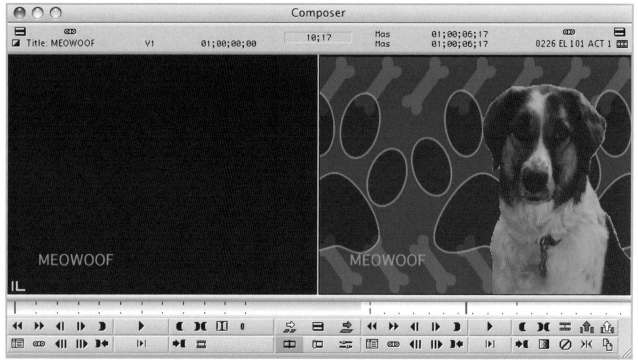

Figure 8-13. Source monitor displays the title created for insertion into the sequence. Record monitor displays the title over a video background.

11. Save both of the bins (Mac: ⌘+S | PC: Ctrl+S).

Creating Crawling and Rolling Titles

Instead of having titles cut on and off from one another, it is possible to have them move in a horizontal line (crawling title) or vertical line (rolling title) over the screen. Many television shows and films have rolling titles at the end of those productions. News productions frequently have a bar that crawls across the bottom of the screen with extra information regarding the newscast.

To create a crawling or rolling title

1. Open the bin containing the sequence that needs a crawling or rolling title, and then double-click the correct sequence.

2. In the Timeline window, locate the first video clip that needs a crawling or rolling title, and then place the position indicator over that video clip.

3. Select Tools≫Title Tool.

4. In the Title Tool window that appears, click the Title tool.

5. Click Crawl or Roll (depending on what type of title you are creating).

6. Do one of the following:

    (a) If the electronic file containing the title text (that is, the credits) exists on the Avid computer, copy (Mac: ⌘+C | PC: Ctrl+C) and paste (Mac: ⌘+V | PC: Ctrl+V) the title text into the Title Tool window and then proceed to Step 7.

    –or–

    (b) Type the text in the Title Tool window and then proceed to Step 7.

7. Select the text, and then modify it using the Text Formatting tools and the Color and Transparency Blend tools.

8. Click the Selection tool, and then modify the control points of the object selection handles to set the boundaries of where the title should be.

9. Position the text in the Title Tool window within the safe title area (also called the title safe area) and outside of the network no-fly-zone area.

10. Save the title. (Remember, save it to the correct bin, on the correct drive, and in the correct resolution.)

11. Close the Title tool.

12. Save the bin (Mac: ⌘+S | PC: Ctrl+S).

Note | Crawling or rolling titles are frequently used to display a large amount of information.

In those situations, instead of typing a lot of text, copy/paste the text into the Title tool.

Copy/paste is only possible if the electronic text file exists on the Avid computer.

Note | Sometimes a rolling title will be on the left side of the screen or a section of the screen.

Modifying the object selection handles allows you to position the title where it needs to go.

For instance, into a small rectangle-shaped text object.

To clarify, the Selection tool allows you to move that small rectangle to different locations within the Title tool.

Overwriting Crawling or Rolling Titles into a Sequence

The duration of a rolling or crawling title is initially dependent on the number of lines of text. Afterward, Avid adjusts the speed of the title to fit within IN and OUT points set in the sequence. Essentially, you set the length and Avid sets the speed.

To overwrite a crawling or rolling title into a sequence

1. Open the bin containing the crawling or rolling title.

2. Double-click the correct crawling or rolling title.

3. Mark Clip (press T).

4. Open the bin containing the sequence that needs the crawling or rolling title.

5. Double-click the correct sequence.

    When a crawling or rolling title plays, it starts with the text off screen at one location and ends with the text off screen in a different location. If you want all of the text within the crawl or roll to appear on screen, it is necessary to Mark Clip on the crawling or rolling title while it is in the Source monitor. Otherwise, the text will stop in the middle of the crawl or roll.

6. Do one of the following:

    (a) If there is only one video track in the sequence, and if the title is to appear without a video background, proceed to Step 7.

    –or–

    (b) If there is only one video track in the sequence, and if the title is to appear with a video background, create a video track (Mac: ⌘+Y | PC: Ctrl+Y), and then proceed to Step 7.

7. Mark IN (press I) and OUT (press O) in the sequence for the desired duration of the crawling or rolling title (for example, 30 seconds).

8. Patch the source video track to the desired record video track.

9. Overwrite (press B) the crawling or rolling title into the sequence.

10. Press Play in the sequence, and then do one of the following:

    (a) If the crawling or rolling title appears after pressing Play, proceed to Step 11.

    –or–

Note | When you play the sequence, it is possible that the crawling or rolling title won't appear—usually an indication that the crawling or rolling title needs to be rendered.

Rendering is necessary for clips that can't play back in real time and rendering creates a media file that enables the crawling or rolling title to play back.

(b) If the crawling or rolling title does not appear after pressing Play, render the crawling or rolling title by doing the following, and then proceed to Step 11.

(i) Select all of the tracks in the sequence (Mac: ⌘+A | PC: Ctrl+A).

(ii) Mark IN (press I) and OUT (press O) around the crawling or rolling title.

(iii) Select Clip≫Render In/Out.

(iv) In the Render Effects dialog box that appears, on the Drive menu, select the correct drive, and then click OK.

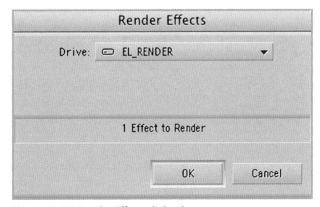

Figure 8-14. Render Effects dialog box.

(v) Play the sequence to view the crawling or rolling title.

11. Save both of the bins (Mac: ⌘+S | PC: Ctrl+S).

Modifying Titles

When you encounter a title that is misspelled or an existing title that needs to have material added, you can choose to create a title from scratch or modify the title that is in the sequence.

To modify a title in a sequence

1. Open the bin containing the sequence that needs to have a title modified, and then double-click the correct sequence.

2. Place the position indicator over the title that needs to be modified.

3. In the Timeline window, enable the video track that has the title that needs to be modified.

4. On the bottom toolbar of the Timeline window, click Effect Mode 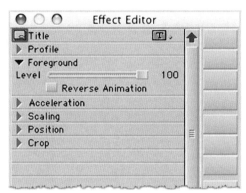 .

5. In the Effect Editor window that appears, click Other Options to open the Title Tool window.

Figure 8-15. Effect Editor window with the Other Options button highlighted.

6. In the Edit Title dialog box that appears, click No, and the Title Tool window appears.

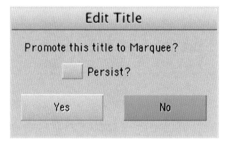

Figure 8-16. Edit Title dialog box.

7. Modify the title using the Title Tool toolbar.

8. Right-click and select Save the Title As.

9. Click Save.

Figure 8-17. Avid Media Composer dialog box prompting you to save the title and exit the Title Tool.

10. Click Save. (Remember, save it to the correct bin, on the correct drive, and in the correct resolution.) The title will update in the sequence.

11. Close the Effect Editor.

12. Save the bin (Mac: ⌘+S | PC: Ctrl+S).

Saving Title Templates

When using the Title tool, you may find yourself using the same font, font size, and font color over and over again. To maintain consistency and to save time, save these parameters, and others such as shadow and border size, in a template. For example, the text in FIGURE 8-18 was created using the following settings:

- Font: American Typewriter
- Font Size: 40
- Font Style: Bold
- Font Just.: Center
- Fill Color: Red
- Border Color: Yellow

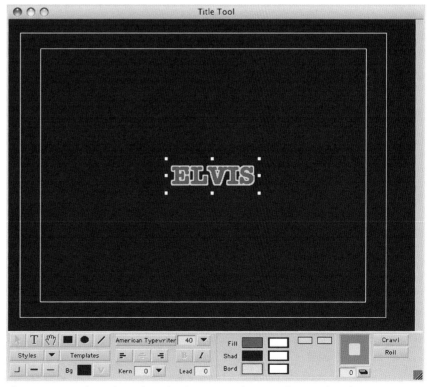

Figure 8-18. Title Tool window displaying text formatted using the aforementioned settings.

To save a title template

1. Select Tools≫Title Tool.

2. Click the text with the Selection tool.

3. Click the Save Style Parameter menu (the down arrow to the right of the Styles button on the Title Tool toolbar), and then select Save As.

4. In the Title Style Sheet dialog box that appears, do the following:

   (a) Select only the parameters that you want to save.

   (b) (Optional) Assign a Function Key.

   (c) Rename the template.

   (d) Click Done.

> **Note** | If you assign a function key to a template, when that function key is pressed while in the Title Tool window, that template is applied to the selected title.

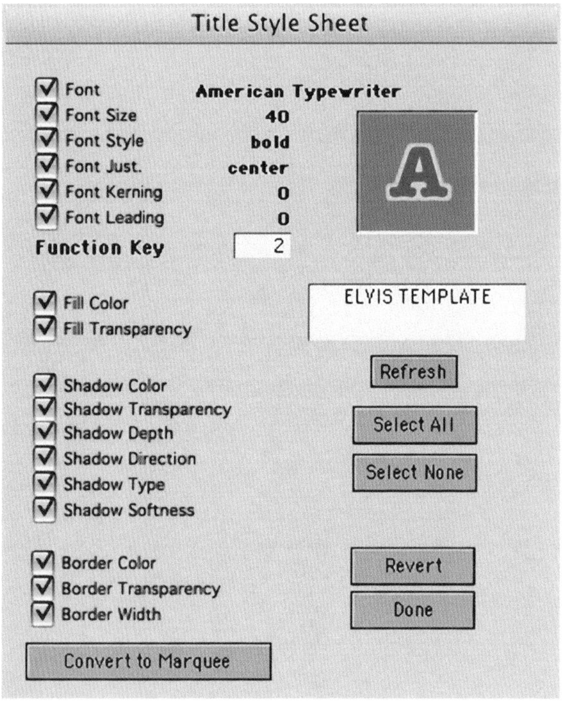

Figure 8-19. Title Style Sheet dialog box.

5. Right-click and select Save the Title As. (Remember, save it to the correct bin, on the correct drive, and in the correct resolution.)

6. Close the Title tool.

Using Title Templates

To use a title template

1. Select Tools≫Title Tool.

2. Click Title tool.

3. Click Text tool.

4. Type the text in the Title Tool window.

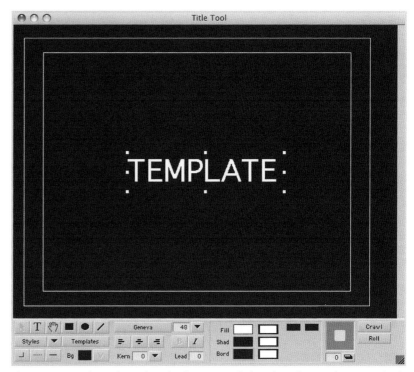

Figure 8-20. Title Tool window displaying text *before* the title template is applied.

5. Click the Selection tool, and then select the text.

6. Click the Save Style Parameter menu (the down arrow to the right of the Styles button on the Title Tool toolbar) and then select the desired template.

Tip | You can also apply the template by pressing the assigned function key.

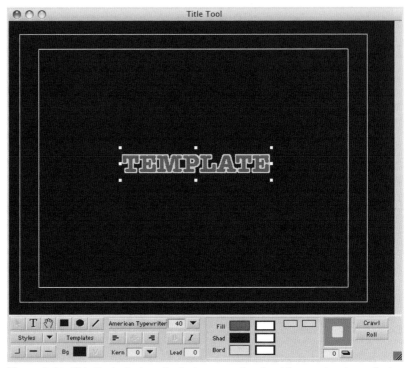

Figure 8-21. Title Tool window displaying text *after* the title template is applied.

7. Right-click and select Save Title As. (Remember, save it to the correct bin, on the correct drive, and in the correct resolution.)

8. Close the Title tool.

Did I Do This Correctly?

■ **Have all of the titles been justified correctly?**

If the object selection handles aren't positioned correctly, any text that is justified within the object selection handles may not be correctly justified to fit on the television screen.

■ **Are all of the titles within the safe title area (also called the title safe area)?**

All of the titles should be contained within the inner grid line of the Title tool.

■ **Are the lower thirds and subtitles consistent?**

All of the lower thirds and subtitles should be in the same color, size, and font and appear at the same place on the screen.

■ **Is each character identified when it is supposed to be?**

A lower third should appear according to your company's specifications.

■ **Are the titles accurate?**

Once the titles are created, they should be checked, preferably by someone who did not create them, to make sure all the text is complete and spelled correctly.

■ **Have all of the titles been saved to the correct drive?**

It is possible to save titles to a local drive, but they will only be available on that specific computer.

CHAPTER 9:
Outputs

Tasks in This Chapter

OUTPUTS RECORD A SEQUENCE onto tape and are used to preserve the episode cuts of a show. Outputs can also be in a digital format, and CHAPTER 10: *Imports and Exports* on page 253 is appropriate for those types of outputs. This chapter discusses how to prepare sequences for outputs to tape, but it should be used in conjunction with CHAPTER 10. This chapter also provides instructions for creating a showbuild template that you can use to efficiently create output sequences for tape.

Settings Needed

Configure the following setting before beginning the tasks in this chapter.

DECK PREFERENCES DIALOG BOX

Navigation: Project window | Settings tab | Select Deck Preferences from the Settings list | Deck Preferences dialog box

Allow assemble edit & crash record for digital cut (selected)—When this option is selected, you can access additional options while using the Digital Cut tool to output a sequence to tape. The options used are dependent on the type of output. For an explanation of the different types of outputs, see APPENDIX 7: *Digital Cut Tool* on page 359.

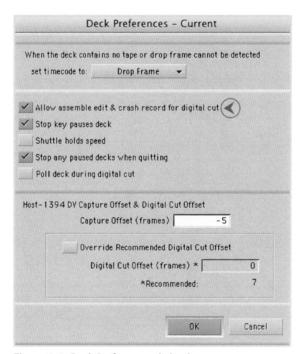

Figure 9-1. Deck Preferences dialog box.

Creating an Output Sequence for Tape

In this section, we are going to create an output sequence for tape. It is common for an output sequence to be circulated among the company executives before it is sent to the network. These output sequences are commonly known as *internal cuts* because they are only seen internally within the company. Output sequences that are sent outside of the company to the network are commonly known as *external cuts*. The naming system for these cuts varies from company to company, so you should understand your company's naming conventions before you begin. To make the process a little bit easier, subheadings have been inserted to break up the steps; however, all of the steps must be performed in the order presented.

Importing Color Bars and Creating Tone Media

To import color bars and create tone media

1. Create a bin (Mac: ⌘+N | PC: Ctrl+N).

2. Rename the new bin with the date, show, episode, and output type (for example, 0613 EL 101 Output).

3. Create a sequence (Mac: Shift+⌘+N | PC: Shift+Ctrl+N).

4. Rename the sequence exactly as the bin.

5. Press Enter.

6. Right-click in the Record monitor, and select Get Sequence Info (Mac: ⌘+I | PC: Ctrl+I).

7. In the Sequence Info dialog box that appears, in the Starting TC box, type "00;59;10;00" and then click OK.

In most companies, the first frame of the episode starts at 01;00;00;00.

What differs among companies is how long the color bars and tone, filler, and slates are before that first frame of video.

In our example, we have 30 seconds of color bars and tone media, 15 seconds of filler (total), and a 5-second slate. Choose semicolons (DF) or colons (NDF) per the requirements of your company.

It is important to choose correctly because the sequence timecode and the digital cut tape timecode must match. This choice has an impact during the outputting process in *To output a sequence to tape*, Step 13, page 245.

> **Tip** | Typing the desired timecode into the sequence's Start column in the bin can also change a sequence's Starting TC. (The Bin View menu must be set to Statistics to see the Start column heading.)

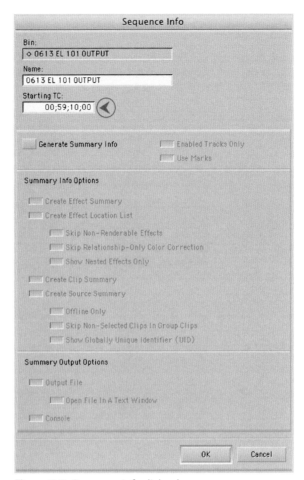

Figure 9-2. Sequence Info dialog box.

8. Click the bin (0613 EL 101 Output).

9. Select File≫Import.

10. In the Select files to Import dialog box that appears, do the following:

    (a) Follow this file path to the color bars file (SMPTE_Bars.pct):

    Mac: Macintosh HD/Applications/Avid editing application/SupportingFiles/ Test_Patterns/SMPTE_Bars.pct

    PC: C:\Program Files\Avid\Avid editing application\SupportingFiles\ Test_Patterns\SMPTE_Bars.pct

    (b) Click Options, and in the Import Settings dialog box that appears, on the Image tab, do the following, and then click OK.

        (i) In the File Pixel to Video Mapping area, click 601 SD or 709 HD (16-235).

Note | Color bars are imported at 601 SD or 709 HD (16-235) because video material should be imported at this setting or risk causing the levels to be incorrect.

(ii) In the Frame Import Duration area, in the Duration (seconds) box, type "30".

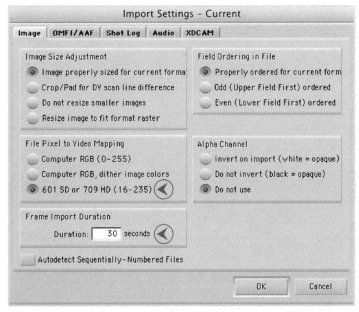

Figure 9-3. Import Settings dialog box | Image tab.

(c) In the Video Resolution menu, select the correct resolution.

(d) In the Video Drive menu, select the correct drive.

(e) Click Open.

11. Click the bin.

12. Open the Audio Tool (Mac: ⌘+1 | PC: Ctrl+1), click PH (peak hold), and then select Create Tone Media.

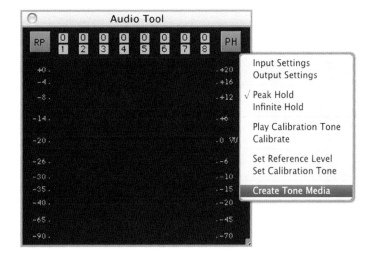

13. In the Create Tone Media dialog box that appears, do the following, and then click OK.

    (a) In the Number of Tracks menu, select 2.

    (b) In the Target Bin menu, select the bin for the tone.

    (c) In the Target Drive menu, select the drive to save the media to.

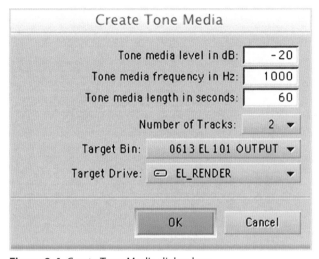

Figure 9-4. Create Tone Media dialog box.

14. Save the bin (Mac: ⌘+S | PC: Ctrl+S).

Creating Slates for Output

A *slate* is a title that gives information about the upcoming video. There are two types of slates—head slates and act slates.

The head slate typically contains more information than the act slates. The head slate information may include the show title, episode, total runtime, date, audio channel splits, version, destination, and many other line items. The act slate information can contain a combination of the elements of a head slate or just the act number. Determine the protocol for your company and follow it.

An output sequence will contain one head slate and various act slates. The number of act slates is equal to the total number of acts less one. So if there are four acts, you will create one head slate and three act slates. The number of act slates created is one less than the number of acts because it is assumed that the act after the head slate is Act 1.

To create slates for output

1. Select Tools≫Title Tool.

2. In the New Title dialog box that appears, click Title Tool.

Figure 9-5. New Title dialog box.

3. In the Title Tool window that appears, click the Text tool.

4. Click in the Title Tool window, and type the slate text.

5. Select the text and modify it using the Text Formatting tools and the Color and Transparency Blend tools.

6. Click the Selection tool and position the title text.

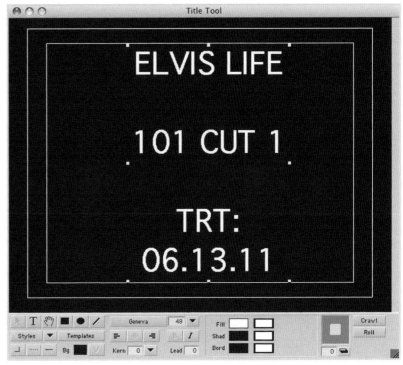

Figure 9-6. Title Tool window with head slate information.

7. Right-click in the Title Tool window, and select Save Title as.

8. In the Save Title dialog box that appears, do the following:

   (a) In the Title Name box, type "Head Slate", or "Act 2", "Act 3", etc., as appropriate.

   (b) Choose the correct bin, on the correct drive, and in the correct resolution.

   (c) Click Save.

Figure 9-7. Save Title dialog box.

9. Repeat Steps 4–8 until there are enough act slates for the acts of the episode.

10. Close the Title tool.

11. Save the bin (Mac: ⌘+S | PC: Ctrl+S).

Assembling the Output Sequence

Accumulating all of the materials for an output sequence in the beginning makes it easier to assemble the output sequence because everything you need is at your disposal. Now that you have color bars, tone media, and slates, you can place everything into a sequence with the acts of the show.

To assemble the output sequence

1. Double-click the 30 seconds of color bars in the bin (SMPTE_Bars.pct).

2. Overwrite (press B) the 30 seconds of the color bars at the beginning of the sequence. (Since you want the entire clip, it isn't necessary to Mark Clip. When there aren't any Mark IN or OUT points, the entire clip is used.)

3. Make sure the position indicator is at the end of the sequence and Mark OUT (press O).

4. Press Home to place the position indicator at the beginning of the sequence.

5. Mark IN (press I).

6. Deselect the video track.

7. Double-click the tone media (see *To import color bars and create tone media*, Step 13, page 226).

8. Overwrite (press B) the tone media into the sequence directly beneath the color bars.

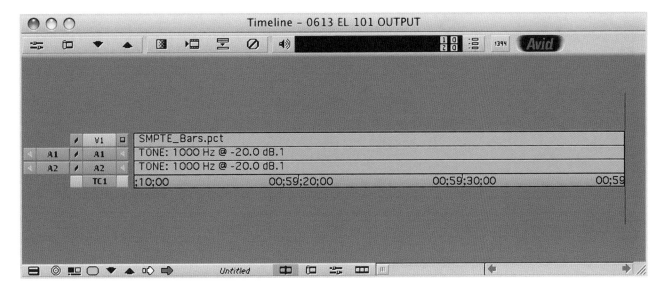

9. Double-click the head slate.

10. Mark IN (press I) and OUT (press O) points of the head slate for 5 seconds using the following method (when you want a specific duration and the material between the IN and OUT points isn't particularly important, it is an easy process):

(a) Mark IN (press I).

(b) On the numeric keypad press + (plus sign).

(c) On the numeric keypad press the desired minutes and frames.

In our example, for 5 seconds, press 429 [4 seconds and 29 frames] because when the Mark OUT point is placed, it adds one frame; therefore, what is typed should be one frame short.

(d) Press Enter.

(e) Mark OUT (press O).

11. Patch the source video track to the record video track.

12. Overwrite (press B) the head slate in directly after the color bars and tone.

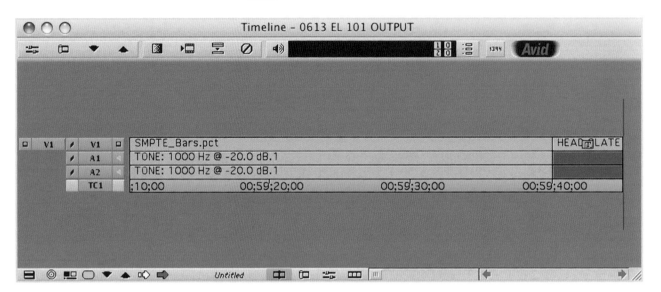

13. In the Composer window, click above the Source monitor, and from the Clip Name menu, select Load Filler.

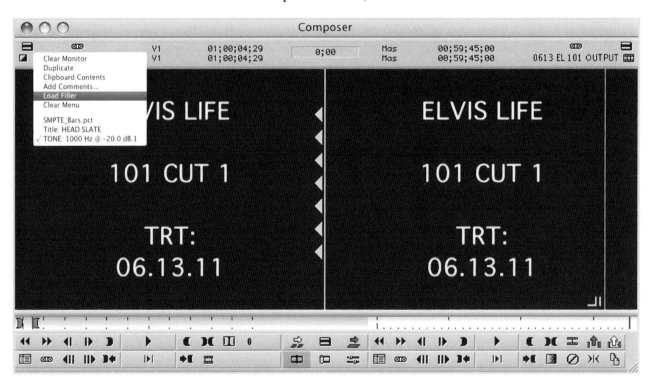

14. Mark IN (press I) and OUT (press O) points for 10 seconds using the following method:

    (a) Mark IN (press I).

    (b) On the numeric keypad press +929 (9 seconds and 29 frames).

    (c) Press Enter.

    (d) Mark OUT (press O).

15. Snap the position indicator to the edit point between the color bars and tone and the head slate (Mac: ⌘+Click | PC: Ctrl+Click).

16. Insert (press V) the 10 seconds of filler between the color bars and tone and the head slate. Make sure sync locks are on!

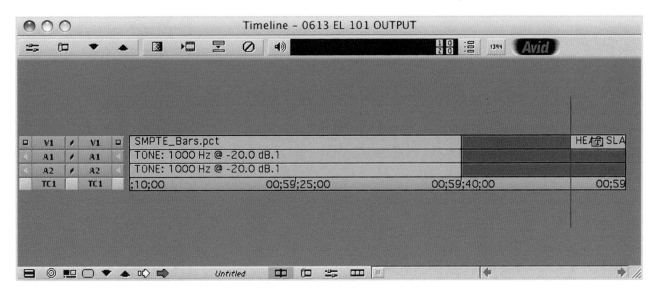

17. Do one of the following:

    (a) If the acts of the episode are saved in separate bins, open the Act 1 bin.

    –or–

    (b) If the acts of the episode are all saved in the same bin, open the master sequence bin.

    –or–

    (c) If all of the acts of the episode are saved in one sequence, in one bin, open that combined sequence bin.

18. Drag—*do not double-click*—the Act 1 sequence or the combined sequence in the bin to the Source monitor.

Tip | Only open one act bin at a time to prevent the oft-repeated mistake of cutting an act into an output sequence more than once.

Make sure the sequences are completely finished before cutting them into the output sequence.

Note | The sequence must be dragged to the Source monitor because double-clicking a sequence automatically loads it in the Record monitor.

19. Mark IN (press I) and OUT (press O) points of the entire act or episode.

    The best way to Mark IN and OUT points of an entire act is to press Home and place an IN point, and then press End and place an OUT point. Do this with caution because there may be filler at the beginning or end of the sequence! If there is filler at the beginning or end of the sequence, zoom in to those locations and move the IN and OUT points to the first and last frame of video, respectively.

20. Patch the source video and audio tracks to the desired record video and audio tracks.

21. In the Timeline window, place the position indicator at the end of the sequence.

22. Overwrite (press B) that sequence into the output sequence after the head slate.

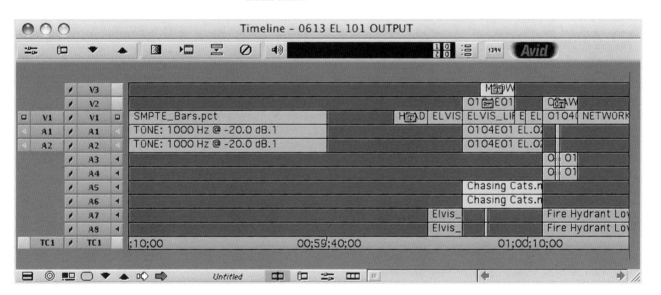

23. Do one of the following:

    (a) Close the Act 1 bin if the acts of the episode are saved in separate bins.

    –or–

    (b) Leave the master sequence bin open, if the acts of the episode are saved in one bin.

    –or–

    (c) Close the combined sequence bin if the acts of the episode are in one sequence.

24. In the Composer window, click above the Source monitor, and from the Clip Name menu, select Load Filler.

25. Mark IN (press I) and OUT (press O) points for 5 seconds using the following method:

    (a) Mark IN (press I).

    (b) On the numeric keypad press +429 (4 seconds and 29 frames).

    (c) Press Enter.

    (d) Mark OUT (press O).

26. Snap the position indicator between the head slate and the beginning of the inserted sequence (Mac: ⌘+Click | PC: Ctrl+Click).

27. Insert (press V) the 5 seconds of filler between the head slate and the first clip of video of the inserted sequence. Make sure sync locks are on!

> **Note** | The Load Filler command on the Clip Name menu retains the last IN and OUT points; therefore, it may not be necessary to Mark IN and OUT every time.
>
> However, in our example, it is necessary because the last time the Load Filler command was used it was for 10 seconds—not the 5 seconds that we require now.

> **Note** | When done correctly, the first frame of video should be at exactly 01;00;00;00.

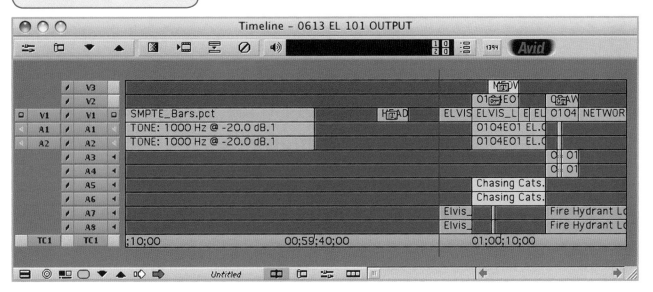

The type of output you are doing determines what should be in an output sequence. In the beginning of a show, an output sequence may only contain the acts. However, the closer that episode gets to completion additional elements may be added that include the following:

- **Previously On**—A section before the main title that describes what happened in the previous episode.

- **Act Bump**—Teaser that appears at the end of acts to describe what is coming up in the rest of the episode.

- **Website Tease**—Portions of the episode that appear throughout the show encouraging viewers to visit the show's website.

- **Next On**—A section at the end of the last act that describes what will happen in the next episode.

- **Credits and End Logo Pages**—These appear at the end of the show.

When doing an output that requires the insertion of these additional elements, navigate to the appropriate bins and add them to the end (or beginning) of the appropriate act. Before doing so, make sure these elements aren't already present in the sequence of the act bin, and if they are present, make sure they are the most current version.

28. Do one of the following:

    (a) If the acts of the episode are saved in separate bins or in a master sequence bin, double-click the Act 2 slate, and then proceed to Step 29.

    –or–

    (b) If the acts of the episode are in one combined sequence, proceed to *Calculating the Output Sequence's Runtime* on page 235.

29. Mark IN (press I) and OUT (press O) points in the Act 2 slate for 5 seconds.

30. In the Timeline window, place the position indicator at the end of the sequence.

31. Patch the source video track to the desired record video track.

32. Overwrite (press B) the Act 2 slate directly after Act 1.

33. Open the Act 2 bin if the acts of the episode are saved in separate bins.

34. Drag the Act 2 sequence from the Act 2 bin or from the master sequence bin to the Source monitor.

35. Mark IN (press I) and OUT (press O) points of the entire act.

36. Patch the source video and audio tracks to the desired record video and audio tracks.

37. In the Timeline window, place the position indicator at the end of the sequence.

38. Overwrite (press B) into the output sequence after the Act 2 slate.

39. Close the Act 2 bin.

40. In the Composer window, click above the Source monitor, and from the Clip Name menu, select Load Filler.

41. Mark IN (press I) and OUT (press O) points for 5 seconds.

42. Snap the position indicator to the edit point between the end of Act 1 and the beginning of Act 2 (Mac: ⌘+Click | PC: Ctrl+Click).

43. Insert (press V) the filler. Make sure sync locks are on!

44. Snap the position indicator to the edit point between the Act 2 slate and the beginning of Act 2 (Mac: ⌘+Click | PC: Ctrl+Click).

45. Insert (press V) the filler. Make sure sync locks are on!

46. Repeat Steps 28(a)–45 until all of the acts have been cut into the sequence.

47. Save the bin (Mac: ⌘+S | PC: Ctrl+S).

Calculating the Output Sequence's Runtime

Despite the presence of filler and slates between the acts, those elements are not included in the final runtime for the output sequence. The cumulative time for those elements needs to be subtracted from the total runtime of the sequence to determine the final runtime of the show.

To calculate the output sequence's runtime

1. Calculate the time of the filler and slates that are present between the acts.

   For example, for a four-act show, it would be 45 seconds calculated as follows:

   5 seconds of filler + 5 second slate + 5 seconds of filler = 15 seconds
   15 second break x 3 act breaks = 45 seconds total filler

2. Mark IN (press I) at 01;00;00;00.

3. Mark OUT (press O) on the last frame of video in the sequence.

4. Select Tools≫Calculator to open the Avid Calculator (Mac: ⌘+2 | PC: Ctrl+2).

5. On the Format menu, select 30 Non-Drop or 30 Drop in accordance with the sequence setting.

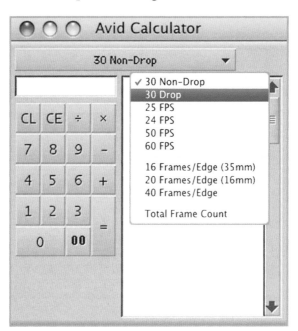

Figure 9-8. Avid Calculator displaying the Format menu.

6. Type the duration of the sequence (found at the top of the Source/Record monitors) into the Avid Calculator.

In our example, the duration of the sequence is 1;02;11—1 minute, 2 seconds, and 11 frames—see FIGURE 9-9.

Figure 9-9. Composer window with the duration between the IN and OUT points highlighted.

7. In the Avid Calculator, subtract the filler from the duration. The difference is the sequence total runtime.

    In our example, the calculation is as follows:

    1 minute, 2 seconds, and 11 frames duration – 15 seconds filler = 47 seconds, 09 frames total runtime.

8. Place the position indicator on the head slate.

9. On the bottom toolbar of the Timeline window, click Effect Mode .

Note | If the position indicator isn't over a title when the Effect Mode button is clicked in the Timeline window, the Other Options button will not display. Additionally, the track the title is on needs to be enabled.

10. In the Effect Editor window that appears, click Other Options to open the Title Tool window.

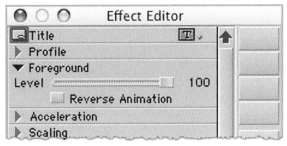

Figure 9-10. Effect Editor window with the Other Options button highlighted.

11. In the Edit Title dialog box that appears, click No.

Figure 9-11. Edit Title dialog box.

12. Modify the title using the Title Tool toolbar.

13. Update the head slate by adding the duration.

14. Right-click and select Save Title As.

15. Click Save.

> **Note** | Most companies don't add frames to the duration—usually just hours, minutes, and seconds.

Figure 9-12. Avid Media Composer dialog box prompting you to save the title and exit the Title Tool.

16. Click Save. (Remember, save it to the correct bin, on the correct drive, and in the correct resolution.)

    The duration will update to the head slate in the sequence.

17. Close the Effect Editor.

18. Save the bin (Mac: ⌘+S | PC: Ctrl+S).

Creating a Showbuild Template

It is helpful to have a showbuild template already created that allows you to quickly assemble the acts into a master sequence that is ready for output. Using a showbuild template drastically cuts down the time it takes to create an output sequence for tape. A showbuild template sequence contains the color bars and tone, slates, and filler. It also contains add edits that are placeholders for the filler in between the slates.

If you want to create a showbuild template later, you can skip this section and continue with the output in *Outputting a Sequence to Tape* on page 242.

To create a showbuild template

1. Repeat *To import color bars and create tone media* on page 223, and rename the bin and sequence Showbuild Template. (It isn't necessary to import color bars or create tone media if you already have those clips available.)

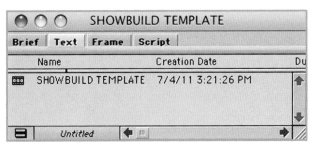

Figure 9-13. Showbuild Template bin displaying the showbuild template sequence.

2. Repeat *To create slates for output* on page 227 until you have created a head slate and act slates for a typical show at your company.

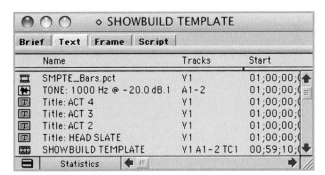

Figure 9-14. Showbuild Template bin displaying the elements needed to create the showbuild template sequence.

3. Repeat Steps 1–8 of *To assemble the output sequence* on page 228 for the color bars and tone.

4. Select the video track.

5. Double-click the head slate.

6. Mark IN (press I) and OUT (press O) points in the head slate for 5 seconds.

7. Overwrite (press B) the head slate in at the end of the sequence.

8. Repeat Steps 5–7 for the rest of the act slates.

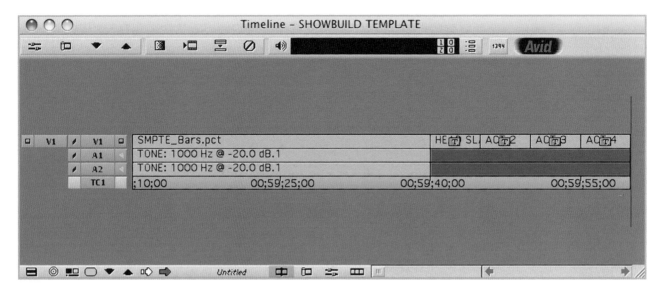

9. In the Composer window, click above the Source monitor, and from the Clip Name menu, select Load Filler.

10. Mark IN (press I) and OUT (press O) points for 10 seconds.

11. Snap the position indicator to the edit point between the color bars and tone and the head slate (Mac: ⌘+Click | PC: Ctrl+Click).

12. Insert (press V) the 10 seconds of filler between the color bars and tone and the head slate. Make sure sync locks are on!

13. Snap the position indicator to the edit point between the head slate and the Act 2 slate (Mac: ⌘+Click | PC: Ctrl+Click).

14. Insert (press V) 10 seconds of filler between the rest of the slates.

15. Deselect the audio tracks.

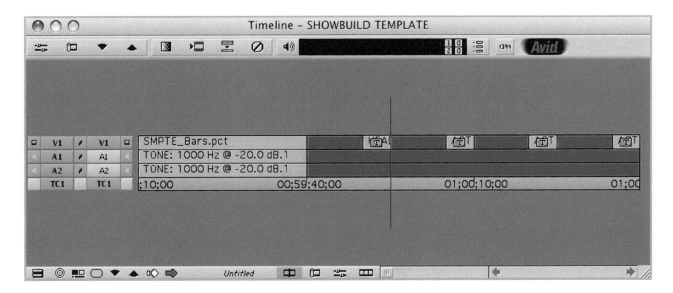

16. Snap the position indicator to the end of the head slate (Mac: ⌘+Click | PC: Ctrl+Click).

17. Type "+500" (5 seconds), and then press Enter.

18. Add Edit (press F8).

19. Repeat Steps 16–18 for the rest of the filler.

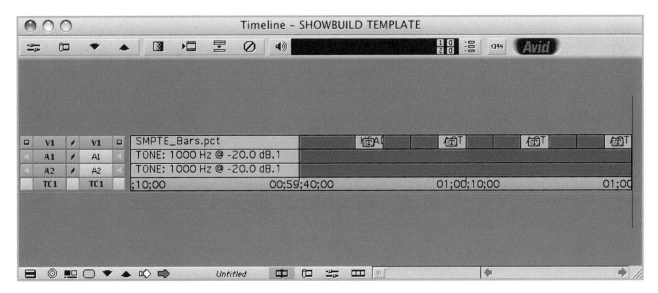

20. Save the bin (Mac: ⌘+S | PC: Ctrl+S).

The showbuild template has now been created and will make completing outputs a little easier and faster. (It may be a good idea to transfer the showbuild template to your own work bin so it is easily accessible.)

When using a showbuild template, building an output sequence involves:

■ Copying and renaming the showbuild template.

■ Opening the act bins.

■ Marking IN and OUT points (and making sure the tracks are patched correctly).

■ Snapping to the add edit points and inserting the acts into the showbuild sequence.

When doing this, make sure you check that the slates and filler are still exactly 5 seconds in duration (or your company's specifications).

Outputting a Sequence to Tape

The steps in this section should be performed immediately before an output. They ensure that Avid is correctly set up and the sequence will be recorded to the tape correctly.

To output a sequence to tape

1. Double-click the output sequence to load it in the Timeline window.

2. Select Tools≫Timecode Window.

3. In the Timecode window that appears, click the black area, and then select Size and select a number to adjust the size of the numbers displayed in the Timecode window. (The Timecode window may have other lines from the last time you used it. This isn't a problem, but you can Remove Line if it bothers you.)

Figure 9-15. Timecode window.

4. Open the Audio Tool window (Mac: ⌘+1 | PC: Ctrl+1), click PH (peak hold), and then select Output Settings.

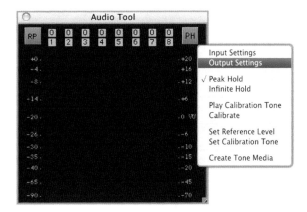

5. In the Audio Project Settings window that appears, on the Output tab, make sure the Mixed Mode Selection button displays Stereo to ensure that the dialogue, music, and sound effects are mixed to all audio channels.

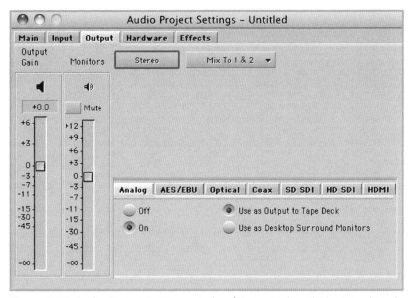

Figure 9-16. Audio Project Settings window | Output tab with the Mixed Mode Selection button highlighted.

6. Close the Audio Project Settings window.

7. Select Tools≫Video Output Tool.

8. In the Video Output Tool window that appears, on the Options tab, in the Sync Lock menu, select either Internal or Reference.

9. Close the Video Output Tool window.

Note | The Sync Lock option for the Video Output Tool is dependent on the setup at your company.

In our example, Reference is chosen because the sync is determined by an external cable and not internally by Avid.

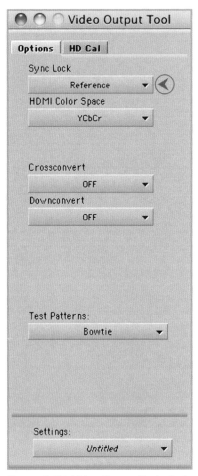

Figure 9-17. Video Output Tool window with the Sync Lock menu highlighted.

10. Make sure the deck is in remote. (This is usually a button or switch on the front of the deck.)

11. Select Output≫Digital Cut. (See APPENDIX 7: *Digital Cut Tool* on page 359, for a review of the tool and its functions.)

12. In the Digital Cut Tool window that appears, the video deck connected to Avid appears in the Deck Selection menu. (If it doesn't, see APPENDIX 2: *Deck Configuration* on page 311.)

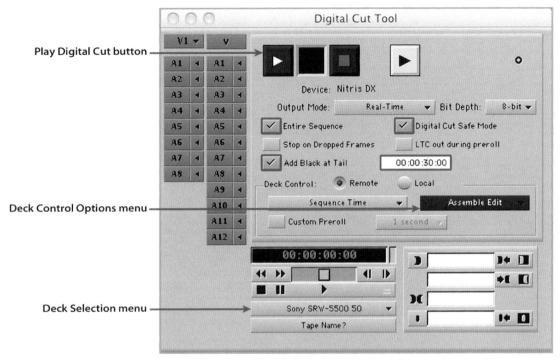

Figure 9-18. Digital Cut Tool window configured for recording an entire sequence onto tape.

13. In the Digital Cut Tool window, do the following:

   (a) Select the Entire Sequence check box.

   (b) Select the Digital Cut Safe Mode check box.

   (c) Select the Add Black at Tail check box, and then in the box to the right, type "00;00;30;00".

   (d) In the Deck Control Options menu, select the record type from Assemble Edit, Crash Record, and Insert Edit.

   Tapes with preexisting timecode are frequently used for outputs because it eliminates the need to record timecode onto a tape immediately before outputting a sequence onto that tape. When using a tape with preexisting timecode, make sure the tape timecode and the sequence timecode are both DF or NDF; otherwise, the digital cut process will generate an error message saying that the tape and sequence timecodes don't match. If you receive that message, switch the sequence to DF or NDF as applicable or use another tape with the correct timecode type.

246

When using tapes with preexisting timecode, some will have timecode on the entire tape and some will only have it on the beginning portion.

If the timecode is on the entire tape, select Insert Edit.

If the timecode isn't on the entire tape, select Assemble Edit, and Avid will regenerate the timecode while it is recording.

If there isn't any timecode on the tape, select Crash Record and Avid will assign timecode to the tape based on whatever timecode is on the video deck.

14. In the Timeline window, and do the following:

    (a) Select all of the tracks in the sequence (Mac: ⌘+A | PC: Ctrl+A).

    (b) Mark IN (press I) at the beginning of the sequence.

    (c) Mark OUT (press O) at the end of the sequence.

    (d) Enable the video monitor for the topmost video track.

    (e) Enable all of the audio track speakers.

    (f) Select Insert Edit, Assemble Edit, or Crash Record.

15. In the Digital Cut Tool window, click Play Digital Cut.

16. Do one of the following:

    (a) If there are unrendered titles, effects, or graphics that would affect the playback of the sequence, in the ExpertRender dialog box that appears asking if you want to render those clips, click OK.

Caution! | The ExpertRender dialog box will only appear if the Digital Cut Safe Mode check box is selected in the Digital Cut Tool window (see Figure 9-18 on page 245).

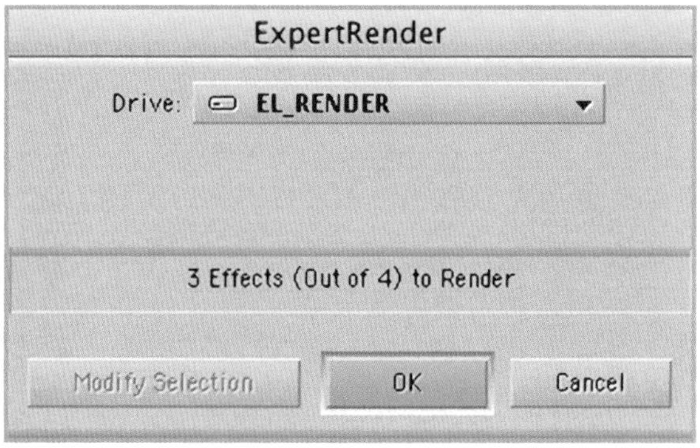

Figure 9-19. ExpertRender dialog box.

–or–

(b) If there are no unrendered titles, effects, or graphics that would affect the playback of the sequence, in the Avid Symphony Nitris dialog box that appears prompting you to mount a destination tape in the deck, insert a tape in the deck, and then click OK.

Figure 9-20. Avid Symphony Nitris dialog box prompting you to mount the destination tape in the video deck.

17. Click OK, and then Avid cues the tape and starts recording video and/or audio to the tape.

18. If the sequence aborts in the middle of a full output—*full output and not an insert edit; this is an important distinction*—do the following:

    (a) In the Timeline window, Mark IN (press I) a new point before the occurrence (on an edit point).

    (b) In the Digital Cut Tool window, clear the Entire Sequence check box.

    (c) Continue with the output.

Insert Editing onto Tape

There will be occasions when it is necessary to insert a section of a sequence onto a tape.

When making an insert edit, Avid is frame accurate. *Frame accurate* means an insertion can be made without having a video glitch. Despite Avid's ability to do this, it is best to find a place where there are hard edit points to minimize any glitches that may occur.

Imagine that the crawling title over the 0104C01 EL clip in FIGURE 9-21 on page 248 was modified to correct a misspelling. The purple circles indicate the best place to Mark IN and OUT points to do an insert edit.

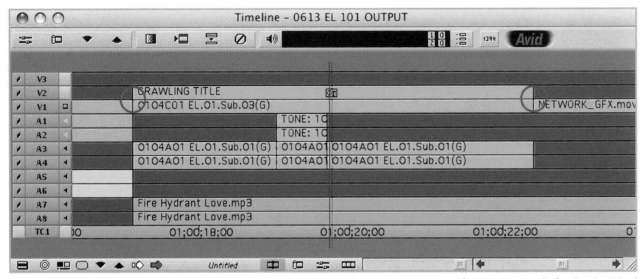

Figure 9-21. Timeline window of 0613 EL 101 Output highlighting the best edit points to perform an insert edit for the described scenario.

To insert a section of a sequence onto a tape

1. Make the correction on the output sequence.

2. Mark IN (press I) and OUT (press O) points around the correction.

3. In the Digital Cut Tool window, do the following:

   (a) Select all of the sequence tracks on the left set of tracks that need to be inserted onto the tape.

   (b) Enable all of the tracks on the right set of tracks that need to be inserted onto the tape.

   (c) Clear the Entire Sequence check box.

   (d) Clear the Add Black at Tail check box.

   (e) Select the Digital Cut Safe Mode check box.

   (f) Select Insert Edit from the Deck Control Options menu.

4. Click Play Digital Cut to insert edit the section onto tape, and then Avid cues the tape, plays the sequence, and records the section at the correct sequence time.

> **Note** | There are three main differences of the setup of the Digital Cut tool for an insert edit vs. recording an entire sequence onto tape.
>
> To set up the Digital Cut tool for an insert edit:
>
> ◆ The Entire Sequence check box is not selected.
> ◆ The Add Black at Tail check box is not selected.
> ◆ Only those tracks that should be inserted are selected (ensuring that only the IN and OUT points of the sequence are inserted).

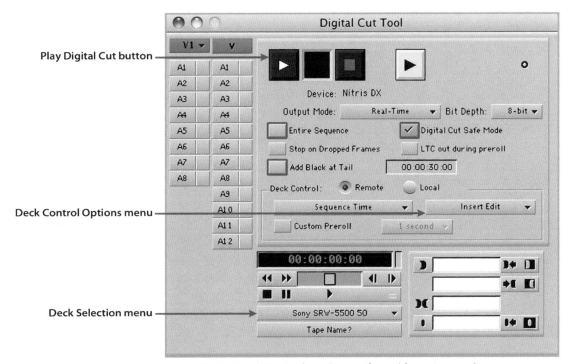

Figure 9-22. Digital Cut Tool window configured for an insert edit.

5. Rewind the tape, and then play the tape to make sure the insert edit is correct.

Finishing the Output Process

After an output is completed, the output sequence should be made available to the editor. This ensures that any notes that are given on the outputted sequence will match the timecodes of the sequence the editor is working on. Depending on the company you work for, the following are the options for the final sequence:

■ The sequence is broken down into acts and placed into bins within the editor's project.

■ The entire output sequence is copied and placed in a new bin within the editor's project, and the editor is alerted to the location.

To finish the output process

1. Open the Act 1 bin.

2. Select all the tracks in the sequence (Mac: ⌘+A | PC: Ctrl+A).

3. Mark IN (press I) and OUT (press O) points at the beginning and end of Act 1 in the output sequence.

4. Subclip (press F7) the sequence.

5. Rename the sequence by the output date, show, episode, and act (for example, 0613 EL 101 Act 1).

6. Drag this subsequence into the Act 1 bin or master sequence bin. (You should move the older acts to another bin for archiving purposes.)

7. Repeat Steps 1–6 for the rest of the output sequence.

8. Save the bins (Mac: ⌘+S | PC: Ctrl+S).

Did I Do This Correctly?

■ **Was any act duplicated in the sequence?**

It is possible to accidentally cut the same act into a sequence twice. If Dupe Detection is enabled in the Timeline Fast menu, this duplication will be evident because there will be continuous dupe lines throughout the sequence. This is best avoided by only opening one act bin at a time.

■ **Was the sequence rendered?**

As long as the Digital Cut Safe Mode check box is selected in the Digital Cut Tool window, unrendered effects will automatically be rendered before outputting.

■ **Does the sequence begin at 01;00;00;00?**

Sequences start at different times. The first frame of video usually starts at 01;00;00;00. However, make sure the starting timecode is according to your company's specifications.

■ **Was the runtime accurately calculated?**

The runtime is accurately calculated by subtracting the total of the filler and slates from the total duration of the sequence. The total duration of the sequence (including filler and slates) can be determined by marking IN at 01;00;00;00 and marking OUT at the very end of the output sequence.

■ **Are additional elements—previously on, act bump, website tease, next on, and credits and end logo pages—and other extra elements in the sequence in the correct place?**

Make sure the most current additional elements are added and are in their correct places.

■ **Are insert edits completely done and checked?**

Insert edits are portions of a sequence that were output to tape to correct a mistake. They should be viewed after insertion to make sure that the tape is free of glitches and flickers.

Chapter 10:
Imports and Exports

Tasks in This Chapter

INPUTTING AND OUTPUTTING MATERIAL to and from Avid can be done via tape, cards, or discs. There are instances when it is more appropriate and convenient to go tapeless. To accommodate those situations, it is possible to import and export clips and sequences.

Avid has numerous import/export options for importing/exporting video, audio, and clip information. These formats include Windows Media®, QuickTime®, MP3, Wave™, and EDL (edit decision list) files. Despite the numerous options available for importing/exporting, the process pretty much remains the same for each format. The main differences are the specific file settings for the current situation.

Importing

To import a file

1. Create a bin (Mac: ⌘+N | PC: Ctrl+N).

2. Rename the bin 0704 Imports, and then press Enter.

3. Click the bin.

4. Select File≫Import.

5. In the Select files to Import dialog box that appears, do the following:

    (a) Navigate to the file.

    (b) Click Options.

        (i) In the Import Settings dialog box that appears, modify the import options as appropriate for the file type.

        (ii) Click OK.

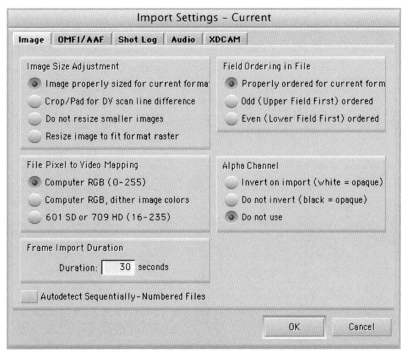

Figure 10-1. Import Settings dialog box | Image tab.

(c) In the Video Resolution menu, select the correct resolution.

(d) In the Video Drive menu, select the correct drive.

(e) Click Open, and the file appears in the bin (the file can be treated as any other video or audio file captured into Avid).

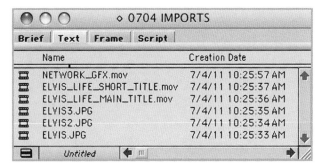

Figure 10-2. 0704 Imports bin displaying imported clips.

6. Save the bin (Mac: ⌘+S | PC: Ctrl+S).

7. Close the bin.

Exporting QuickTime Movies

It is infinitely more convenient to export a movie of a clip or sequence and then email it rather than deal with a tape. In this fashion, producers aren't tied to a conventional television setup and can view an episode on a computer or other electronic devices with relative ease and portability.

To export a QuickTime movie

1. Create a bin (Mac: ⌘+N | PC: Ctrl+N).

2. Rename the new bin 0704 EL 101 QuickTime, and then press Enter.

3. Open the bin that contains the sequence to be exported.

4. Click the sequence.

5. Copy the sequence to the 0704 EL 101 QuickTime bin (Mac: Option+Drag | PC: Alt+Drag).

6. Rename the sequence 0704 EL 101 QuickTime.

7. Double-click the sequence.

    Sometimes companies will want burned-in timecode (BITC—sometimes pronounced "bitsy") on the sequence. BITC allows you to view the export and see the master timecode of the sequence.

8. Do one of the following:

    (a) If BITC is not required, proceed to Step 9.

    –or–

    (b) If BITC is required, complete the following steps and then proceed to Step 9.

        (i) Create a new video track (Mac: ⌘+Y | PC: Ctrl+Y).

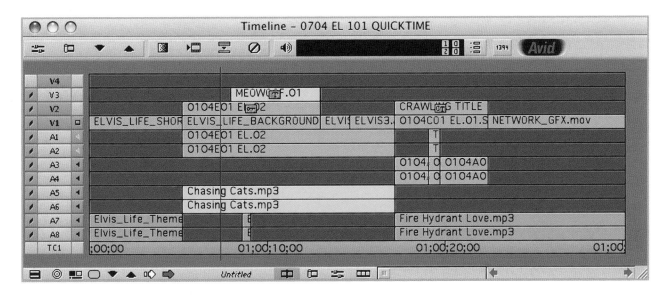

(ii) Open the Effect palette (Mac: ⌘+8 | PC: Ctrl+8).

(iii) On the left pane of the Effect palette, click Generator in the Effect Category list.

(iv) In the right pane, drag the Timecode Burn-In effect onto the newly created video track, and the Timecode Burn-In effect appears on the track displaying the sequence timecode.

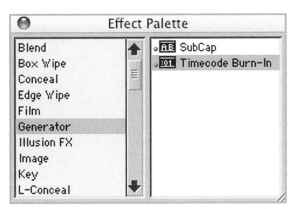

Figure 10-3. Effect Palette window with Generator | Timecode Burn-In selected.

9. Select all of the tracks of the sequence that need to be exported (Mac: ⌘+A | PC: Ctrl+A).

10. Enable the Record Monitor Track button for the top track of the sequence.

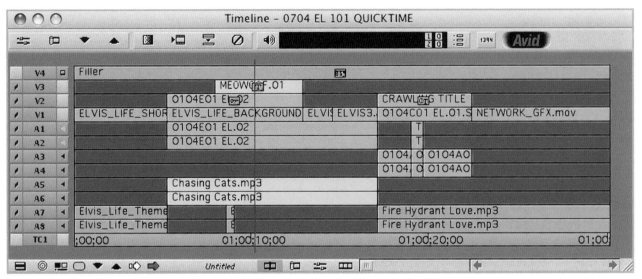

Figure 10-4. Timeline window of 0704 EL 101 QuickTime displaying the Timecode Burn-In effect icon on video track 4 (V4).

> **Note** | Mark IN/OUT at the beginning and end of the sequence assumes that the whole sequence is to be exported; otherwise, Mark IN/OUT around the section that is to be exported.

11. Mark IN (press I) at the beginning of the sequence.

12. Mark OUT (press O) at the end of the sequence.

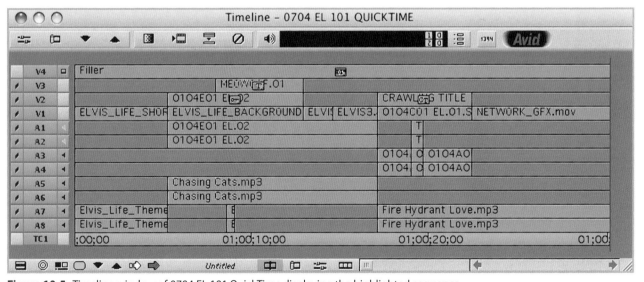

Figure 10-5. Timeline window of 0704 EL 101 QuickTime displaying the highlighted sequence.

13. Select Clip≫Render In/Out.

14. In the Render Effects dialog box that appears, select the render drive from the Drive menu.

15. Click OK.

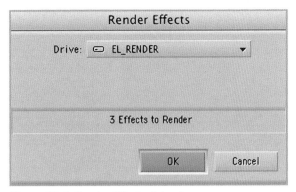

Figure 10-6. Render Effects dialog box.

16. Click the sequence in the bin.

17. Select File≫Export.

18. In the Export As dialog box that appears, select Untitled from the Export Setting menu.

> **Tip |** Right-clicking on the sequence in the bin also opens the Export As dialog box.

> **Caution! |** Select Untitled as the Export Setting to ensure that you are working with an unsaved export setting.
>
> Since it is possible to save frequently used export settings, it is also possible to unintentionally choose a saved setting, modify it, and save over the original setting.

Figure 10-7. Export As dialog box.

When the Export As dialog box opens, the file extension defaults to that of the last file that was exported. Once a new setting is chosen, the file extension updates.

19. Click Options, and the Export Settings dialog box appears.

> **Note** | The Export Settings dialog box retains the settings that were last used, so if a QuickTime movie was the last export, Step 20 can be skipped. However, it is prudent to make sure the settings are correct.
>
> There are numerous settings that can be modified to create a QuickTime movie, and the settings described in Step 20 are one combination.
>
> Find out what export settings your company uses for the different export file types.

20. In the Export Settings dialog box, select QuickTime Movie from the Export As menu, and then do the following:

   (a) Select the Use Marks check box.

   (b) Select the Use Enabled Tracks check box.

   (c) Select Custom.

   (d) Click Format Options.

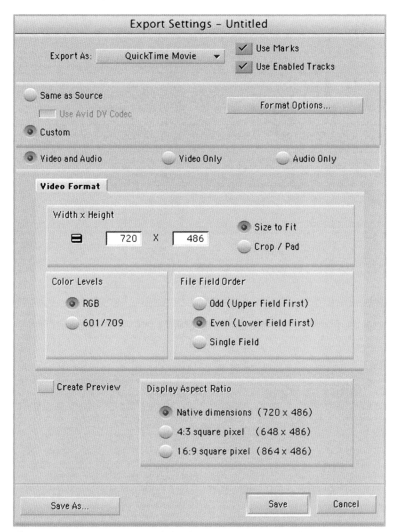

Figure 10-8. Export Settings dialog box displaying example export settings for QuickTime Movies.

   (e) In the Movie Settings dialog box that appears, do the following:

      (i) In the Video area, click Settings.

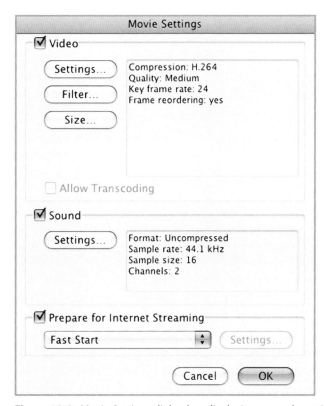

Figure 10-9. Movie Settings dialog box displaying example settings.

(ii) In the Standard Video Compression Settings dialog box that appears, choose the video settings appropriate for your export, and then click OK.

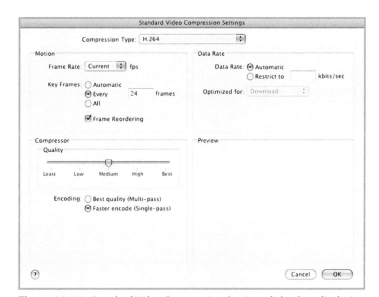

Figure 10-10. Standard Video Compression Settings dialog box displaying example video compression settings.

Different combinations of these settings result in QuickTime movies that range in size, video quality, and playability. Typically, the lower the quality, the faster the export resulting in a lower quality video.

(iii)In the Sound area, click Settings.

(iv) In the Standard Audio Compression Settings dialog box that appears, select the audio settings appropriate for your export, and then click OK.

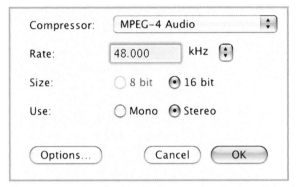

Figure 10-11. Standard Audio Compression Settings dialog box displaying example audio compression settings.

21. Click OK.

22. Click Save.

23. Navigate to the destination for the file.

24. Click Save, and then the file exports.

25. Play the QuickTime movie to make sure it has video and audio.

Saving and Deleting Export Settings

It is possible to save export settings to make the exporting process easier and faster. Once you create and save an export setting, you can select it in the Export Settings dialog box, from the Export As list. You can also delete saved export settings on the Settings tab of the Project window.

To save export settings

1. Click the sequence in the bin.

2. Select File≫Export.

3. In the Export As dialog box that appears, select Untitled from the Export Setting menu.

Select Untitled as the Export Setting to ensure that you are working with an unsaved export setting.

4. Click Options, and in the Export Settings dialog box that appears, do the following:

    (a) In the Export As menu, select a setting.

    (b) Modify the options in the Export Settings dialog box.

    (c) Click Save As.

    (i) In the Save Export Setting dialog box that appears, in the Setting Name box, type a name for the setting.

    (ii) Click OK.

Figure 10-12. Save Export Setting dialog box.

5. Click Save.

6. Click Save.

Figure 10-13. Export As dialog box displaying saved export setting.

If an export setting (or just about any user-created setting) is mistakenly saved or no longer of use, it is possible to delete it.

To delete a saved export setting

1. In the Project window, on the Settings tab, scroll down to Export.

2. Highlight the setting.

3. Press Delete.

    If there is a check mark next to the name of the saved setting you won't be able to delete it (see FIGURE 10-14 for the message displayed in this circumstance). In those situations, click another inactive setting (that is, one without a check mark), and then highlight and delete the desired setting.

Figure 10-14. Avid Media Composer dialog box.

Exporting AAF/OMF Files

During the onlining process (see CHAPTER 11: *Onlining* on page 275), audio from a sequence may be separated from the video and exported in two formats: AAF (Advanced Authoring Format) and OMF (Open Media Framework).

These two file formats allow an audio mix house to "see" the audio tracks exactly as they are in the Avid sequence. AAF/OMF files contain clip names, timecodes, and other miscellaneous information to help audio mixers determine the best way to mix the cut.

The audio mix house takes creative liberties with the audio inserting sound effects into the audio sequence to make it sound as believable, comical, or serious as required. A finalized cut of the final offline sequence—either on tape or in a digital format—is sent to the audio mix house as a video reference to make sure the audio and video are in sync.

Exporting AAF/OMF files requires two tasks: (1) Consolidating the Media and (2) Exporting. Creating AAF/OMF files are the same process to a point. In our example, we used an AAF file.

Consolidating the Media

For both AAF and OMF files, the procedure for consolidating the media is the same.

To consolidate the media

1. Create a bin (Mac: ⌘+N | PC: Ctrl+N).

2. Rename the bin 0704 EL 101 AAFs, and then press Enter.

3. Open the bin that contains the final sequence.

4. Click the sequence.

5. Copy the sequence to the 0704 EL 101 AAFs bin (Mac: Option+Drag | PC: Alt+Drag).

6. Rename the sequence 0704 EL 101 AAFs, and then press Enter.

7. Double-click the sequence.

8. Deselect all of the tracks of the sequence (Mac: Shift+⌘+A | PC: Shift+Ctrl+A).

9. Select the video tracks of the sequence.

10. Press Delete.

11. In the Delete Track dialog box that appears, click OK.

Figure 10-15. Delete Track dialog box.

12. Select all of the audio tracks (Mac: ⌘+A | PC: Ctrl+A).

13. Mark IN (press I) at the beginning of the sequence.

14. Mark OUT (press O) at the end of the sequence.

15. Click the Bin Fast menu.

16. Choose Select Offline Items to make sure nothing is offline. (The sequence will be highlighted if anything is offline.)

You shouldn't consolidate a sequence that has offline clips because once those clips are sent to the audio mix house, the clips will be offline there as well. You should find the missing media for the offline clips and once the sequence is entirely online, proceed with the consolidating process.

17. Click the sequence in the bin.

18. Select Clip≫Consolidate/Transcode.

19. In the Consolidate/Transcode dialog box that appears, do the following:

> **Note** | The settings in Step 19 are an example of the options you can choose. Check with your company for the specific consolidate settings required.

    (a) **Consolidate (selected)**—When this option is selected, the media is consolidated. If Transcode is selected, the media is transcoded.

    (b) **Target Drive(s) area: Video and audio on same drive(s) (selected)**—When this option is selected, the video and audio are copied to the same target drive. When this option is not selected, the video and audio are copied to separate target drives.

    (c) **Target Drive area: Video list**—The location the consolidated clips are copied to.

    (d) **Handle length box**—Type the number of frames to extend the IN and OUT points of the consolidated clips. (60 frames is the default value.)

    (e) **Create new sequence (not selected)**—When this option is selected, a copy of the consolidated sequence is created. When this option is not selected, a copy of the consolidated sequence is not created.

    (f) **Delete original media files when done (not selected)**—When this option is selected, the media on the original drive is deleted during the consolidation process. When this option is not selected, the media on the original drive is not deleted during the consolidation process.

    (g) **Skip media files already on the target drive (selected)**—When this option is selected, the consolidation process disregards any duplicate clips that may exist on the target drive. When this option is not selected, all of the clips from the sequence are consolidated possibly creating duplicate clips on the target drive.

    (h) **Relink selected clips to target drive before skipping (selected)**—When this option is selected, all of the consolidated clips are linked to the media on the target drive. When this option is not selected, consolidated clips may not be relinked to media on the target drive.

(i) **Consolidate all clips in a group edit (not selected)**—When this option is selected, all of the clips in a group are consolidated. When this option is not selected, only the clips present in the sequence are consolidated.

(j) **Convert Audio Sample Rate (not selected)**—When this option is selected, the sample rates of the consolidated clips are modified. When this option is not selected, the consolidated clips retain their original sample rate.

(k) **Convert Audio Sample Bit Depth (not selected)**—When this option is selected, the audio sample bit depth of the consolidated clips is modified. When this option is not selected, the consolidated clips retain their original audio sample bit depth.

(l) **Convert Audio Format (not selected)**—When this option is selected, the audio format of the consolidated clips is modified. When this option is not selected, the consolidated clips retain their original audio format settings.

Note | The Consolidate/ Transcode function takes the sequence and separates all of the clips from their master files and creates new and sometimes smaller clips.

Consolidating copies media from one drive to a new (target) drive while preserving the media's original format.

Transcoding copies media from one drive to a new (target) drive while converting the media to a different format.

It is possible to complete the AAF process without consolidating the audio, but that is not recommended. If the audio is not consolidated, the process takes considerably longer and is prone to errors. (Largely dependent on the length and complexity of the sequence.)

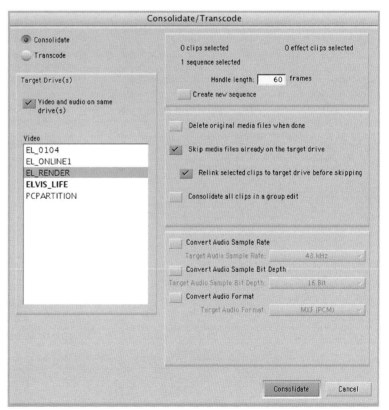

Figure 10-16. Consolidate/Transcode dialog box displaying Consolidate settings.

20. Click Consolidate, and then clips will appear in the bin (these clips are the smaller sections of the master clips that were contained in the sequence).

21. Save the bin (Mac: ⌘+S | PC: Ctrl+S).

Exporting

After consolidating the sequence, it is ready to export. If a sequence exceeds the 2 GB file size limit for exporting an AAF/OMF file, break the sequence into smaller sections (known as *subsequences*) by exporting two to three tracks at a time or by acts.

Depending on the setup at your company, AAF/OMF files can be created as acts become available from the editors. This is a significantly faster workflow because you can export files as they are completed. Some audio mix houses may not desire this workflow, however, so make sure to check if there is a preference.

To export an AAF file

1. Double-click the consolidated sequence in the bin.

2. Snap the position indicator to the beginning of the first act (Mac: ⌘+Click | PC: Ctrl+Click).

3. Mark IN (press I).

4. Snap the position indicator to the end of the first act (Mac: ⌘+Click | PC: Ctrl+Click).

5. Mark OUT (press O).

6. Subclip (press F7) the act into a subsequence.

7. Rename the subsequence according to the act.

8. Repeat Steps 1–7 for the remaining acts until the entire consolidated sequence has been subclipped.

9. Double-click the first subsequence.

10. Mark IN (press I) at the beginning of the subsequence.

11. Mark OUT (press O) at the end of the subsequence.

12. Click the subsequence in the bin.

13. Select File≫Export.

Caution! | Select Untitled as the Export Setting to ensure that you are working with an unsaved export setting.

14. In the Export As dialog box that appears, select Untitled from the Export Setting menu, and then click Options.

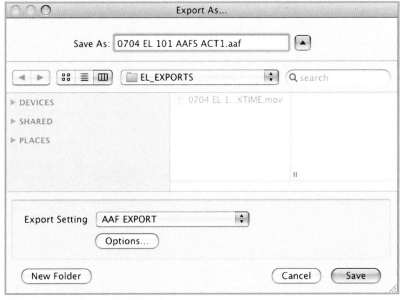

Figure 10-17. Export As dialog box.

15. In the Export Settings dialog box that appears, do the following:

(a) In the Export As menu select AAF.

Note | Find out what export settings your company uses for the different export file types.

(b) Modify the options in the Export Settings dialog box.

The Export Settings dialog box retains the settings that were last used, so if an AAF file was the last export, Step 15(b) can be skipped. However, it is prudent to make sure the settings are correct because there are numerous settings that can be modified to create an AAF file.

(c) Click Save As.

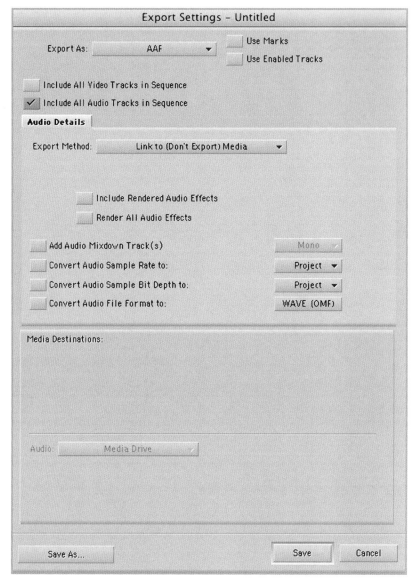

Figure 10-18. Export Settings dialog box.

(i) In the Save Export Setting dialog box that appears, in the Setting Name box, type a name for the setting.

(ii) Click OK.

Figure 10-19. Save Export Setting dialog box.

16. Click Save.

17. Click Save.

18. Double-click the next subsequence.

19. Mark IN (press I) at the beginning of the subsequence.

20. Mark OUT (press O) at the end of the subsequence.

21. Click the subsequence in the bin.

22. Select File≫Export.

23. In the Export As dialog box that appears, select the export setting you named in Step 15(c)(i) from the Export Setting menu, and then click Save.

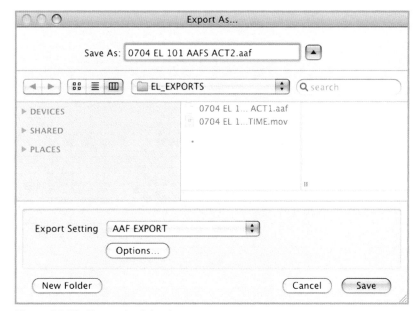

Figure 10-20. Export As dialog box.

24. Repeat Steps 18–23 for the remaining subsequences.

Export Settings Dialog Box Options

AAF/OMF export settings are very much like those for QuickTime movie exports. There are many choices allowing for numerous export combinations. Whether exporting an AAF or an OMF, the setting choices are the same; however, you need to know the requirements of the audio engineer to send a correctly exported AAF or OMF. Check with your company for the specific export settings required, and use this discussion of the Export Settings dialog box options to supplement the information received from your company.

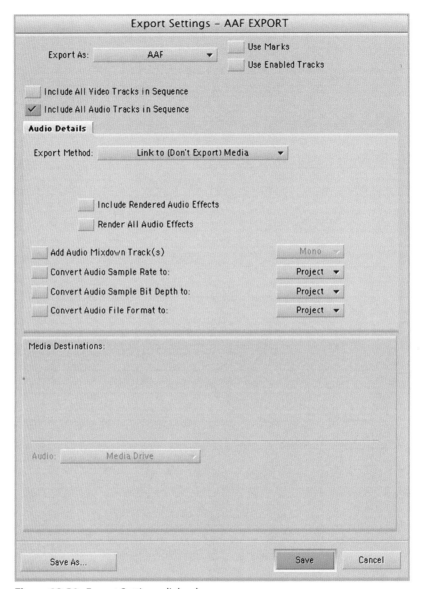

Figure 10-21. Export Settings dialog box.

- **Export As**—Notice that AAF is selected.

- **Use Marks (not selected)**—When this option is selected, anything within the current Mark IN/OUT points, is exported. When this option is not selected, the entire clip or sequence is exported.

- **Use Enabled Tracks (not selected)**—When this option is selected, all enabled tracks are exported. When this option is not selected, all tracks are exported.

- **Include All Video Tracks in Sequence (not selected)**—When this option is selected, all video tracks are exported, and the Video Details tab appears; however, this option is unnecessary.

- **Include All Audio Tracks in Sequence (selected)**—When this option is selected, all audio tracks from the sequence are exported, and the Audio Details tab appears.

AUDIO DETAILS TAB

- **Export Method menu**—There are three options for exporting an AAF.

  - ◆ **Link to (Don't Export) Media (default selection)**—When this option is selected, the AAF information but not the media is exported. Select this option if the audio mixer already has the files and only needs the sequence information.

  - ◆ **Copy All Media (not selected)**—When this option is selected, the media is copied to a drive and the exported AAF/OMF links to the copied media.

  - ◆ **Consolidate Media (not selected)**—When this option is selected, portions of the media are copied to a drive and the exported AAF/OMF links to the consolidated media.

- **Include Rendered Audio Effects (not selected)**—When this option is selected, all rendered effects (dissolves, filters, etc.) in the sequence are exported.

- **Render All Audio Effects (not selected)**—When this option is selected, all unrendered effects in the sequence are rendered during the AAF export process. (This can be very time consuming, and some audio engineers remove Avid effects. Check with your company for the protocol.)

- **Add Audio Mixdown Track(s) (not selected)**—When this option is selected, an audio mixdown track is added during export, for which you select mono or stereo as the track type.

- **Convert Audio Sample Rate to (not selected)**—When this option is selected, the audio sample of the project is converted to a new sample rate. Select this option if the sequence has multiple sample rates and the exported AAF/OMF needs to have one, or if the application that you are exporting to doesn't support the current sample rate.

- **Convert Audio Sample Bit Depth to (not selected)**—When this option is selected, the sample bit depth is converted to a new sample bit depth.

Select this option if the sequence has multiple sample bit depths and the exported AAF/OMF needs to have one, or if the application that you are exporting to doesn't support the current sample bit depth.

■ **Convert Audio File Format to (not selected)**—When this option is selected, the audio file format is converted to a new audio file format. There needs to be a single audio file format to include media in an AAF/OMF export.

■ **Media Destinations**—Determines where the media (if there is media) is located. The Audio menu has three options.

◆ **Media Drive**—Places the exported media in a drive.

◆ **Folder**—Places the exported media in a folder.

◆ **Embedded in AAF**—Creates self-contained AAFs with the exported media files.

Did I Do This Correctly?

■ **Does the export file have video and audio?**

Play the movie on a computer different from the computer the movie was created on, and it should have video and audio (if it is supposed to have video and audio).

■ **Was the sequence completely online before the AAF/OMF was created?**

On the Bin Fast menu, Select Offline Items should have been selected to see if the sequence was offline before creating the AAF/OMF because if the sequence was not completely online, some of the files within the AAF/OMF will be offline at the audio mix house.

CHAPTER 11:
Onlining

~ **With the collaboration of Online Editor and Colorist Josh Petok**

Tasks in This Chapter

—**If your company works in a full-resolution environment, this chapter is optional**—

**(You should still read this chapter to familiarize yourself with new concepts
that could help you in other assistant editing situations.)**

W HEN IT COMES TO editing an episode of a show, speed is of the essence and drive space is of concern. Therefore, editors typically work in an environment where the footage is captured at a low resolution because it is quicker to work with and it takes up less drive space. However, when it comes time to deliver an episode of a show to the network, it must be delivered in full resolution, so the low-resolution episode is re-captured (*uprezzed*) to full resolution. Full resolution depends on the type of project your episode is in. It can be 1:1, DNxHD 145, or some other type.

After an episode of a show has been re-captured to full resolution, the online editor, or colorist, does a pass on it to make sure that the colors and luminance (brightness) levels are consistent and within NTSC standards. Given the inevitable delays against a hard delivery date, colorists usually work under tight deadlines, and they rely on you to ensure that the only thing left for them to do is to color the show. You should handle, among other things, graphic importing, titles, footage at the correct video resolution, and correctly timed act breaks. If you work with the colorist in this manner, the colorist will have the maximum time available to make the episode picture perfect.

The setup of an online project varies greatly from company to company. No matter how your company chooses to set up an online project, here are a few helpful hints to help you set up your own.

- The only item in the online sequence bin should be the sequence.

- Bins should contain only one type of item. For example, titles, graphics, clips, and the offline reference copy should be in separate bins.

- Folders should separate your work from colorist work. Your work includes clips, titles, and graphics. Colorist work includes different cuts, special keys, and effects.

Settings Needed

Configure the following settings before beginning the tasks in this chapter.

Capture Settings Dialog Box

BATCH TAB

Navigation: Project window | Settings tab | Select Capture from the Settings list | Capture Settings dialog box | Batch tab

- **Eject tape when finished (selected)**—When the tape is finished, it automatically ejects—a time saver when monitoring several decks.

■ **Capture the tracks logged for each clip (selected)**—Whatever tracks were first selected during capturing, Avid automatically selects those tracks to be batch captured, so you won't have to remember to.

Figure 11-1. Capture Settings dialog box | Batch tab.

Prepping for Onlining

Two tasks are required to prep for onlining: (1) creating a reference copy of the offline sequence and (2) dropping all possible video clips to the lowest video track.

■ **Creating a reference copy of the offline sequence.** Create a reference copy of the offline sequence you are working with for the online editor to use as a copy to make sure that the sequence they are working with is the final version. The reference copy given to the online editor must *exactly* match the offline sequence you are working with.

■ **Drop all possible video clips to the lowest video track.** Drop all possible video clips to the lowest video track to reduce the number of clips that need to be re-captured, thereby shortening the re-capturing process. Notice the use of "all possible" video clips. Not all video clips can be dropped to the lowest video track because sometimes there are effects present that are deleted if there aren't two (or more) tracks of video.

To create a reference copy of the offline sequence

1. Create a bin in the offline project (Mac: ⌘+N | PC: Ctrl+N).

2. Rename the new bin according to date, show, episode, and type of cut (0828 EL 101 Final Cut).

3. Open the bin containing the final sequence.

4. Click the sequence.

5. Copy that sequence to the new bin (Mac: Option+Drag | PC: Alt+Drag).

6. Rename the sequence exactly as the bin.

7. Close the bin containing the final sequence.

8. Double-click the sequence in the new bin (0828 EL 101 Final Cut).

9. In the Timeline window, select all of the tracks (Mac: ⌘+A | PC: Ctrl+A).

10. Mark IN (press I) at the beginning of the sequence.

11. Mark OUT (press O) at the end of the sequence.

12. Click the sequence in the new bin (0828 EL 101 Final Cut).

13. Output this sequence to tape or export it as a movie.

    See CHAPTER 9: *Outputs* on page 221 for information on outputting a sequence to tape or CHAPTER 10: *Imports and Exports* on page 253 for information on exporting a sequence as a movie.

14. Save the 0828 EL 101 Final Cut bin (Mac: ⌘+S | PC: Ctrl+S).

To drop all possible video clips to the lowest video track

1. Click Lift/Overwrite Segment Mode ⏵ .

2. Hold down Ctrl and click and move all unnecessary video clips to video track 1 (V1).

    Look at the clip *before and after* the unnecessary video clips have been dropped to the lowest track (see FIGURE 11-2 and FIGURE 11-3, respectively). Sometimes there are effects present that are deleted if there aren't two tracks of video.

> **Note** | The reference copy can be brought into the online editor's project by tape or as a movie; however, whatever format is given to the online editor, it must exactly match the sequence the assistant editor is working with.
>
> This is very important—*it must exactly match!*

> **Caution!** | Be careful when dropping all possible video clips to the lowest video track because sometimes effects are present that are deleted if there aren't two tracks of video.

For example, in FIGURE 11-3, the title remains on video track 3 (V3) because moving it to video track 1 (V1) will delete the video beneath it.

Figure 11-2. Timeline window of 0828 EL 101 Final Cut *before* unnecessary video tracks are dropped.

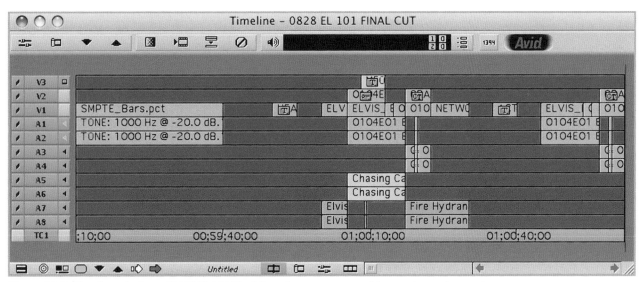

Figure 11-3. Timeline window of 0828 EL 101 Final Cut *after* unnecessary video tracks are dropped.

3. Click Lift/Overwrite Segment Mode to exit the function.

4. Save the 0828 EL 101 Final Cut bin (Mac: ⌘+S | PC: Ctrl+S).

Decomposing the Sequence

Decomposing the sequence takes all of the clips associated with the sequence and breaks their links with the original media files and creates new and smaller clips that are linked to the current sequence. This achieves two purposes: (1) you can immediately see the clips associated with the sequence and the durations they have in the sequence, and (2) if the sequence exists in a shared media environment, there is a possibility that the smaller clips can be relinked to media files at the higher resolution.

At your company, there should be a distinct separation of the offline low-resolution footage and online full-resolution footage. If the offline and online footage are not separated, it is possible to have low-resolution and full-resolution footage in the final delivery sequence. When performing this next task, make sure the sequence doesn't have access to the low-resolution footage and make sure the low-resolution footage is completely offline.

To decompose the sequence

1. Create a bin (Mac: ⌘+N | PC: Ctrl+N).

2. Rename the new bin EL 101 Online Video Only, and then press Enter.

3. Click the final sequence in the final online bin (0828 EL 101 Final Cut).

4. Copy that sequence to the new bin (Mac: Option+Drag | PC: Alt+Drag).

5. Close the final online bin (0828 EL 101 Final Cut).

6. Double-click the final sequence in the new bin (EL 101 Online Video Only).

7. In the Timeline window, deselect all tracks (Mac: Shift+⌘+A | PC: Shift+Ctrl+A).

8. Select only the audio tracks of the sequence.

9. Press Delete.

10. In the Delete Track dialog box that appears, click OK.

Figure 11-4. Delete Track dialog box.

11. Click the sequence in the bin (EL 101 Online Video Only).

12. Select Clip≫Decompose.

13. In the Decompose dialog box that appears, do the following:

    (a) Select the Offline media only check box.

    (b) For Clip Types, select Captured clips only.

    (c) In the Handle Length box, type "15". (Frame handles allow an editor to extend an edit because additional frames are added at the beginning and end of the clip and captured during the onlining process.)

    (d) Select the Extend handles beyond Master Clip edges check box.

    (e) Click OK, and then master clips, subclips, and groups may appear in the bin.

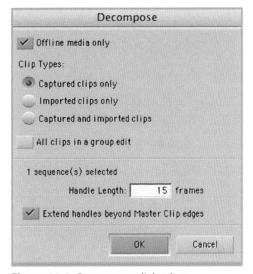

Figure 11-5. Decompose dialog box.

14. Select all of the objects in the bin (Mac: ⌘+A | PC: Ctrl+A).

15. Press Delete.

16. In the Delete dialog box that appears, delete everything except for sequences and master clips. For our example, do the following:

    (a) Select the Delete 3 subclip(s) check box.

    (b) Select the Delete 2 group(s) check box.

17. Click OK.

> **Caution!** | Do not delete sequences and master clips.

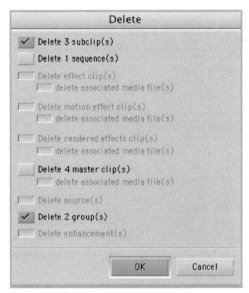

Figure 11-6. Delete dialog box.
(Do not delete sequences and master clips.)

18. Save the EL 101 Online Video Only bin (Mac: ⌘+S | PC: Ctrl+S).

Relinking Decomposed Clips to Full-Resolution Clips

The clips remaining in the new bin (EL 101 Online Video Only) need to be re-captured (uprezzed) at the full resolution. You can save time if any of the remaining clips in the new bin have been used in previous sequences (meaning that a full-resolution version of them exists) by linking to those full-resolution clips and only re-capturing the clips that are left.

If you are certain there are no full-resolution clips that can be linked to this sequence, proceed to *Gathering Source Tapes* on page 289.

To relink decomposed clips to full-resolution clips

1. Open the EL 101 Online Video Only bin.

2. Select all of the objects in the bin (Mac: ⌘+A | PC: Ctrl+A).

3. Press Delete.

> **Caution!** | Do not delete sequences.

4. In the Delete dialog box that appears, delete everything except for sequences. For our example, do the following:

   (a) Select the Delete 4 master clip(s) check box.

   (b) Click OK.

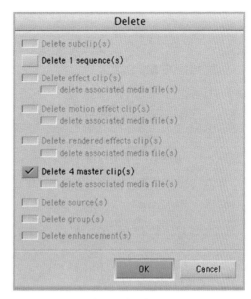

Figure 11-7. Delete dialog box.
(Do not delete sequences.)

5. Select Tools≫Media Tool.

6. In the Media Tool Display dialog box that appears, do the following, and then click OK.

   (a) Click All Drives.

   (b) Click All Projects.

   (c) Select the Master Clips check box.

   (d) Clear the Precompute Clips check box.

   (e) Clear the Media Files check box.

> **Note |** The Media tool keeps track of all of the clips brought into Avid.
>
> Using the Media tool, check to see if any clips from the current sequence can relink to clips that have already been re-captured at full resolution from previous projects.

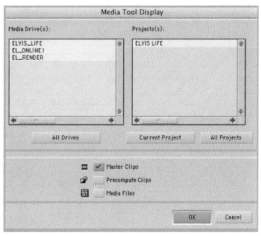

Figure 11-8. Media Tool Display dialog box.

7. In the Media Tool bin that appears, click the Text tab.

8. On the Bin View menu, select Statistics.

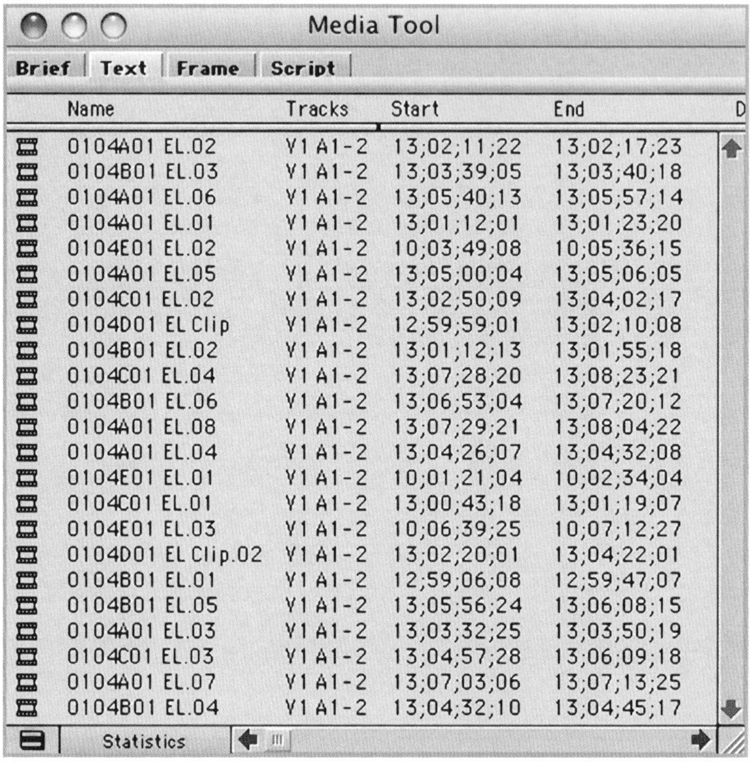

	Name	Tracks	Start	End	D
	0104A01 EL.02	V1 A1-2	13;02;11;22	13;02;17;23	
	0104B01 EL.03	V1 A1-2	13;03;39;05	13;03;40;18	
	0104A01 EL.06	V1 A1-2	13;05;40;13	13;05;57;14	
	0104A01 EL.01	V1 A1-2	13;01;12;01	13;01;23;20	
	0104E01 EL.02	V1 A1-2	10;03;49;08	10;05;36;15	
	0104A01 EL.05	V1 A1-2	13;05;00;04	13;05;06;05	
	0104C01 EL.02	V1 A1-2	13;02;50;09	13;04;02;17	
	0104D01 EL Clip	V1 A1-2	12;59;59;01	13;02;10;08	
	0104B01 EL.02	V1 A1-2	13;01;12;13	13;01;55;18	
	0104C01 EL.04	V1 A1-2	13;07;28;20	13;08;23;21	
	0104B01 EL.06	V1 A1-2	13;06;53;04	13;07;20;12	
	0104A01 EL.08	V1 A1-2	13;07;29;21	13;08;04;22	
	0104A01 EL.04	V1 A1-2	13;04;26;07	13;04;32;08	
	0104E01 EL.01	V1 A1-2	10;01;21;04	10;02;34;04	
	0104C01 EL.01	V1 A1-2	13;00;43;18	13;01;19;07	
	0104E01 EL.03	V1 A1-2	10;06;39;25	10;07;12;27	
	0104D01 EL Clip.02	V1 A1-2	13;02;20;01	13;04;22;01	
	0104B01 EL.01	V1 A1-2	12;59;06;08	12;59;47;07	
	0104B01 EL.05	V1 A1-2	13;05;56;24	13;06;08;15	
	0104A01 EL.03	V1 A1-2	13;03;32;25	13;03;50;19	
	0104C01 EL.03	V1 A1-2	13;04;57;28	13;06;09;18	
	0104A01 EL.07	V1 A1-2	13;07;03;06	13;07;13;25	
	0104B01 EL.04	V1 A1-2	13;04;32;10	13;04;45;17	

Figure 11-9. Media Tool bin displaying Statistics from the Bin View menu.

9. Click the Media Tool Bin Fast menu, and then select Custom Sift.

10. In the Custom Sift dialog box that appears, in the Find clips that meet these criteria area, in the topmost row, do the following, and then click OK.

(a) For the Criterion, select Contains from the menu.

(b) In the Text to Find text box, type the full resolution that applies to the project (in our example, the full resolution is 1:1).

(c) For the Column or Range to Search, select Video from the menu. (This instructs the Media tool to search for all 1:1 video media.)

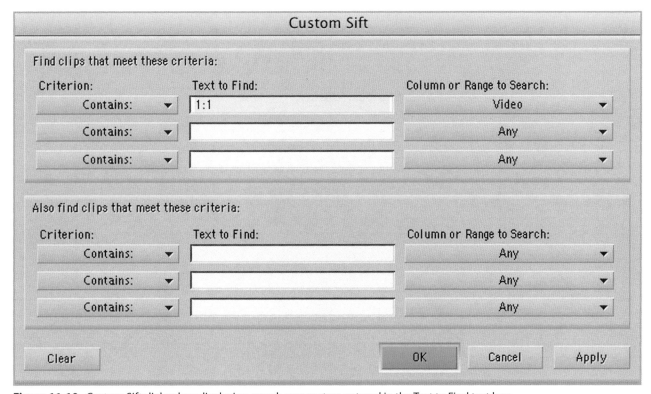

Figure 11-10. Custom Sift dialog box displaying search parameters entered in the Text to Find text box.

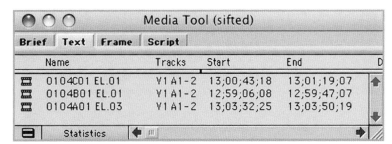

Figure 11-11. Media Tool bin after sifting. Notice that "(sifted)" displays after the bin name and that there are three clips that fit the requirements specified in the Custom Sift dialog box in Figure 11-10.

11. Do one of the following:

   (a) If there aren't any clips in the Media Tool bin, proceed to Step 20.

   –or–

   (b) If there are clips in the Media Tool bin, proceed to Step 12.

12. Select all of the clips in the Media Tool bin (Mac: ⌘+A | PC: Ctrl+A), and then move the clips to the EL 101 Online Video Only bin. (When dragging clips from the Media Tool bin, it automatically makes copies.)

13. Close the Media Tool bin.

14. In the EL 101 Online Video Only bin, select all of the clips and the sequence (Mac: ⌘+A | PC: Ctrl+A).

15. Select Clip≫Relink.

16. In the Relink dialog box that appears, do the following:

   (a) In the Relink by menu, select Source Timecode and Tape.

   (b) Select Relink all non-master clips to selected online items.

   (c) In the Relink to media on volume menu, select All Available Drives (assuming full-resolution media is separated from low-resolution media).

   (d) Make sure all other options are not selected.

   (e) Click OK, and then some clips may come online.

> **Note |** This option instructs Avid to relink the media to the clips that have a common relationship with the sequence and clips in the bin.
>
> By deselecting all of these options and choosing All Available Drives, Avid will look to see if any commonalities exist between the clips and the sequence.

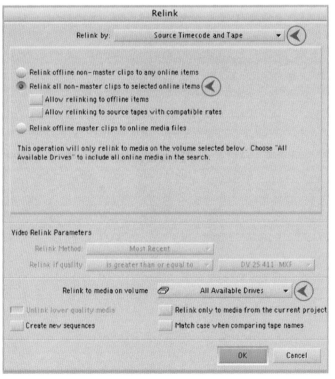

Figure 11-12. Relink dialog box.

17. Select all of the clips in the EL 101 Online Video Only bin (Mac: ⌘+A | PC: Ctrl+A).

18. Press Delete.

Caution! |
Do not delete sequences.

And be very careful not to delete the media files associated with the master clips!

That is, for master clips, select the first option only—Delete 3 master clip(s).

Do not select the second option—delete 9 associated media file(s)—because if you do, all of the media you just relinked will be deleted.

19. In the Delete dialog box that appears, delete everything except for sequences and media files associated with master clips. For our example, do the following:

    (a) Select the Delete 3 master clip(s) check box.

    (b) Click OK.

Figure 11-13. Delete dialog box.
(Do not delete sequences and associated media files.)

20. Click the sequence in the EL 101 Online Video Only bin.

21. Select Clip≫Decompose.

Note | The sequence is intentionally decomposed twice.

Once to create smaller clips that are linked to the newly created online sequence and determine if those smaller clips will relink to any full-resolution media.

Again to re-create any clips from the sequence that are still offline from the relinking function for use during the uprezzing process.

22. In the Decompose dialog box that appears, do the following:

    (a) Select the Offline media only check box.

    (b) For Clip Types, select Captured clips only.

    (c) In the Handle Length box, type "15".

    (d) Select the Extend handles beyond Master Clip edges check box.

    (e) Click OK, and then master clips, subclips, and groups may appear in the bin.

Figure 11-14. Decompose dialog box.

23. Select all of the objects in the EL 101 Online Video Only bin (Mac: ⌘+A | PC: Ctrl+A).

24. Press Delete.

25. In the Delete dialog box that appears, do the following:

    (a) Select the Delete 3 subclip(s) check box.

    (b) Select the Delete 2 group(s) check box.

26. Click OK.

Caution! | Do not delete sequences and master clips.

Figure 11-15. Delete dialog box.
(Do not delete sequences and master clips.)

27. Save the bin (Mac: ⌘+S | PC: Ctrl+S).

28. Close the bin.

Gathering Source Tapes

When shooting footage for a show, a production company can use a lot of tapes. In addition to the tapes specifically shot for the show, the production company may use tapes from its tape library. Due to this tape sharing, it is nearly impossible to know exactly what tapes have been used in an episode. As a result, the final sequence is used to show what tapes came from where, and all of those tapes should be assembled in a central location for easier re-capturing.

To gather source tapes

1. Create a bin (Mac: ⌘+N | PC: Ctrl+N).

2. Rename the new bin EL 101 Decomp 1, and then press Enter.

3. Open the EL 101 Online Video Only bin.

4. Select all of the clips in the EL 101 Online Video Only bin (Mac: ⌘+A | PC: Ctrl+A), and then Shift+Click the sequence to deselect it.

5. Move the clips to the EL 101 Decomp 1 bin.

6. In the Bin window, click the Text tab.

7. On the Bin View menu, select Statistics.

8. Click the Name column.

9. Sort the Name column in ascending order (Mac: ⌘+E | PC: Ctrl+E).

10. Select all of the clips in the EL 101 Decomp 1 bin (Mac: ⌘+A | PC: Ctrl+A), and drag them into the Timeline window, and then *the offline clips automatically create a sequence within the Timeline window*.

11. Rename the sequence EL 101 Source Tapes, and then press Enter.

12. Make sure all of the video tracks are enabled.

13. In the EL 101 Decomp 1 bin, click the EL 101 Source Tapes sequence.

14. Select Output≫EDL, and then the Avid EDL Manager window opens. (It is empty until a sequence is brought into the program.)

> **Note |** An EDL can be created from the video-only sequence; however, it will contain all of the sources for the entire show, not just the offline sources.

15. Select File≫Get Current Sequence (Mac: ⌘+G | PC: Ctrl+G), and then the offline sequence in the Timeline window loads in the Avid EDL Manager.

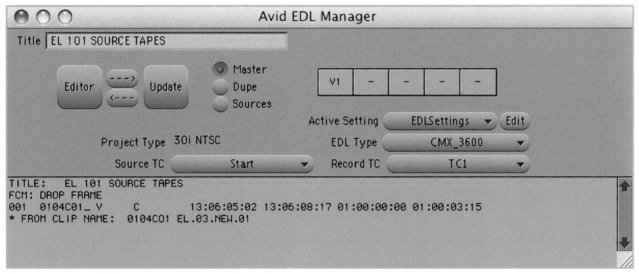

Figure 11-16. Avid EDL Manager window (see Table 11-1).

At first glance, the EDL appears to be a jumble of letters and numbers, but once you are familiar with the information, an EDL can be very useful. We do not need to use the EDL information now, but let's briefly go over the aspects of this EDL (see TABLE 11-1).

TABLE 11-1. AVID EDL MANAGER CLIP INFORMATION (SEE FIGURE 11-16)

001	0104C01	V	C	13;06;05;02 / 13;06;08;17	01:00:00:00 / 01:00:03:15
Clip number in the sequence	Clip name	Clip tracks in the sequence	Clip edit type (cut, dissolve, etc.)	Clip IN / OUT points	Clip timecode location in the sequence

16. Do one of the following:

    (a) If the EDL Type menu is set to CMX_3600, proceed to Step 17.

    –or–

    (b) If the EDL Type menu is not set to CMX_3600, select it from the EDL Type menu, and then proceed to Step 17.

17. Click Edit.

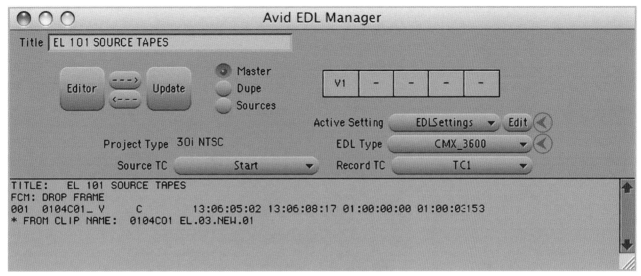

Figure 11-17. Avid EDL Manager window with EDL Type menu set to CMX_3600.

18. In the Options window that appears, displaying the Options tab, confirm that the Tapename truncation menu is set to the option that best suits your situation (see FIGURE 11-18 on page 292).

An EDL can only display eight characters for the clip name, so depending on your company's tape naming convention, you may have to remove the beginning, middle, or end of the tape name so that the EDL provides the necessary information to retrieve the tapes from the library.

■ If your tape naming convention is shorter than the EDL's restrictions (eight characters), the entire tape name is displayed.

■ If the important portion of the tape name is at the beginning, select Tapename truncation Remove End.

■ If the important part of the tape name is at the beginning and end, select Tapename truncation Remove Middle.

■ If the important part of the tape name is at the end, select Tapename truncation Remove Beginning.

■ If the important part of the tape is at the end while preserving the first character, select Tapename truncation Keep First Character, End.

19. Click Update (if changes were made).

20. Close the Options window.

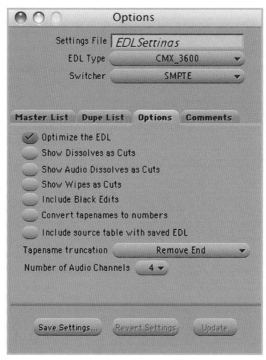

Figure 11-18. Options window | Options tab.

21. Select Sources in the Avid EDL Manager window.

    All of the sources for the clips in the sequence will be listed in the Sources pane of the Avid EDL Manager. Despite clips being in the sequence more than once, the Sources pane will only display the tape name once.

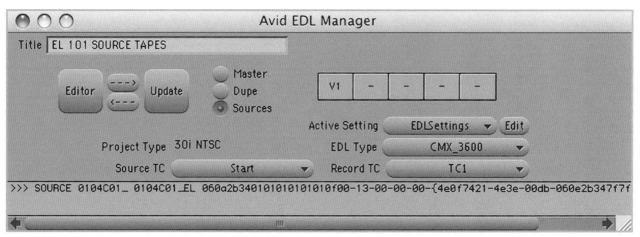

Figure 11-19. Avid EDL Manager window with Sources selected.

22. Select File≫Save As.

23. Give the EDL to the tape library to pull the tapes. (When the file is saved, it will have a .EDL file extension. This file type is usually opened in a spreadsheet program.)

24. Close the Avid EDL Manager window.

25. Create the same number of bins as there are edit suites available (Mac: ⌘+N | PC: Ctrl+N)—do not include EL 101 Decomp 1 bin in this calculation. (For example, if there are four edit suites, create three bins.)

26. Rename the bins in ascending order as follows: EL 101 Decomp 2, EL 101 Decomp 3, etc. (For example, if there are four edit suites, the bin names are EL 101 Decomp 1 through EL 101 Decomp 4.)

27. Click the Tape column in the bin. (You may need to resize the bin to see the tape column.)

28. Sort the Tape column in ascending order (Mac: ⌘+E | PC: Ctrl+E).

29. Lasso a set of clips for one source (all the clips for tape 0104C01 EL, for example).

30. Move those clips to EL 101 Decomp 2.

31. Lasso another set of clips for one source (all the clips for tape 0104A01 EL, for example).

32. Move those clips to EL 101 Decomp 3.

33. Repeat Steps 29–30 until the clips are evenly distributed in the bins created in Step 25.

34. Save all of the bins.

35. Close all of the bins.

> **Note** | If your company has multiple edit suites to re-capture the clips in, create the same number of bins as there are edit suites and then drag an even amount of clips into each of the new bins. Each bin will be opened in its own edit suite for re-capturing, thereby shortening the re-capturing process.

> **Note** | This process doesn't need to be done one source at a time. These steps are just to give a general idea of the process.
>
> The clips should be divided up by source tape so each suite receives a certain number of tapes, instead of moving the tapes from room to room.

Re-capturing Decomposed Clips

To re-capture decomposed clips

1. Open EL 101 Decomp 1 bin created in *To gather source tapes*, Step 1, page 289.

2. Open the Capture tool (Mac: ⌘+7 | PC: Ctrl+7), and then do the following:

(a) Confirm the video deck connected to Avid is displayed in the Deck Selection menu. If the name of the video deck connected to Avid is not displayed, see APPENDIX 2: *Deck Configuration* on page 311.

(b) In the Res (Resolution) menu, select the video resolution.

(c) In the Drive menu, select the capture drive.

(d) Select the Custom Preroll check box, and then in the menu to its right, select 1 second.

> **Note** | When Avid looks for a timecode, it is preset to scroll backward (preroll) five seconds from that timecode and then batch capture at the appointed time.
>
> If you set the Custom Preroll option to one second, Avid takes less time to complete a batch capture because for each clip captured, four seconds are saved.

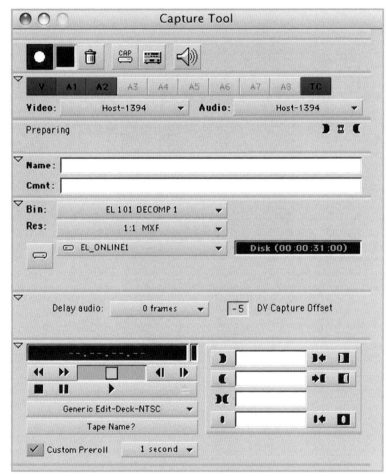

Figure 11-20. Capture Tool window configured for Batch Capture.

3. Click the bin opened in Step 1.

4. Select all of the clips in the bin (Mac: ⌘+A | PC: Ctrl+A). (Make sure not to select the EL 101 Source Tapes sequence that is in the EL 101 Decomp 1 bin.)

5. Select Clip≫Batch Capture.

6. In the Batch Capture dialog box that appears, select the Offline media only check box, and then click OK.

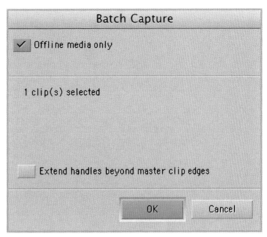

Figure 11-21. Batch Capture dialog box displaying the total number of clips selected in the bin to be re-captured (uprezzed).

7. Insert the correct tape/disc into the deck.

8. In the Avid Media Composer dialog box that appears, click Mounted (Avid begins capturing the clips in the bin), and then do one of the following:

Figure 11-22. Avid Media Composer dialog box prompting you to mount the tape/disc into the deck.

(a) If the Avid Media Composer dialog box does not appear with an error message, proceed to Step 9.

–or–

(b) If the Avid Media Composer dialog box appears with the error message below, do the following, and then proceed to Step 9.

"Halted on clip '<clipname>':
Exception: Failed to find pre-roll point on tape.
Number of clips remaining to re-capture: <number>
Do you want to continue?"

Note | Avid will cue the deck to the correct timecode and capture all of the clips from that tape. However, there will be instances when the correct tape is inserted in the deck, but Avid isn't able to find the clip on the tape.

Since a deck holds the memory of the last tape that was in it, if a tape that is not rewound is inserted in a deck, the Capture tool may mistakenly fast forward the tape looking for a timecode (when it should rewind instead) causing the deck to fail to find the preroll point on the tape.

This results in the message displayed in the Avid dialog box in Figure 11-23 on page 296.

(i) Take the deck out of remote (this setting is usually a button or switch on the front of the deck).

(ii) Rewind (or fast forward) the tape until the correct timecode is displayed.

(iii) Put the deck back into remote, click Try Again, and then Avid should start batch capturing.

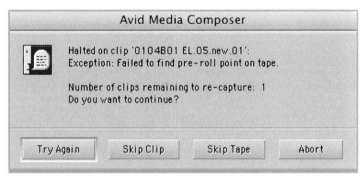

Figure 11-23. Avid Media Composer dialog box.

9. Save the bin (Mac: ⌘+S | PC: Ctrl+S).

10. Close the bin.

11. Rewind the tape/disc.

12. Repeat Steps 1–11 for each of the remaining decomp bins created in *To gather source tapes* on page 289.

13. Look at the clips in the sequence to make sure they are online. If the clips appear offline, that is, if you see Media Offline in the Record monitor, reopen all of the decomp bins, including the EL 101 Decomp 1 bin, while the EL 101 Online Video Only bin is open (now the clips should appear online in the sequence), and then close all of the bins.

> **Note** | When Avid finishes capturing the offline clips from a tape, a dialog box will appear asking you to mount the next tape.

> **Note** | Once all of the clips have been re-captured, the video of the sequence should be completely online. Although the decomposed clips are in separate bins in different edit suites, a link still exists to the sequence.

Re-creating Titles and Importing Graphics

After all video clips have been brought into the sequence, it is likely that there will still be offline clips in the sequence. These clips are either titles or graphics. The titles need to be re-created in the sequence at full resolution, and the graphics need to be imported into the sequence at full resolution.

To re-create titles in full resolution

1. Create a bin (Mac: ⌘+N | PC: Ctrl+N).

2. Rename the new bin EL 101 Titles, and then press Enter.

3. Open the EL 101 Online Video Only bin.

4. Double-click the sequence in the EL 101 Online Video Only bin.

5. In the Timeline window, Mark IN (press I) and OUT (press O) points at the beginning and end of the sequence.

6. Select Clip≫Re-create Title Media.

7. In the Select a Bin dialog box that appears, select the EL 101 Titles bin, as the destination, and then click OK.

Figure 11-24. Select a Bin dialog box.

8. In the Re-create Title Media dialog box that appears, do the following, and then click OK.

(a) In the Drive menu, select the drive.

(b) In the Title Resolution menu, select the resolution.

(c) In the Re-create area, select the Title Media check box.

Figure 11-25. Re-create Title Media dialog box.

> **Note |** The bin with the final sequence should only contain the sequence. All other items, such as titles, graphics, and clips should be in separate bins for each type of media.

9. Save the EL 101 Titles bin (Mac: ⌘+S | PC: Ctrl+S).

10. Close the EL 101 Titles bin.

To batch import graphics into the sequence at full resolution

1. Do one of the following:

    (a) If you do not have XDCAM footage, proceed to Step 2.

    –or–

    (b) If you have XDCAM footage, complete Steps 1–9 in CHAPTER 3: *File-Based Media: To bring XDCAM footage into Avid with AMA disabled* on page 61, and then proceed to Step 2.

> **Note |** It is important that the entire sequence is online before batch importing. The Batch Import dialog box may list clips to be imported that are currently being uprezzed. After batch importing, make sure to check the Video column in the bin and ensure that all of the clips are full resolution.

    In Step 8 on page 62, in the Import Settings dialog box, on the XDCAM tab, make sure the Batch Import High-resolution Video option is selected. This ensures that any batch imported XDCAM clips are imported with the high-resolution files and *not* the low-resolution proxy files.

2. Create a bin (Mac: ⌘+N | PC: Ctrl+N).

3. Rename the new bin EL 101 Graphics, and then press Enter.

4. Click the sequence in EL 101 Online Video Only bin.

5. Select Clip≫Batch Import.

6. In the Avid Media Composer dialog box that appears displaying "Import clips with offline media only?" click Offline only.

7. In the Batch Import dialog box that appears (see FIGURE 11-26 on page 300), do one of the following:

7. In the Batch Import dialog box that appears (see FIGURE 11-26 on page 300), do one of the following:

   (a) If all of the clip names are displayed in black and you are sure that each clip is the current version, proceed to Step 8.

   –or–

   (b) If a clip name is displayed in black, and it is not the current version, or if a clip name is displayed in red because the imported file is not in its original location, do the following, and then proceed to Step 8.

   (i) Click the clip.

   (ii) Click Set File Location.

   (iii) Navigate to the file. Make sure it is the most updated file!

   (iv) Click Open, and then the file path is displayed in the Batch Import dialog box as the Import File Location for that clip.

   (v) Repeat Steps 7(b)(i)–7(b)(iv) for each clip that needs to be updated.

Note | In the Batch Import dialog box (Figure 11-26 on page 300), clip names displayed in red are the graphics that Avid can't find.

This usually means the graphic isn't in the location it was when it was initially imported.

Clip names that are displayed in black are graphics that Avid has been able to find and are ready to import.

Note | As a rule, graphics should be centrally located and not imported off of flash drives or desktops.

Note | Once you click Import, if there are any XDCAM clips that need to be uprezzed, a dialog box appears prompting you to insert the XDCAM disc. Otherwise, Avid immediately starts batch importing the clips at the chosen resolution and to the specified drive.

8. In the Batch Import dialog box, in the Import Target area, do the following, and then click Import (see FIGURE 11-26 on page 300).

   (a) In the Video Resolution menu, select the resolution that the video clips will be uprezzed to.

   (b) In the Video Drive and Audio Drive menu, select the drive that the video clips will be uprezzed to.

9. In the EL 101 Online Video Only bin, select the graphics and move them to the EL 101 Graphics bin.

10. Save the EL 101 Graphics bin and the EL 101 Online Video Only bin (Mac: ⌘+S | PC: Ctrl+S).

11. Close the EL 101 Graphics bin.

> **Note |** If you can't find the full
> resolution files for any clips in
> red, click each clip name and
> click Skip This Clip. Once those
> clips are located, you can repeat
> Steps 4–11 on page 298 to batch
> import the remaining clips.

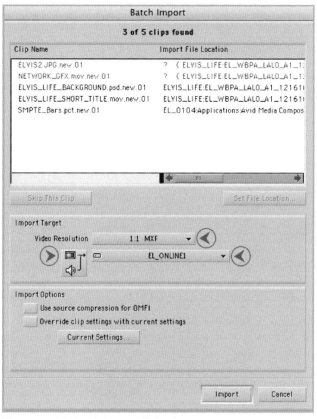

Figure 11-26. Batch Import dialog box.

Importing/Capturing the Offline Reference

It is impossible for a colorist to know what a cut is supposed to look like. The offline reference copy is used to check the online sequence against to ensure that the correct shots are in place and that the cut is in sync. (The offline reference can be a tape or an exported movie.)

This is the last step of the onlining process because it enables you to put your eyes on every inch of the sequence. Tiny offline clips, misspelled titles, and missing graphics should all be found and corrected during this process. Remember, it is your responsibility to give as complete of a sequence as possible to the colorist so that they can start coloring and not get tied up with other time-consuming tasks.

To create the offline reference

1. Create a bin (Mac: ⌘+N | PC: Ctrl+N).

2. Rename the new bin EL 101 Offline Ref, and then press Enter.

Note | Some companies capture or import the offline reference at a lower resolution rather than the full resolution.

Capturing the offline reference at full resolution isn't wise because it takes up a lot of drive space. Also, given that the offline reference is one long clip that has never existed before, it won't relink to any existing clips.

This is one of the few instances when low-resolution video should be mixed with full-resolution video.

3. Capture or import the video and audio of the offline reference into the 101 Offline Ref bin at a low resolution.

   See CHAPTER 2: *Capturing* on page 17 for information on capturing from a tape or CHAPTER 10: *Imports and Exports* on page 253 for information on importing a movie.

4. Create a bin (Mac: ⌘+N | PC: Ctrl+N).

5. Rename the new bin EL 101 Online Sequence, and then press Enter.

6. Click the sequence in the EL 101 Online Video Only bin.

7. Copy the sequence to the EL 101 Online Sequence bin (Mac: Option+Drag | PC: Alt+Drag).

8. Rename the sequence EL 101 Online Sequence, and then press Enter.

9. Double-click the EL 101 Online Sequence.

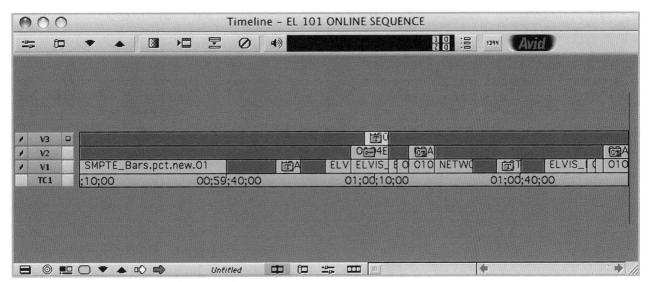

Figure 11-27. Timeline window of EL 101 Online Sequence.

10. Double-click the 101 Offline Ref clip.

11. In the Timeline window, create a video track (Mac: ⌘+Y | PC: Ctrl+Y).

    In our example it is video track 4 (V4).

12. Create two audio tracks (Mac: ⌘+U | PC: Ctrl+U).

    In our example they are audio tracks 1 and 2 (A1 and A2, respectively).

13. Place the position indicator at the beginning of the sequence.

14. Patch the source tracks of the 101 Offline Ref clip to the newly created record video and audio tracks.

15. Make sure sync locks are enabled.

16. Deselect any other enabled tracks.

17. Overwrite (press B) the 101 Offline Ref clip to the EL 101 Online Sequence.

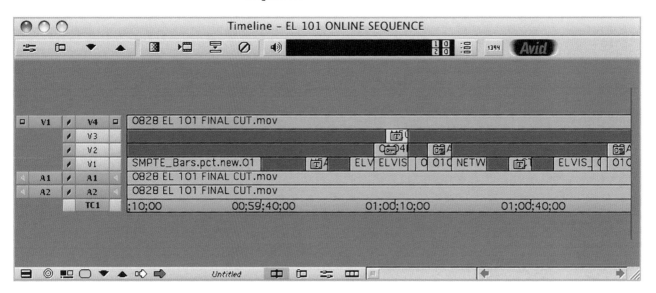

18. Open the Effect palette (Mac: ⌘+8 | PC: Ctrl+8).

19. In the left pane of the Effect palette, click the Edge Wipe category.

20. Drag the Vert Open effect onto the video of the offline reference (see FIGURE 11-29).

The Vert Open effect allows the full-resolution and low-resolution video to be viewed simultaneously by splitting the screen into three parts. The full-resolution video is displayed in the middle of the screen and the offline video reference borders the full-resolution video on both the top and the bottom (see FIGURE 11-30 on page 304).

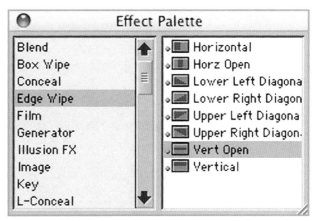

Figure 11-28. Effect palette with Edge Wipe selected in the Effect Category list and Vert Open selected in the right pane.

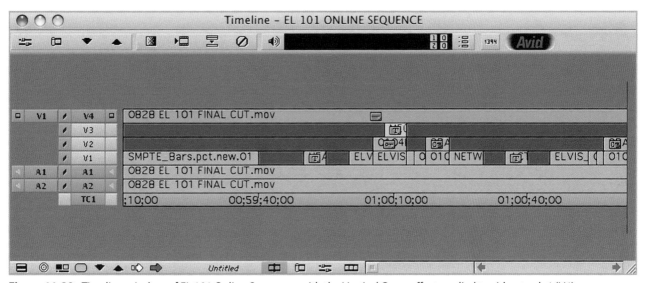

Figure 11-29. Timeline window of EL 101 Online Sequence with the Vertical Open effect applied to video track 4 (V4).

Figure 11-30. An example of the full-resolution clip (top and bottom portions) being out of sync with the low-resolution offline video reference (middle portion).

21. Go through the entire sequence and snap to every single edit point to make sure it is completely online and in sync (Mac: ⌘+Click | PC: Ctrl+Click).

22. Save the bins (Mac: ⌘+S | PC: Ctrl+S).

23. Close the bins.

There are several reasons why the online sequence might not be in sync with the offline reference. The most common reasons are as follows:

■ The wrong tape was inserted into the deck during the re-capturing process.

■ The offline reference does not exactly conform to the online sequence because changes were made to the final sequence after the offline reference copy was made.

Did I Do This Correctly?

■ **Are all of the clips, titles, and graphics online?**

Click the online bin's Fast menu and choose Select Offline Items, and the sequence shouldn't be highlighted. If the sequence is highlighted, that means there is a clip in the sequence that is still offline.

■ **Are all of the elements online at full resolution?**

The bin column headings should show Video and Offline only and Set Bin Display should be set to Show Reference Clips. This displays everything related to the sequence including the decomposed clips of the sequence. By clicking the Video and Offline column headings and sorting (Mac: ⌘+E | PC: Ctrl+E), all of the various resolution clips will appear together and the Offline column should be empty.

■ **Have unneeded locators been removed?**

Locators that were added by the editors should be deleted, unless they contain information that the colorist needs to know.

■ **Have informational locators been added?**

Any information that the colorist needs to know should have locators added with specific information.

■ **Is the offline reference completely captured and in the sequence with audio?**

The offline reference should be on the top video track of the sequence and the audio on tracks A1 and A2. This allows the colorist to confirm that the video and audio are in sync.

Appendix 1:
Capture Tool

T HE CAPTURE TOOL IS used to convert information from tapes/discs into digital format to bring footage into Avid. Tapes/discs are controlled through the Capture tool. The shortcut for the Capture tool is Mac: ⌘+7 | PC: Ctrl+7. The Capture tool is frequently referred to as the Digitize tool. The two terms are interchangeable and you will hear people use both.

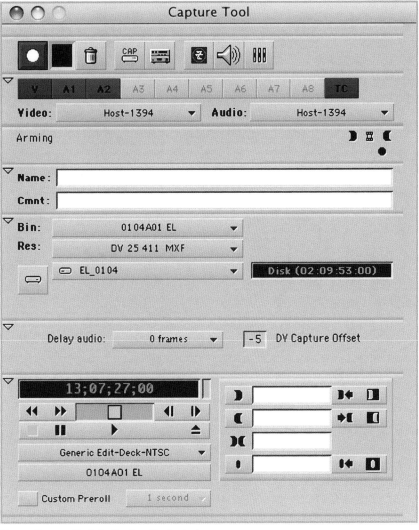

Figure Appendix 1-1. Capture Tool window.

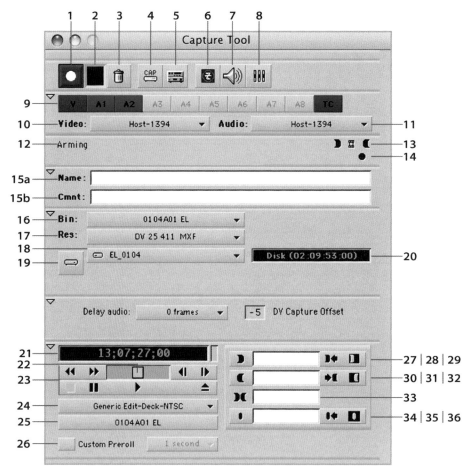

Figure Appendix 1-2. Capture Tool with numbered components
(see Table Appendix 1-1).

TABLE APPENDIX 1-1. CAPTURE TOOL COMPONENTS/FUNCTIONS (SEE FIGURE APPENDIX 1-2)

	Component	Function
1	Record button	Click to begin capturing.
2	Capture indicator	Flashes when the Capture tool is capturing.
3	Trash	Click to abort capturing.
4	Capture/Log Mode button	Toggles between Capture mode (for capturing) and Log mode (for logging clips).
5	Toggle Source button	Allows you to capture when a deck cannot be controlled by Avid. In these instances, Avid creates its own timecode.
6	Video Tool button	Allows you to monitor the video levels as the tape/disc is being captured.
7	Audio Tool button	Allows you to monitor the audio levels as the tape/disc is being captured. (Shortcut to open Audio tool: Mac: ⌘+1│PC: Ctrl+1)
8	Passthrough Mix Tool button	Allows you to monitor and adjust the audio being captured. This tool only monitors the captured audio—the audio on the tape/disc is not affected.
9	Channel Selection buttons	Allows you to select the tracks to be captured, making it possible to capture video and audio separately.

TABLE APPENDIX 1-1. CAPTURE TOOL COMPONENTS/FUNCTIONS (CONTINUED)

	Component	Function
10	Video (Input) menu	Displays how the video signal is coming from the deck into Avid.
11	Audio (Input) menu	Displays how the audio signal is coming from the deck into Avid.
12	Message bar	Displays the status of the Capture tool.
13	Subclip status indicators	Icons are highlighted when creating subclips during capturing.
14	Video Lock icon	Displays green when there is a valid video signal and Avid recognizes that signal.
15a 15b	Clip Name text box Clip Comment text box	◆ Before capturing begins, click the arrow to display the Clip Name text box and the Clip Comment text box. ◆ During capturing, type the clip name, press Tab, and then type the clip comments. ◆ After capturing, the clip name and clip comments appear in the project's bin.
16	Bin menu	Displays the name of the bin being captured to.
17	Res (Resolution) menu	Displays the resolution of the clips being captured.
18	Target Drive menu	Displays the drive the media will be captured to.
19	Single/Dual Drive Mode button	Allows you to capture video and audio to one drive or across several drives.
20	Time Remaining on Target Drives display	Displays the space left on the drive while capturing at the selected resolution. The numbers represent hours, minutes, seconds, and frames available at that resolution.
21	Timecode display	Displays the timecode of the tape/disc. Semicolons (;) indicate drop-frame video and colons (:) indicate non-drop-frame video.
22	Shuttle button	Use to rewind and fast forward through a tape/disc, instead of using Rewind and Fast Forward buttons.
23	Deck controls	Use to control the video deck through the Capture tool.
24	Deck Selection menu	Displays the name of the deck Avid believes is connected to the computer. (If the deck name is displayed in italic, the deck is offline.)
25	Source Tape display	Displays the tape/disc name.
26	Custom Preroll option	Displays how much time the tape/disc will play after a timecode break before capturing again.
27	Mark IN button	Marks the beginning of a section of the tape/disc to be captured.
28	Go to IN button	Moves the deck's playhead to the Mark IN point on the tape/disc.
29	Clear IN button	Clears the Mark IN point.
30	Mark OUT button	Marks the end of a section of the tape/disc to be captured.
31	Go to OUT button	Moves the deck's playhead to the Mark OUT point on the tape/disc.
32	Clear OUT button	Clears the Mark OUT point.
33	Duration display	Displays the duration between the Mark IN and Mark OUT timecodes.
34	Mark Memory button	Adds a temporary locator to a point on the tape/disc for later reference. Only one memory mark can be present on a tape/disc.
35	Go to Memory button	Moves the deck's playhead to the memory mark.
36	Clear Memory button	Clears the memory mark. (Removing the tape/disc from the deck also clears the memory mark.)

APPENDIX 2:
Deck Configuration

Task in This Appendix

OCCASIONALLY, A VIDEO DECK will appear to be connected to Avid, but Avid won't see it. There are a number of reasons why Avid won't see a video deck, and they fall into two categories—hardware and software.

Hardware

■ The deck remote cable is not connected.

■ The deck is connected to a switcher, and the switcher is on the wrong deck.

Software

■ The deck is looking at the wrong port.

■ The wrong deck is assigned in the deck configuration.

Hardware

Any video deck that you want to use with Avid should be connected to Avid before starting the application. Connecting a video deck to an Avid computer can be a complicated venture, and normally, video engineers connect decks to Avid computers for you. There will be situations when you may need to connect a video deck by yourself, but it is not advised because connecting the deck could cause issues with Avid or injury to yourself.

If you suspect that the deck is not correctly connected to Avid, ask an informed assistant editor or a video engineer for assistance. During that time, ask if it is okay to connect decks on your own, and if yes, then ask for that instruction.

One of the most common reasons a deck that appears to be connected to Avid isn't working, and therefore the deck configuration isn't working, is because the deck remote cable is not connected. The deck remote cable connects the Avid computer to the deck, and this connection allows you to control the deck through Avid. Without a deck remote cable connection, it is impossible to control the deck through Avid.

Another reason you may not be able to control a deck through Avid is because a switcher is being used, and the physical selector on the switcher is switched to the wrong deck (that is, a deck other than the one Avid is currently configured to look for). A switcher allows multiple decks to be hooked up to one computer. Since Avid can only look at one deck at a time, if the switcher is physically switched to a deck other than the one Avid is looking for, you won't be able to control the deck through Avid.

Software

Once the video deck is correctly connected to Avid, you still may not be able to control it through Avid. The biggest indicators that Avid does not see the deck is when the Capture tool doesn't display a specific deck name in the Deck Selection menu or the Timecode display is "NO DECK."

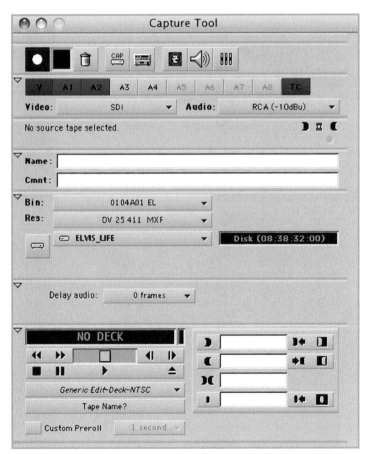

Figure Appendix 2-1. Capture Tool window incorrectly configured.

This usually occurs when the deck is looking at the wrong port and/or the wrong deck has been assigned in a previous deck configuration process. The following steps can resolve both of these issues.

To configure a video deck to be controlled through Avid

1. Write down the manufacturer and the model number that are printed on the physical video deck.

2. Make sure the video deck is on and set to remote.

    The video deck must be set to remote (not to local) for you to control it through Avid. This is usually a button or switch on the front of the video deck. On the Capture tool, if the deck is not in remote, the Timecode display is "Local Mode."

3. Open the Capture tool (Mac: ⌘+7 | PC: Ctrl+7), and do the following:

    (a) On the Deck Selection menu, select Check Decks.

         The Check Decks option instructs Avid to check all connected ports and wiring to see if it can find the video deck. You know this action is successful when the name of the video deck (that is, the manufacturer and model number you wrote down in Step 1) is displayed in the Deck Selection menu.

         For our example, let's assume that the Check Decks instruction is unsuccessful.

    (b) On the Deck Selection menu, select Adjust Deck.

         (i) In the Deck Settings dialog box that appears, do the following, and then click OK.

              (1) On the left Device menu, select the deck manufacturer (reference the information from Step 1).

              (2) On the right Device menu, select the deck model number (reference the information from Step 1).

> **Note** | The Deck Settings dialog box allows you to select the video deck that is connected to Avid.
>
> It displays the last selected deck manufacturer and model number.

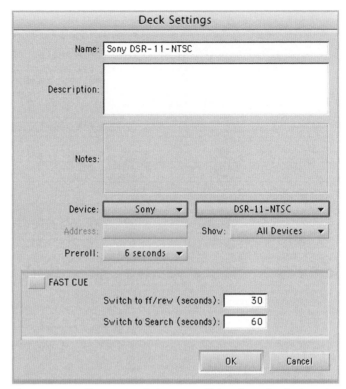

Figure Appendix 2-2. Deck Settings dialog box displaying the last selected deck manufacturer and model number.

You will know this action was successful when the name of the video deck is displayed in the Deck Selection menu of the Capture tool.

For our example, let's assume that the Adjust Deck instruction was unsuccessful.

4. In the Project window, click the Settings tab.

5. Double-click the Deck Configuration setting, and then the Deck Configuration window appears.

In the Deck Configuration window, two things need to happen: the channel must be configured and a video deck must be added to that configured channel. A channel consists of two parts: channel type (the type of connection used) and port (the Avid port that connection is hooked up to).

6. Click Add Channel.

If the Deck Configuration window already has a configured channel in it, disregard it because it may apply to a video deck previously connected to that Avid computer.

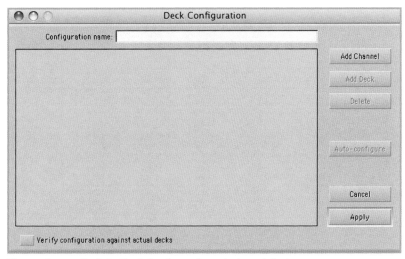

Figure Appendix 2-3. Deck Configuration window: default.

7. In the Channel dialog box that appears, do the following, and then click OK.

    (a) In the Channel Type menu, select the channel type consistent with the deck's connection to Avid (ask someone if you don't know).

    (b) In the Port menu, select the port consistent with the deck's connection to Avid (ask someone if you don't know).

Figure Appendix 2-4. Channel dialog box.

Note | Autoconfiguring the channel can be a reliable way to determine what video deck is connected to Avid. However, for this exercise, it is best to know how to do the entire process and then incorporate shortcuts as you see fit.

8. In the Avid Media Composer dialog box that appears with the message "Do you want to autoconfigure the channel now?" click No. (Notice that the default selection is Yes, but you should click No.)

9. In the Deck Configuration window, click on the channel that you selected in Step 7 (it is outlined with a red border), and then click Add Deck.

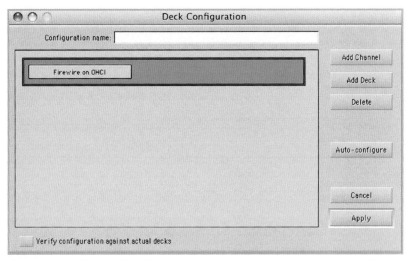

Figure Appendix 2-5. Deck Configuration window displaying a partially configured channel. It is missing the connected deck.

10. In the Deck Settings dialog box that appears, modify the settings consistent with the deck connected to Avid, and then click OK.

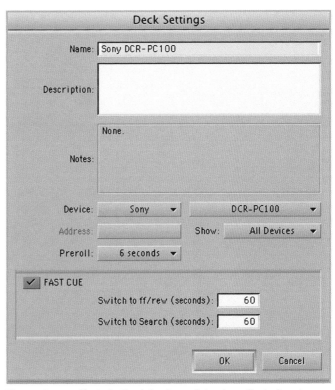

Figure Appendix 2-6. Deck Settings dialog box displaying the currently selected deck manufacturer and model number.

11. In the Deck Configuration window, notice that the correctly selected deck is displayed, and then click Apply.

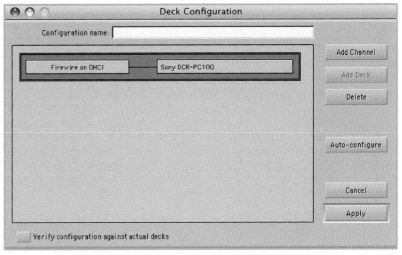

Figure Appendix 2-7. Deck Configuration window displaying a configured channel.

You will know the deck configuration is successful if the name of the video deck is displayed in the Deck Selection menu of the Capture tool and the Timecode display is showing numbers.

If Avid doesn't recognize the deck, either the options chosen in the Deck Configuration window are incorrect or the deck is not correctly connected to Avid. (There could be a faulty cable, for example.) In either case, find a video engineer.

APPENDIX 3:
Keyboard Setting

Tasks in This Appendix

U SE THE KEYBOARD SETTING to optimize your editing workflow by mapping Avid buttons and menu commands to the keys on your physical keyboard. This keyboard customization makes editing faster and easier.

Mapping a Keyboard: 'Button to Button' Reassignment

Customizing your physical keyboard through mapping via 'Button to Button' Reassignment requires the Command palette and the Keyboard setting. The Command palette contains all of the editing functions available for use in customizations. The Keyboard setting displays the Keyboard layout. The Keyboard layout is a graphical representation of a physical keyboard with user-selectable buttons for use in customizations.

The buttons on the Command palette are being *assigned from*, and the Keyboard layout buttons are being *assigned to*. For example, reassigning the Fast Forward command from the Command palette to the PDn button on the Keyboard layout allows you to press Page Down on your physical keyboard to fast forward a clip.

To map a keyboard via 'Button to Button' Reassignment

1. In the Project window, on the Settings tab, double-click Keyboard, and the Avid Keyboard appears.

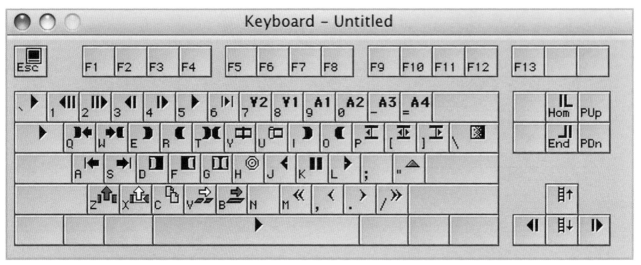

Figure Appendix 3-1. Avid Keyboard: default.

2. Open the Command palette (Mac: ⌘+3 | PC: Ctrl+3).

3. On the Command palette, select 'Button-to-Button' Reassignment.

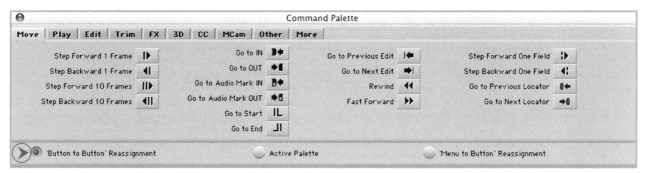

Figure Appendix 3-2. Command palette with 'Button to Button' Reassignment selected.

4. Drag a shortcut from any tab of the Command palette to a key on the Keyboard, and the shortcut icon appears on the mapped Keyboard key.

5. Close the Avid Keyboard and Command palette.

Using the Active Palette Option

The Active Palette option on the Command palette allows you to click the Command palette buttons to perform the commands.

To use the Active Palette option

1. Open the Command palette (Mac: ⌘+3 | PC: Ctrl+3).

2. On the Command palette, select Active Palette.

3. Click the tab of the Command palette that displays the desired command.

4. Click the icon for the desired command to manipulate clips and sequences.

Figure Appendix 3-3. Command palette with Active Palette selected.

Mapping a Keyboard: 'Menu to Button' Reassignment

Customizing your physical keyboard through mapping via 'Menu to Button' Reassignment requires the Command palette and the Keyboard setting. The Command palette contains the 'Menu to Button' Reassignment option. The Keyboard setting displays the Keyboard layout. The Keyboard layout is a graphical representation of a physical keyboard with user-selectable buttons for use in customizations.

The menu options are being *assigned from*, and the Keyboard layout buttons are being *assigned to*. For example, reassigning Rewind from the Move menu to the F1 button on the Keyboard layout allows you to press F1 on your physical keyboard to move backward in the sequence or clip.

To map a keyboard via 'Menu to Button' Reassignment

1. In the Project window, on the Settings tab, double-click Keyboard, and the Avid Keyboard appears.

2. Open the Command palette (Mac: ⌘+3 | PC: Ctrl+3).

3. On the Command palette, click 'Menu to Button' Reassignment.

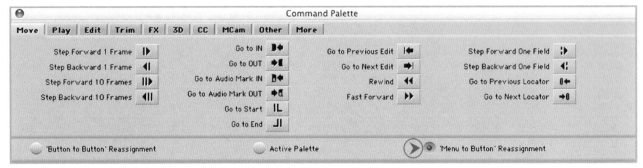

Figure Appendix 3-4. Command palette with 'Menu to Button' Reassignment selected.

4. On the Keyboard layout, click the button to be reassigned, and the button appears highlighted.

   In our example, we chose the F11 key.

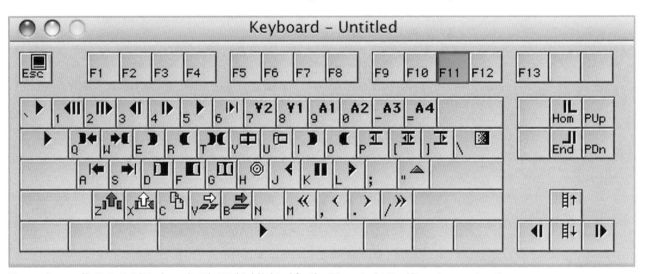

Figure Appendix 3-5. Avid Keyboard with F11 highlighted for the 'Menu to Button' Reassignment option.

5. Select the menu option to be assigned to the Keyboard layout, and a two-letter abbreviation appears on the Keyboard layout button indicating that the key is reassigned.

   In our example, we assigned the MultiGroup command (Mu) to the F11 key. Now, pressing F11 on the physical keyboard is equivalent to selecting Bin≫MultiGroup from the menu.

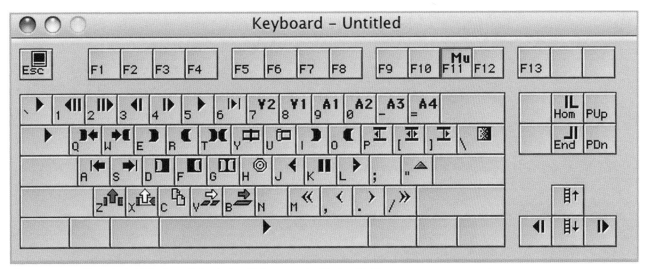

Figure Appendix 3-6. Avid Keyboard displaying F11 mapped with the Multigroup menu command.

6. Close the Avid Keyboard and Command palette.

Keyboard Layout: Default Key Mappings

With dozens of keys on a keyboard, there is ample opportunity for customization. If you take the time to learn the default key mappings and enhance them with some of your own, you will thank yourself at every editing session. Over time, you will be amazed by how much time you save through just this one technique. TABLE APPENDIX 3-1 on page 324 provides a description of the command assigned to each key.

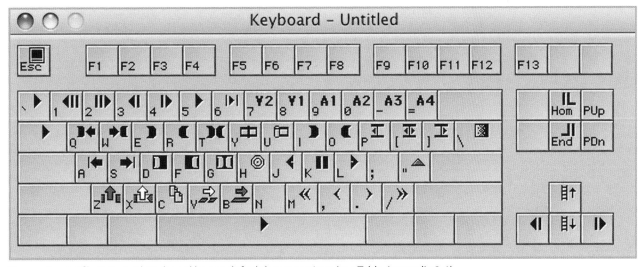

Figure Appendix 3-7. Avid Keyboard layout default key mappings (see Table Appendix 3-1).

Table Appendix 3-1. Avid Keyboard Layout Default Key Mappings (see Figure Appendix 3-7)

Key	Command	Result
Esc	Toggle Source/Record	Switches between the Source monitor and the Record monitor.
`	Play	Start and stop playback.
1	Step Backward 10 Frames	Plays clips backward 10 frames at a time.
2	Step Forward 10 Frames	Plays clips forward 10 frames at a time.
3	Step Backward 1 Frame	Plays clips backward 1 frame at a time.
4	Step Forward 1 Frame	Plays clips forward 1 frame at a time.
5	Play	Start and stop playback.
6	Play IN to OUT	Plays a section in a loop from an IN point to an OUT point.
7	V2	Selects source or record video track 2.
8	V1	Selects source or record video track 1.
9	A1	Selects source or record audio track 1.
0	A2	Selects source or record audio track 2.
–	A3	Selects source or record audio track 3.
=	A4	Selects source or record audio track 4.
Tab	Play	Start and stop playback.
Q	Go to IN	Takes the position indicator to an IN point.
W	Go to OUT	Takes the position indicator to an OUT point.
E	Mark IN	Marks the beginning of a section of a clip or sequence, and it is known as an IN point. That frame may not necessarily be at the beginning of a clip.
R	Mark OUT	Marks the end of a section of a clip or sequence, and it is known as an OUT point. That frame may not necessarily be at the end of a clip.
T	Mark Clip	Sets IN and OUT points at the very beginning and very end of a clip. Selects the entire clip.
Y	Source/Record Mode	Moves in and out of the default editing mode.
U	Trim Mode	Moves in and out of the trim editing mode.
I	Mark IN	Marks the beginning of a section of a clip or sequence, and it is known as an IN point. That frame may not necessarily be at the beginning of a clip.
O	Mark OUT	Marks the end of a section of a clip or sequence, and it is known as an OUT point. That frame may not necessarily be at the end of a clip.
P	Trim A Side	Trims the video of an outgoing clip.
[	Trim AB Sides	Simultaneously trims the video of clips at an edit point.
]	Trim B Side	Trims the video of an incoming clip.
\	Quick Transition	Puts effects, such as dissolves, on clips.
A	Go to Previous Edit	Moves position indicator backward to the closest edit of an enabled track or tracks.
S	Go to Next Edit	Moves position indicator forward to the closest edit of an enabled track or tracks.

TABLE APPENDIX 3-1. AVID KEYBOARD LAYOUT DEFAULT KEY MAPPINGS (CONTINUED)

Key	Command	Result
D	Clear IN Mark	Removes an IN point.
F	Clear OUT Mark	Removes an OUT point.
G	Clear Both Marks	Removes both marks.
H	Focus	Zooms in to the portion of a sequence where the position indicator is located.
J	Play Reverse	Plays footage backward at a normal speed. Pressing this key multiple times increases the rate of play.
K	Pause	Halts the footage.
L	Play	Plays footage at a normal speed. Pressing this key multiple times increases the rate of play.
;	(Unassigned)	
"	Add Keyframe	Places a keyframe on the enabled audio or video track.
Z	Lift	Removes a portion of the sequence that is selected with IN and OUT points. Leaves a gap in the sequence. Sequence duration is not changed.
X	Extract	Removes a portion of the sequence that is selected with IN and OUT points. Does not leave a gap in the sequence. Sequence duration is shortened.
C	Copy to Clipboard	Copies a portion of the sequence to the clipboard without affecting the sequence.
V	Splice-In	Places a clip into a timeline shifting any existing clips further down the sequence. Shift is equal to the length of the clip being cut in.
B	Overwrite	Places a clip into a timeline and cuts over or overwrites any clips that are present in the sequence without shifting any of the clips.
N	(Unassigned)	
M	Trim Left 10 Frames	◆ In Lift/Overwrite Segment mode, moves a clip 10 frames to the left. ◆ In Trim mode, moves the edit point 10 frames to the left.
,	Trim Left 1 Frame	◆ In Lift/Overwrite Segment mode, moves a clip 1 frame to the left. ◆ In Trim mode, moves the edit point 1 frame to the left.
.	Trim Right 1 Frame	◆ In Lift/Overwrite Segment mode, moves a clip 1 frame to the right. ◆ In Trim mode, moves the edit point 1 frame to the right.
/	Trim Right 10 Frames	◆ In Lift/Overwrite Segment mode, moves a clip 10 frames to the right. ◆ In Trim mode, moves the edit point 10 frames to the right.
Space bar	Play	Start and stop playback.
Home	Go to Start	Moves to the beginning of a clip or sequence.
End	Go to End	Moves to the end of a clip or sequence.
PUp	(Unassigned)	
PDn	(Unassigned)	
Up Arrow	Previous in Group	Goes to the previous video track in a group or multigroup.
Down Arrow	Next in Group	Goes to the next video track in a group or multigroup.
Left Arrow	Step Backward 1 Frame	Plays clips backward 1 frame at a time.
Right Arrow	Step Forward 1 Frame	Plays clips forward 1 frame at a time.

APPENDIX 4:
Multigrouping Helpful Hints

Task in This Appendix

THE STEPS OUTLINED FOR syncing in CHAPTER 4: *Multigrouping* on page 71, won't work every single time. In fact, you should treat each time that you sync two clips as a unique circumstance—just because X worked on a previous sync doesn't necessarily mean X will work on this sync.

You will find that most of the time that you spend syncing will be spent trying to figure out where each camera is and what needs to be synced to what. This section presents a collection of advice and hints that will teach you to produce flawless groups in a fraction of the time it takes you now.

Where Is the Audio?

Inevitably, you will receive a clip with no audio from a camera that is clearly in the same room as another camera. Unfortunately, you still need to sync them, and this is tricky at best. Persevere in these situations because it is possible to sync when there isn't any audio!

The first thing to check is if the clip has audio on tracks 3 and 4. Remember, the layouts have tracks 1 and 2, and that isn't always the best audio. Match frame to the clip, listen to the audio on tracks 3 and 4, and if it is usable, overwrite it into your sequence.

If the clip does not have audio on tracks 3 and 4, find a few frames of video with very distinct motion and see if the other camera has the same action in frame at a good angle to pick out a specific frame. Usually hand, arm, or leg motion works best for this. Follow the arc of an arm movement until it reaches its peak and starts back down—use the frame when it's at its peak. Watch for a frame where a finger bends a certain way. Something in the scene with erratic motion works well too. As does flashing or blinking lights, shadows, or any monotonous motion such as a ceiling fan's blades or a computer's screen saver. Just be creative and with a little patience, you can get the clips in sync.

What Is That Audio Doing Over Here?

It is a common mistake to move the video of a clip without its corresponding audio tracks. (The reverse happens as well.) You will immediately know if there are *sync breaks* because *sync break numbers* will appear on the clips (see FIGURE APPENDIX 4-1). The numbers on the clips tell how far out of sync the video and audio tracks are from one another. Undoing the action restores the clip to its proper form.

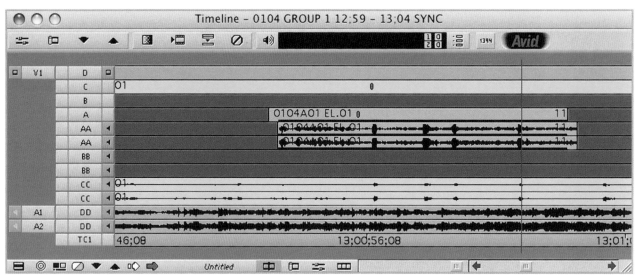

Figure Appendix 4-1. Timeline window displaying clips showing sync break numbers.

What Did You Say?

A common scenario: Camera A is covering a shouting match between two people on the first floor of a house. Camera B is on the other side of the house upstairs shooting a person reading in bed. Camera B's microphone picks up the shouting from downstairs.

This scenario can be difficult to sync and even more difficult to find. Missing these types of sync points is a common mistake.

To avoid this, always be mindful of where all of the cameras are in relation to one another. Also, look out for loud moments in one area and consider that other cameras may have picked them up.

If you have come across one of these moments, you probably noticed that it doesn't sync up nicely. Most of the time, camera B's audio will be at least one-half frame behind camera A's because the sound had to travel farther to reach camera B. So when syncing this scenario, make sure that the sound on camera B follows the sound on camera A. If you think about it, it doesn't make sense to hear the echo before the clap, does it? (Make sure Caps Lock is enabled on your keyboard to hear the audio during scrubbing.)

Waveforms Take Time

When marking IN and OUT points for viewing audio waveforms, do not set them for the entire sequence. Since Avid tends to draw waveforms agonizingly slowly, the less there is to draw, the quicker the waveforms will load. If possible, mark a small section around the sound you are syncing to.

Figure Appendix 4-2. Timeline window displaying audio waveforms between Mark IN and OUT points (that is, not on the entire sequence).

B-roll Is Your Friend

Note | When scrubbing video for camera locations, *always scrub from the beginning of the clip to the end*.

Cameras are often moved from place to place while rolling, and as a result, they may become syncable to cameras that they were previously unsyncable to.

Never assume cameras stay in the same place.

Scan video first to determine if the clip is comprised entirely of B-roll. This is important because B-roll does not need to be synced, since it is usually away from the main action. Add a different color locator to B-roll clips (and to any clip that doesn't need to be synced) to highlight clips that you can skip by and to verify that you didn't accidentally skip that clip. Also, when you are done syncing, every clip in the sequence will have a locator on it.

Know Your Location

It is always easier to figure out which cameras to sync if you look at the video first. Scrub all overlapping cameras to get an idea of where each camera is. Over the course of a show, you will get to know the layout of the set. So for example, you will know instantly that camera A will not sync to camera B because camera A is three floors above camera B.

Sync More Not Less

A common mistake is syncing B to D and then C to D, B to C, and finally A to B. It saves time and improves accuracy to sync A–D after all of the cameras are present in the Timeline tracks. In situations where clips A–D overlap one another, you may discover that a few of them are already in sync and you only need to move one or two clips to sync A–D. Keep an eye out for situations like this, and you'll see a significant reduction in the number of syncs you do in a group.

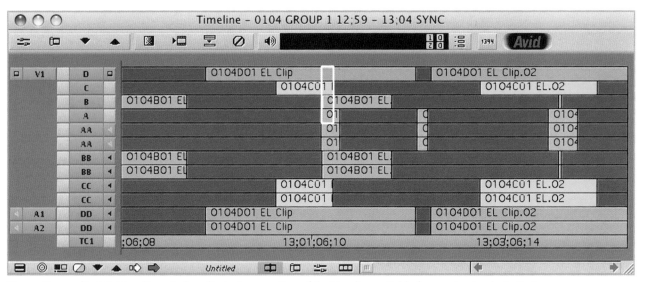

Figure Appendix 4-3. Timeline window displaying a section of the Timeline suitable for syncing tracks A–D at once.

Moving Whole Tapes/Discs/Cards

If you find that you have to move the first C clip back three frames to be in sync with A, it is usually safe to assume that you can move the rest of the C clips from that tape/disc/card back three frames as well. Note that you only need to move the clips from that tape/disc/card—the rest of the clips on the track do not need to be moved. Just look at the names of the clips you are moving and make sure that the tape/disc/card numbers are the same.

Which Clip Do I Move?

The first time you find yourself knee-deep in a monster group, you will probably ask yourself, which clip do I move? You know that once a clip is synced to another, moving one will break the sync—*so once a clip is synced, never move it.* To simplify: *never move a clip that already has a locator.*

Often there are gaps in a group that will allow you to choose which clips to move and which clips not to move. Sometimes it's easier to leave the longest clip in its position and move all of the shorter clips. While at other times, it's easier to move the longer clip and leave the shorter clips in their positions. Over time as you can gain experience, you will know what method works best in certain situations. For this example (see FIGURE APPENDIX 4-4), it might be better to leave the clips on video track 4 (D) in their locations and move the clips on video tracks 1–3 (A, B, and C) into sync with the clips on V4.

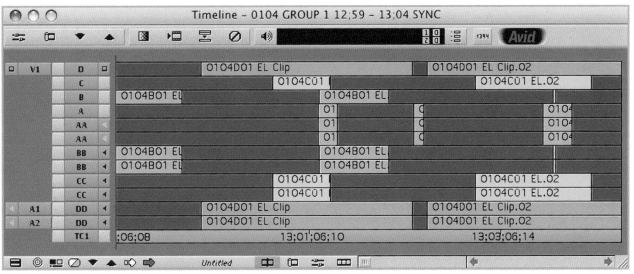

Figure Appendix 4-4. Timeline window displaying clips for syncing.

Where Did It Go?

It isn't uncommon for tapes/discs/cards to come back from the field mislabeled and a crucial clip may be missing from your group. Don't assume there isn't another angle of the scene. Do a little investigative work to see if the missing angle exists and where it is—you may even see the missing camera in another shot. It is an easily avoided mistake to make sure that multigroups contain all of the footage from the shoot. Just remember, if six cameras are filming, there should be six tracks of video unless there is a reasonable explanation.

To Drop or Not to Drop?

On occasion, you will come across a clip that won't match the timecode format of your sequence. Whether it is drop-frame timecode or non-drop-frame timecode, don't worry because it can still be grouped! The layout, sync, and Add Edit function still work the same, and the only difference is in creating subclips. For example, when you create the subclip for a non-drop-frame clip in a drop-frame sequence, the subclip will stand out from the rest because its auxiliary timecode will have colons instead of semicolons. To fix it, when typing the auxiliary timecode in the Auxiliary TC1 column, change the colons to semicolons or vice versa if working in a non-drop-frame sequence and a drop-frame clip is encountered. Just remember that all of the subclips need to all be non-drop-frame or all drop-frame.

Record-Run Timecode and the Chaos It Creates

It is the norm to film footage with time-of-day (TOD) timecode, but there will be those, hopefully, rare instances when you will receive a tape/disc that has record-run timecode. *Record-run timecode* differs from TOD timecode because the camera records continuous timecode on the tape/disc regardless of when the camera starts and stops recording. This creates one long clip on the tape/disc, and that clip won't account for any breaks in filming (see FIGURE APPENDIX 4-5).

Figure Appendix 4-5. Timeline window displaying intact record-run clip (0104D01 EL Clip).

When you receive a tape/disc that has record-run timecode, you will need to manually go through the clip and create individual clips.

To separate one (record-run) clip into individual clips

1. Load the clip in the Source monitor.

2. Mark IN (press I) at the start of one clip.

3. Mark OUT (press O) at the end of one clip.

   You will know you are at the end of a clip because the footage will jump from one frame to another—an indication that the camera stopped recording and then started recording at another time.

4. Subclip (press F7).

5. Repeat Steps 2–4 for the rest of the clip.

Once the record-run timecode clip is broken into separate clips, you can proceed with the multigrouping process. This is a very time-consuming but necessary step to take because an intact record-run timecode clip is difficult, if not impossible, to sync other clips to, as clips from other cameras will overwrite one another (see FIGURE APPENDIX 4-6).

Figure Appendix 4-6. Timeline window displaying intact record-run clip and clips from the cameras overlapping one another to sync with the record-run clip.

The clips from other cameras will have breaks in filming, and they may not all start and stop recording at the same time. For example, imagine that four cameras are recording a 30-minute boat race—one camera with record-run timecode and three cameras with TOD timecode. The intact record-run clip condenses the events of the shoot and the multiple clips created from the other cameras may not line up perfectly with the intact record-run clip. If you persist in trying to sync the TOD clips with the intact record-run clip, you will definitely overwrite some of the clips.

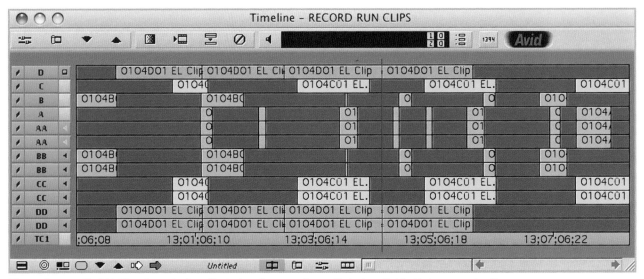

Figure Appendix 4-7. Timeline window displaying the record-run clip being divided into separate clips.

Figure Appendix 4-8. Timeline window displaying the divided record-run clip being synced with the other clips.

Half-Frames (Fields)

Here are a few facts you should know about video:

- An NTSC video image is made of 525 horizontal lines.

- Those lines are scanned in two "waves"—even first and then odd. (Other video formats can scan odd first and then even.)

- It takes approximately 1/60th of a second to display a field. The combination of the two fields is known as *interlacing,* and it produces an image.

What this means for you is that two video clips from two separate cameras could be one and one-half frames out of sync, but within Avid, you can only move clips one frame at a time and possibly leave the two clips one-half frame (field) out of sync.

Bottom Line: There isn't anything you can do about that, and 1/60th of a second is imperceptible. Listen to it one way, then bump it one frame and listen to it again. The decision should be made by allowing the quieter sound to follow the louder sound.

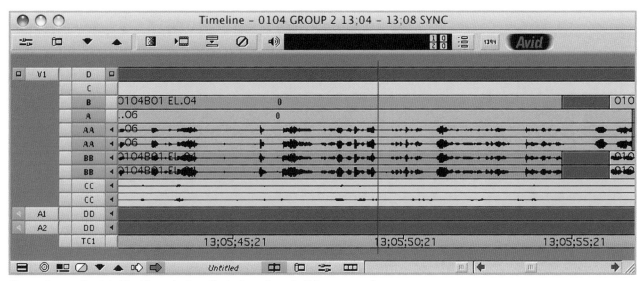

Figure Appendix 4-9. Timeline window displaying clips a half-frame out of sync.

Aren't There Any Shortcuts?

A number of shortcuts can be deployed to make multigrouping easier and faster. If you are considering introducing a multigrouping shortcut into your workflow, do so with the following caveats: (1) not all multigrouping shortcuts are created equally, and (2) a multigrouping shortcut in the wrong hands is a dangerous (read likely to cause problems and time-consuming to fix) thing. Do explore different avenues for completing groups, but just be aware that some things are not as good as they seem.

While some multigrouping shortcuts work very well, others don't work well at all. Take the Auto-Sequence function, for example, where you select a group of clips and Avid automatically lays them into a sequence at the appropriate timecode—terrific, right? Unfortunately, Auto-Sequence cannot account for clips that have incorrect timecodes, nor can it determine if a clip at 01;09;11;00 is before or after a clip that starts at 00;01;14;10 (for example, during a shoot that began at midnight and continued for 24 hours).

Using multigrouping shortcuts—even the ones that work well—without a firm grasp of multigrouping concepts and techniques is very likely to result in problematic scenarios that are difficult to fix and require a grouper to start the multigrouping process from the beginning.

Additionally, there is software that can be programmed to perform multigrouping functions such as assigning auxiliary timecode and creating subclips. Again, these programs can be very helpful; however, if a grouper does not have a clear understanding of the multigrouping process, it will be very difficult to locate and fix the mistakes that are likely to occur.

APPENDIX 5:
Mark IN and OUT

Tasks in This Appendix

You can Mark IN and OUT in the Source monitor, the Timeline, or a combination of the two. It is largely dependent on what you are trying to achieve. This section presents scenarios of the more frequent combinations as follows:

Scenario 1—Source Monitor IN and OUT Points and Timeline IN Point

Scenario 2—Source Monitor IN Point and Timeline IN and OUT Points

Scenario 3—Source Monitor OUT Point and Timeline IN and OUT Points

Scenario 4—Source Monitor Mark Clip

Scenario 5—Timeline Mark Clip

It is a good idea to do run through these scenarios with your own test clips and sequences. All you need is a test sequence and one clip with video and at least two tracks of audio (see FIGURE APPENDIX 5-1 on page 338). The sequence and clip can be used over and over for these scenarios.

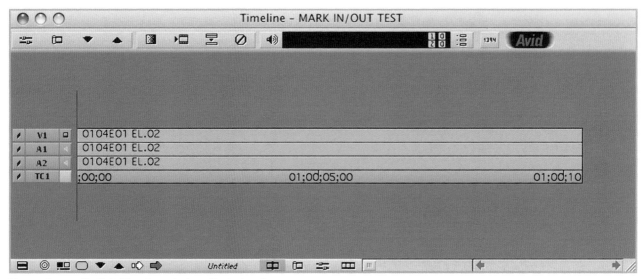

Figure Appendix 5-1. Timeline window displaying the test sequence.

Scenario 1: Source Monitor IN and OUT Points and Timeline IN Point

In this scenario, a clip has specific IN and OUT points because you want to insert edit that clip at a certain point in the sequence. Performing this function requires IN and OUT points in the Source monitor and an IN point in the Timeline sequence.

To insert edit a clip with IN and OUT points to a sequence with an IN point

1. Double-click the correct sequence, and it loads in the Timeline window.

2. Double-click the correct clip and it loads in the Source monitor.

3. In the Source monitor, do the following:

    (a) Play the clip (press L).

    (b) Mark IN (press I) at the beginning of the first word of the desired portion of the clip.

    (c) Mark OUT (press O) at the end of the last word of the desired portion of the clip.

Figure Appendix 5-2. Composer window displaying IN and OUT points in the Source monitor.

4. In the Timeline window, do the following:

   (a) Patch the source video and audio tracks to the desired record video and audio tracks.

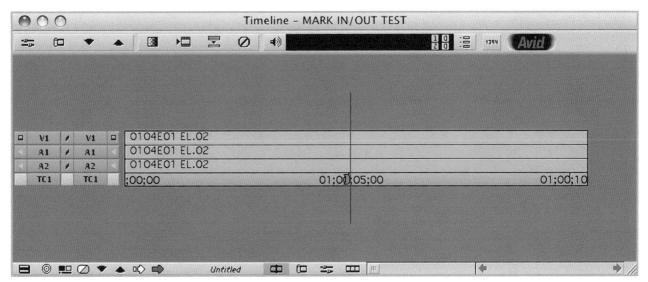

Figure Appendix 5-3. Timeline window displaying an IN point.

   (b) Mark IN (press I) on the Timeline.

   (c) Ensure that sync locks are selected.

(d) Insert (press V) the clip into the sequence.

Figure Appendix 5-4. Timeline window displaying an inserted clip.

Scenario 2: Source Monitor IN Point and Timeline IN and OUT Points

In this scenario, there is a portion of the Timeline that needs video. Performing this function requires IN and OUT points in the Timeline and an IN point in the Source monitor.

Since there are IN and OUT points in the Timeline, in the Source monitor, you can Mark IN or Mark OUT or Mark neither IN nor OUT. (When there isn't an IN or OUT point in the Source monitor, the first frame of the clip in the Timeline will be wherever the Source monitor position indicator is located.) This scenario requires the first frame in the sequence to be a specific first frame from the Source monitor—for example, Elvis looking at Ellie—and an IN point should be placed at that moment.

To overwrite a clip with an IN point to a sequence with IN and OUT points

1. Double-click the correct sequence, and it loads in the Timeline window.

2. In the Timeline window, do the following:

    (a) Mark IN (press I) on the sequence where you want to overwrite the first frame of video.

    (b) Mark OUT (press O) on the sequence where you want to overwrite the last frame of video.

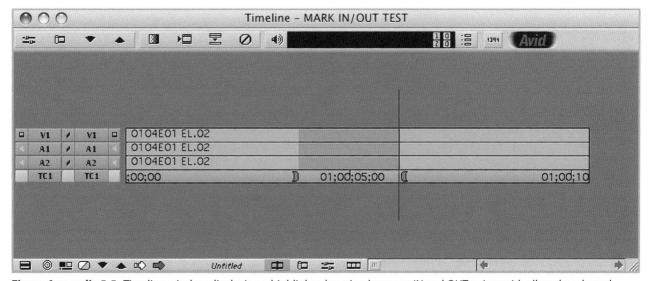

Figure Appendix 5-5. Timeline window displaying a highlighted section between IN and OUT points with all tracks selected.

3. Double-click the correct clip, and it loads in the Source monitor.

4. In the Source monitor, Mark IN (press I) on the clip.

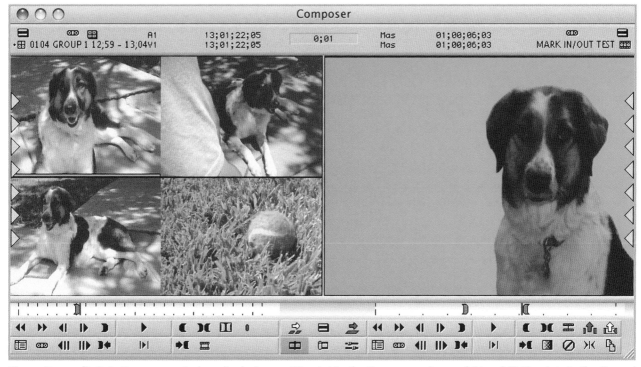

Figure Appendix 5-6. Composer window displaying an IN point in the Source monitor and IN and OUT points in the Record monitor.

5. In the Timeline window, do the following:

    (a) Patch the source video track to the desired record video track.

(b) Deselect the audio tracks.

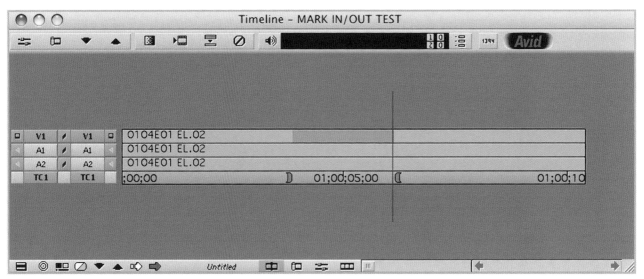

Figure Appendix 5-7. Timeline window displaying a highlighted section between IN and OUT points with video track 1 (V1) selected.

(c) Overwrite (press B) the clip to the sequence.

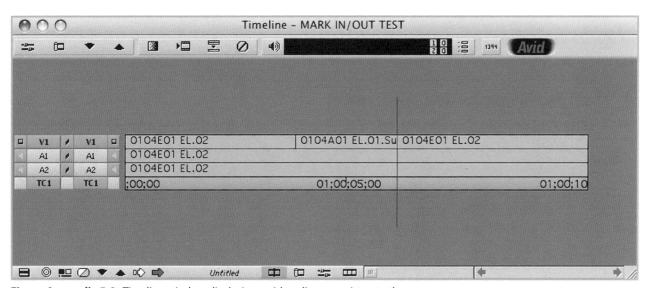

Figure Appendix 5-8. Timeline window displaying a video clip overwritten to the sequence.

Be careful when placing a Mark IN point in the Source monitor when there are IN and OUT points in the sequence. There will be occasions where the IN and OUT duration in the sequence is longer than the remaining time in the Source monitor clip. For example, sequence IN and OUT duration is 5 seconds, and the Source monitor clip is 7 seconds long. If the Mark IN point on the Source monitor clip is at second 3, and the entire clip duration is 7 seconds, that leaves only 4 seconds to place the clip into the

Timeline. In this instance, the solution is to place the Mark IN point at second 2 in the Source monitor.

Scenario 3: Source Monitor OUT Point and Timeline IN and OUT Points

In this scenario, there is a portion of the Timeline that needs video. Performing this function requires IN and OUT points in the Timeline and an OUT point in the Source monitor.

This scenario requires a specific frame in the Source monitor—when the camera pans down as Elvis barks at Ellie—to be the last frame you overwrite into the sequence. Since there are IN and OUT points in the Timeline, an OUT point should be placed at that moment.

To overwrite a clip with an OUT point to a sequence with IN and OUT points

1. Double-click the correct sequence, and it loads in the Timeline window.

2. In the Timeline window, do the following:

    (a) Mark IN (press I) on the sequence where you want to overwrite the first frame of video.

    (b) Mark OUT (press O) on the sequence where you want to overwrite the last frame of video.

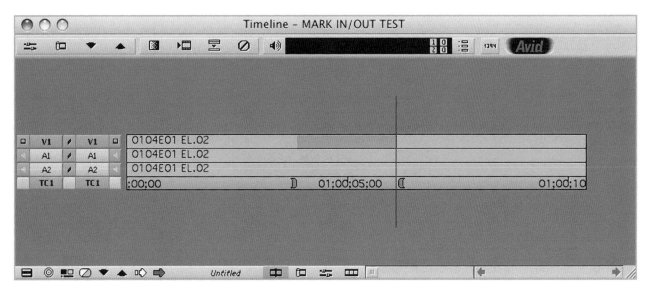

Figure Appendix 5-9. Timeline window displaying a highlighted section between IN and OUT points with video track 1 (V1) selected.

3. Double-click the correct clip, and it loads in the Source monitor.

4. In the Source monitor, Mark OUT (press O) on the clip.

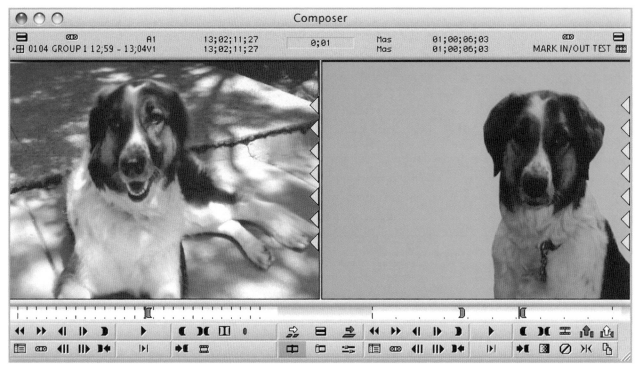

Figure Appendix 5-10. Composer window displaying an OUT point in the Source monitor and IN and OUT points in the Record monitor.

5. In the Timeline window, do the following:

   (a) Patch the source video track to the desired record video track.

   (b) Deselect the audio tracks.

   (c) Overwrite (press B) the clip to the sequence.

   The result of a clip in the Timeline is the same as if a Mark IN point had been used. However, since a specific last frame was desired, Avid back times from that point to fill the duration between the IN and OUT points.

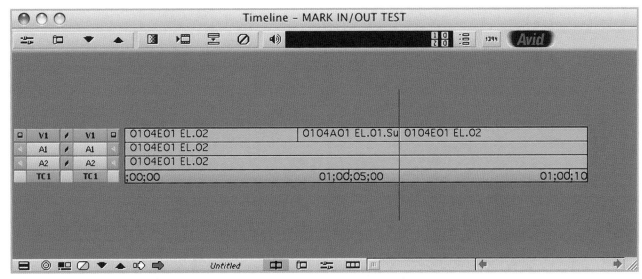

Figure Appendix 5-11. Timeline window displaying a video clip overwritten to the sequence.

Scenario 4: Source Monitor Mark Clip

When Mark Clip is clicked in the Source monitor, an IN point is placed at the first frame of video and an OUT point is placed at the last frame of video.

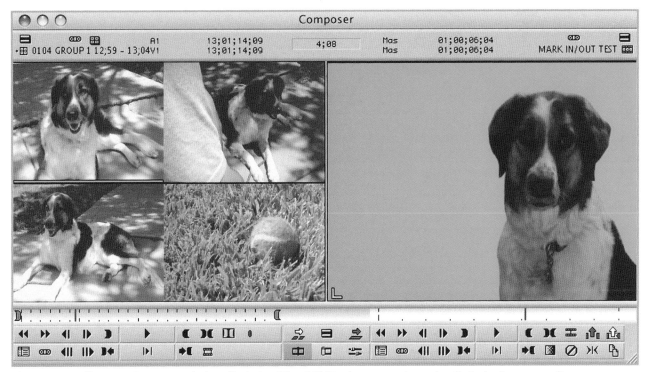

Figure Appendix 5-12. Composer window displaying IN and OUT points across the entire clip in the Source monitor.

Scenario 5: Timeline Mark Clip

When Mark Clip is pressed in the Timeline window, what gets marked for selection is dependent on the video and audio tracks enabled, common edit points, and the position indicator's location. Four exercises are provided for you to practice with using your own test clips and sequences. To begin, create a sequence that looks like FIGURE APPENDIX 5-13.

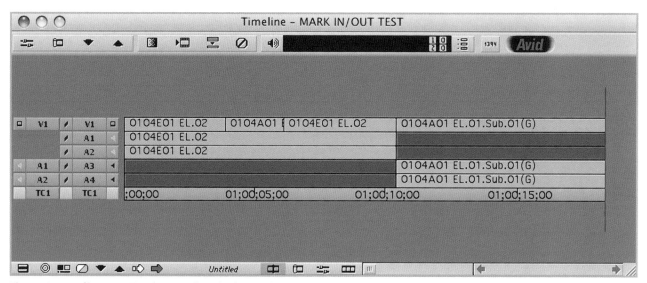

Figure Appendix 5-13. Timeline window displaying the test sequence.

Exercise 1

To mark clip with one video track selected

1. In the Timeline window, enable video track 1 (V1).

2. Deselect the audio tracks.

3. Place the position indicator on the clip on V1.

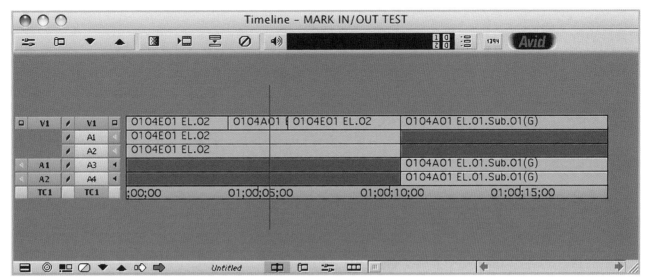

Figure Appendix 5-14. Timeline window displaying the position indicator over the clip on video track 1 (V1).

4.   Mark Clip (press T) and the clip on V1 is marked for selection.

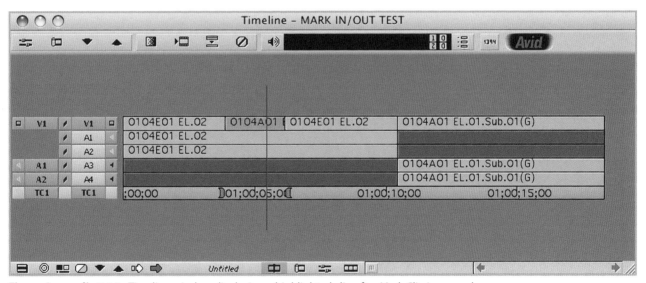

Figure Appendix 5-15. Timeline window displaying a highlighted clip after Mark Clip is pressed.

Exercise 2

To mark clip with one video track and two audio tracks selected

1.   In the Timeline window, enable video track 1 (V1) and audio tracks 1 and 2 (A1 and A2, respectively).

2.   Place the position indicator on the clip on V1.

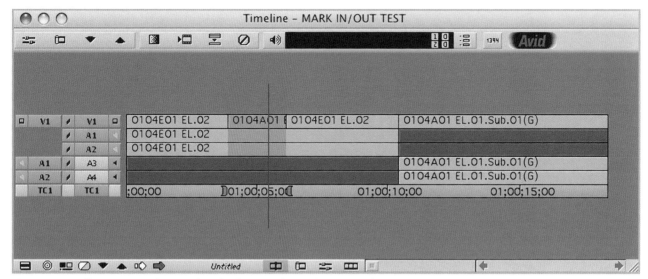

Figure Appendix 5-16. Timeline window displaying video track 1 (V1) and audio tracks 1 and 2 (A1 and A2, respectively) selected.

3. Mark Clip (press T), and the clip on V1, the surrounding video, and the associated audio tracks for the clip are marked for selection.

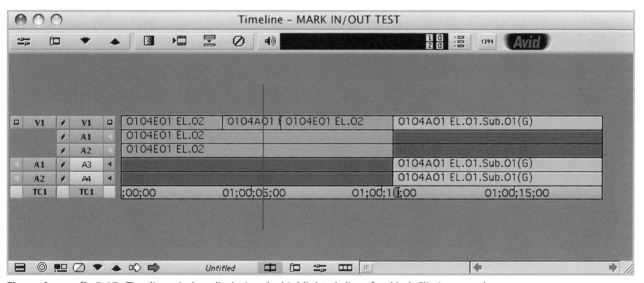

Figure Appendix 5-17. Timeline window displaying the highlighted clips after Mark Clip is pressed.

When using Mark Clip, there is a relationship between the active tracks and any common edit points. This section was selected because there is a common edit point between the beginning of the sequence and the second clip.

Exercise 3

To mark clip with all video and audio tracks selected

1. In the Timeline window, enable video track 1 (V1) and audio tracks 1, 2, 3, and 4 (A1–A4, respectively).

2. Place the position indicator on the clip on V1.

3. Mark Clip (press T), and the clip on V1, the surrounding video, the associated audio tracks for the clip, and the unused audio tracks (A3 and A4) are marked for selection.

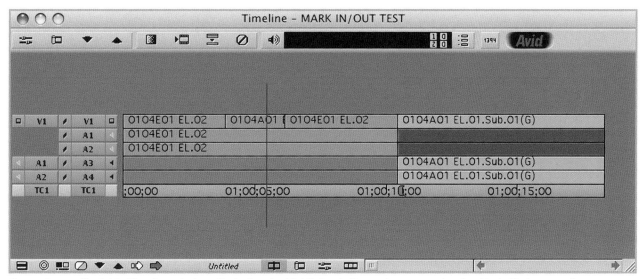

Figure Appendix 5-18. Timeline window displaying the highlighted clips and empty tracks after Mark Clip is pressed.

When using Mark Clip, there is a relationship between the active tracks and any common edit points. This section was selected because there is a common edit point between the beginning of the sequence and the second clip.

Exercise 4

To mark clip with overlapping video and audio tracks selected

1. Click Lift/Overwrite Segment Mode.

2. Shift+Click the video and corresponding audio of the second clip in the sequence (0104A01 EL.01).

3. Move the clip a little to the left so that it overlaps with the first clip (0104E01 EL.02).

4. Click Lift/Overwrite Segment Mode to exit the function.

5. In the Timeline window, enable video track 1 (V1) and audio tracks 1, 2, 3, and 4 (A1–A4, respectively).

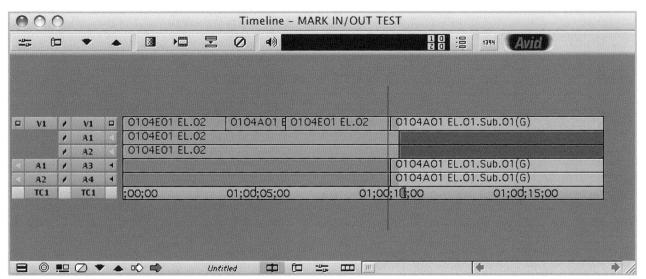

Figure Appendix 5-19. Timeline window displaying the highlighted clips and empty tracks after Mark Clip is pressed (from previous exercise).

6. Place the position indicator on the last clip in the sequence (0104A01 EL.01.Sub.01(G)).

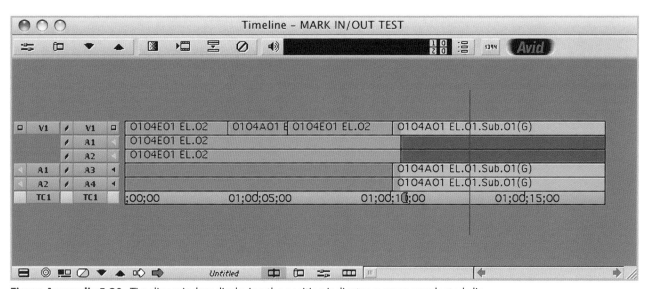

Figure Appendix 5-20. Timeline window displaying the position indicator over an unselected clip.

7. Mark Clip (press T), and all of the clips and tracks for the sequence are marked for selection.

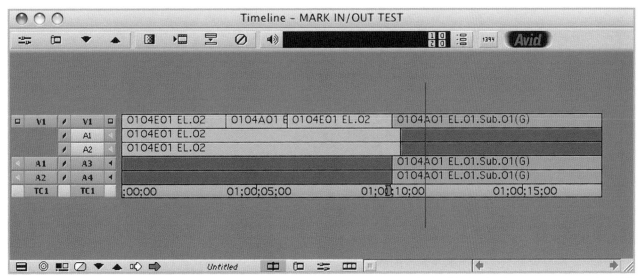

Figure Appendix 5-21. Timeline window displaying the entire highlighted sequence after Mark Clip is pressed.

As mentioned, Mark Clip looks at the relationships between the active tracks and common edit points. Since the second clip was moved over a little bit, there aren't any common edit points when Mark Clip is pressed and all of the tracks are active. This is why the entire sequence was selected.

If (for example) only video track 1 (V1) and audio tracks 3 and 4 (A3 and A4, respectively) were active, the position indicator was over the 0104A01 EL.01.Sub.01(G) clip, and Mark Clip was pressed, then just the clip at the end of the sequence would be selected.

Figure Appendix 5-22. Timeline window displaying the position indicator over the highlight clip (0104A01 EL.01.Sub.01(G)) after Mark Clip is pressed with only video track 1 (V1) and audio tracks 3 and 4 (A3 and A4, respectively) selected.

These examples show how Mark Clip functions, and the more you use it, the more you will be able to achieve the results you are looking for.

APPENDIX 6:
Title Tool

Tasks in This Appendix

THE TITLE TOOL CAN be a powerful supplement to your Avid software—if you know how to use it. Play around and get creative with your text, and remember that the Title tool functions similarly to a lot of word processing software.

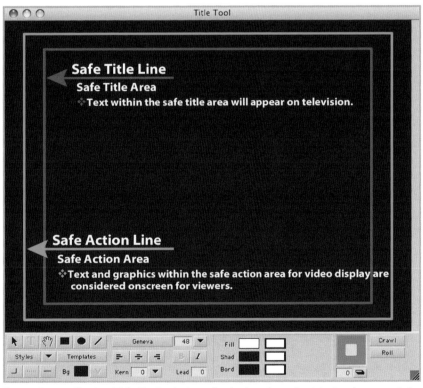

Figure Appendix 6-1. Title Tool window displaying the safe title line/area and the safe action line/area.

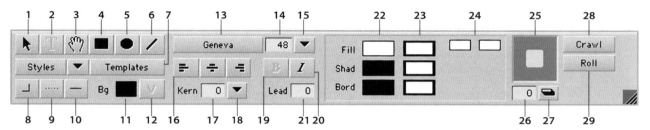

Figure Appendix 6-2. Title Tool toolbar with numbered components (see Table Appendix 6-1).

TABLE APPENDIX 6-1. TITLE TOOL TOOLBAR COMPONENTS/FUNCTIONS (SEE FIGURE APPENDIX 6-2)

	Component	Function
1	Selection tool	Use to select/adjust text and whole objects.
2	Text tool	Use to create/edit text.
3	Video Placement tool	Use to move objects.
4	Square and Rectangle tool	Use to create squares and rectangles.
5	Oval tool	Use to create ovals and circles.
6	Line tool	Use to create lines.
7	Styles and Templates buttons	Use to create styles and templates to give projects a consistent look.
8	Box Corner button	Use to create round corners.
9	Border Width button	Use to place borders on text or graphics.
10	Arrowhead button	Use to create arrows.
11	Background Color window	Use to change the color of backgrounds.
12	Video Background button	Use to switch between a video background and a black background.
13	Font Selection button	Use to format text by changing the font type.
14	Point Size text box	Use to format text by changing the font size.
15	Point Size button	Use to format text by changing the font size.
16	Text Justification buttons (Left, Center, and Right)	Use to format text by changing the justification.
17	Kerning text box	Use to format text by changing the kerning.
18	Kerning button	Use to format text by changing the kerning.
19	Bold button	Use to format text by applying bold attributes.
20	Italic button	Use to format text by applying italic attributes.
21	Leading text box	Use to format text by changing the leading.
22	Color Selection boxes	Use to specify the colors for the fills, shadows, and borders of text and graphics.
23	Transparency Level boxes	Use to specify the opacity for the fills, shadows, and borders of text and graphics.
24	Color and Transparency Blend tools	Use to blend between two colors for the fill, shadow, and/or border.

	Component	Function
TABLE APPENDIX 6-1. TITLE TOOL TOOLBAR COMPONENTS/FUNCTIONS (CONTINUED)		
	Component	**Function**
25	Shadow Depth and Direction button	Use to adjust the depth and direction of a shadow.
26	Shadow Depth text box	Use to adjust the depth and direction of a shadow by typing in numerical values.
27	Drop and Depth Shadow button	Use to switch between a drop or depth shadow.
28	Crawling Title button	Use to create crawling titles (titles that crawl horizontally across the screen from left to right or right to left).
29	Rolling Title button	Use to create rolling titles (titles that scroll vertically onscreen from bottom to top or from top to bottom).

Creating and Modifying Text Objects

Using the Text tool to type in the Title tool creates a text object. Copying and pasting text into the Title tool also creates a text object. Text objects are surrounded by eight small boxes (known as *object selection handles*) and are used to resize text objects.

To create a text object

1. Click the Text tool.

2. Click in the Title tool and type or cut and paste text.

When text objects are created by typing or cutting and pasting text into the Title tool, the object selection handles are fit to the text as shown in FIGURE APPENDIX 6-3 and FIGURE APPENDIX 6-4 on page 356.

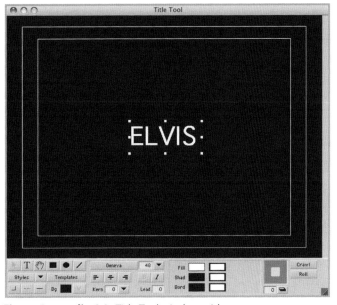

Figure Appendix 6-3. Title Tool window with text.

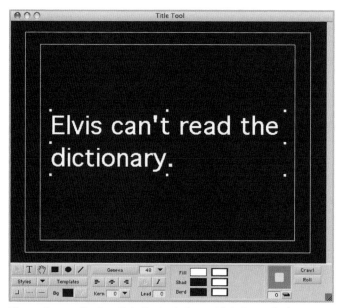

Figure Appendix 6-4. Title Tool window with left justified text in a normal text object. (Notice that the text object's selection handles are fitted to the newly created text object.)

When resizing text objects, you can only resize the width—the height is automatically adjusted based on the text size and number of characters. The text size of resized text objects is not affected. However, the text re-wraps to fill the resized text object.

To modify the width of a text object

1. Click the Selection tool, and click the text object.

2. Click an object selection handle for width (a dotted line appears connecting all of the control points) and drag it to the desired width.

Since the width of the text object determines how text will display, notice in Figure Appendix 6-5 that because the object selection handle was dragged to the left making the width smaller, the longest word in the text object—"dictionary"—no longer fits on one line. As a result, the "y" is separated from the rest of "dictionary," and outside of the safe title area, and thus, off screen for viewing purposes.

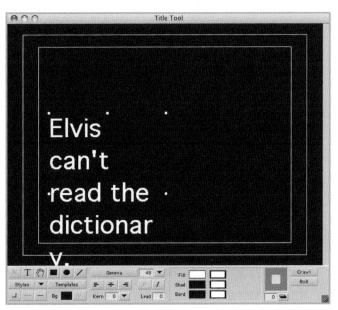

Figure Appendix 6-5. Title Tool window with left justified text in a text object set outside the safe title area.

When text is added and later deleted from text objects, the text objects do not automatically resize causing them to be larger than required by the remaining text as shown in FIGURE APPENDIX 6-6.

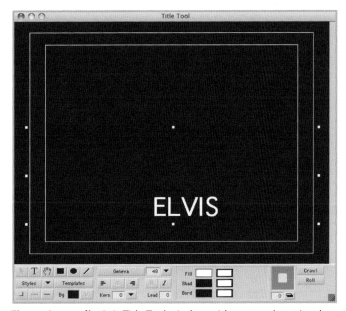

Figure Appendix 6-6. Title Tool window with centered text in a large text object.

Within a text object, text can be left, center, or right justified. However, if the text object's selection handles are not all within the safe title area, depending on the size and placement of the text object and the type of text justification in use, the text may be justified right off the screen.

Best practice when justifying text in the Title tool is to ensure that the text's object selection handles are aligned with the safe title area and that extra space around the text is deleted as shown in Figure Appendix 6-7. Using this technique, if you click Center, Left , or Right Text Justification, the text will remain on a viewer's television screen.

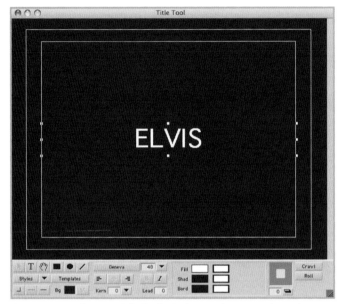

Figure Appendix 6-7. Title Tool window with centered text in a normal text object.

APPENDIX 7:
Digital Cut Tool

T HE DIGITAL CUT TOOL is used to record Avid sequences to tape or disc. Like the Capture tool, the Digital Cut tool is dependent on Avid being aware that a properly configured video deck is connected to the system. Other functions of the Digital Cut tool will help you decide which tracks of a sequence to record to tape or disc and in what format.

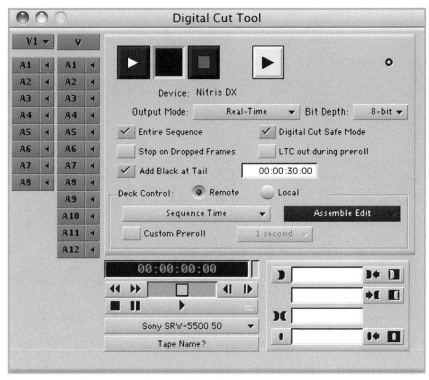

Figure Appendix 7-1. Digital Cut Tool window.

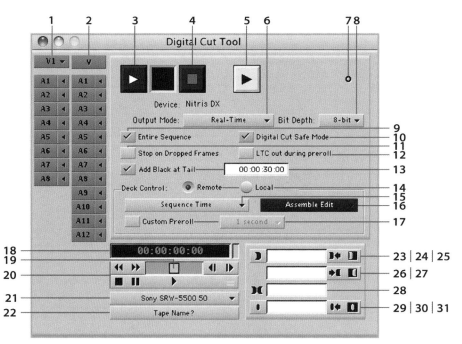

Figure Appendix 7-2. Digital Cut Tool with numbered components (see Table Appendix 7-1).

TABLE APPENDIX 7-1. DIGITAL CUT TOOL COMPONENTS/FUNCTIONS (SEE FIGURE APPENDIX 7-2)

	Component	Function
1	Sequence Track buttons	Represent the tracks of the sequence. Make sure the correct tracks are selected.
2	Enable Track buttons	Represent the tracks that will be laid onto the tape. Make sure the correct tracks are selected. In this example, the one video track and eight audio tracks of the sequence will be laid onto the tape.
3	Play Digital Cut button	Starts the digital cut process.
4	Halt Digital Cut button	Stops the digital cut process at any time.
5	Preview Digital Cut button	Plays a preview of the output before it is recorded onto tape.
6	Output Mode menu	Options available depend on the project type and the deck attached to Avid.
7	Ref Lock icon	Displays green when there is a valid video signal and Avid recognizes that signal.
8	Bit Depth menu	Options available depend on the project type and the deck attached to Avid.
9	Entire Sequence option	Selected: The entire sequence is laid onto tape. Not Selected: A portion of a sequence can be laid onto tape.
10	Digital Cut Safe Mode option	Selected: Analyzes all effects in a sequence and identifies which ones need to be rendered to ensure accurate playback. It also checks the sequence and alerts you to any high-definition clips in a standard-definition sequence that need to be transcoded. (Digital Cut Safe Mode option is similar to ExpertRender option.)
11	Stop on Dropped Frames option	Selected: Aborts the Digital Cut process if any frames are skipped.
12	LTC out during preroll option	Filler added to the beginning of a sequence to give external devices time to synchronize with the sequence immediately before the output. (The filler is not recorded to the tape.)

TABLE APPENDIX 7-1. DIGITAL CUT TOOL COMPONENTS/FUNCTIONS (CONTINUED)

	Component	Function
13	Add Black at Tail option	Selected: Black is added at the tail so that the timecode on the tape does not end on the last frame of video. (00:00:30:00 represents 30 seconds of filler recorded to the end of the tape after the last frame of the sequence.)
14	Deck Control	Determines whether Avid (Remote option) or you (Local option) have control of the deck.
15	Deck Control area: Options menu on the left	The menu options—Sequence Time, Record Deck Time, Mark In Time, and Ignore Time—determine where to start recording on the tape. ◆ Sequence Time: Matches the sequence start time to an existing timecode on the tape. ◆ Record Deck Time: Records the sequence onto the tape at the timecode where it is currently cued. ◆ Mark In Time: Allows you to set an IN point on the tape, and that is the timecode where the sequence will be laid onto tape. ◆ Ignore Time: Disregards the sequence's start timecode and uses the timecode on the deck.
16	Deck Control area: Options menu on the right	The menu options—Insert Edit, Assemble Edit, and Crash Record—determine how to record the sequence onto the tape. To gain access to the Assemble Edit option and the Crash Record option on this menu, select Allow assemble edit & crash record for digital cut option in the Deck Preferences dialog box (Project window | Settings list). ◆ Insert Edit: Select if there is timecode on the entire tape. ◆ Assemble Edit: Select if there is only a section of the tape with timecode on it. Avid will create timecode for the rest of the tape. ◆ Crash Record: Select if the output doesn't need to start at a certain timecode.
17	Custom Preroll option	Selected: Displays how much time the tape will play after a timecode break before capturing again.
18	Timecode display	Displays the timecode of the tape/disc. Semicolons (;) indicate drop-frame video and colons (:) indicate non-drop-frame video.
19	Shuttle button	Use to rewind and fast forward through a tape/disc, instead of using Rewind and Fast Forward buttons.
20	Deck controls	Use to control the video deck through the Capture tool.
21	Deck Selection menu	Displays the name of the video deck Avid believes is connected to the computer. (If the deck name is displayed in italics, the deck is offline.)
22	Source Tape display	Displays the tape/disc name.
23	Mark IN button	Marks the beginning of a section of the tape/disc to be captured.
24	Go to IN button	Moves the deck's playhead to the Mark IN point on the tape/disc.
25	Clear IN button	Clears the Mark IN point.
26	Go to OUT button	Moves the deck's playhead to the Mark OUT point on the tape/disc.
27	Clear OUT button	Clears the Mark OUT point.
28	Duration display	Displays the duration between the Mark IN and Mark OUT timecodes.
29	Mark Memory button	Adds a temporary locator to a point on the tape/disc for later reference. Only one memory mark can be present on a tape/disc. The memory mark is cleared from the Capture tool through the Clear Memory button or when the tape/disc is removed from the deck.

TABLE APPENDIX 7-1. **DIGITAL CUT TOOL COMPONENTS/FUNCTIONS (CONTINUED)**

	Component	Function
30	Go to Memory button	Moves the deck's playhead to the memory mark.
31	Clear Memory button	Clears the memory mark.

APPENDIX 8:
Assistant Editor Checklist

As a new assistant editor, you will have a lot of questions regarding your responsibilities. The questions on the Assistant Editor Checklist on the following two pages are designed to give you a framework for those questions. The Assistant Editor Checklist's formatting/placement is an intentional departure from the rest of the book. Designed so you can easily make copies of it and use it as a place to store critical company-specific and show-specific information, the Assistant Editor Checklist will accommodate any Avid editing environment you encounter.

I wish you the best of luck on your new career path, and I would love to hear from you about your experiences, frustrations, or questions regarding *The Avid Assistant Editor's Handbook* or this field in general. The more we all know and share, the better assistant editors, and eventually editors, we all will become.

Never hesitate to email me at Kyra@AvidAsstEditor.com, and don't forget to check out the book's website at www.AvidAsstEditor.com. If Twitter or Facebook are more your style, you can find me at Twitter.com/AvidAsstEditor or Facebook.com/AvidAsstEditor.

Thank you.

Assistant Editor Checklist

1 Capturing

How are the decks connected to Avid?

_____

Am I allowed to connect/disconnect decks to/from Avid?

_____

What are the deck preference settings for connecting a deck to Avid?

_____

_____

Is low-resolution footage separated from full-resolution footage?

_____

_____

How do I rename bins when capturing footage from tapes/discs?

_____

How do I name tapes/discs when capturing footage?

_____

Do I mark tapes with a colored circle, an X, or another mark to indicate it has been captured?

_____

What do I do with tapes after they have been captured?

_____

2 Rough Cuts Scripts

What tracks should I overwrite interview and reality audio to?

_____

3 Multigrouping

Are there sync "helpers" on set such as clapping or a loud beep?

_____

Are interviews included in multigroups?

_____

Are surveillance clips, such as car or house, included in multigroups?

_____

How are multigroups divided? by scene? by day?

_____

Once I complete a multigroup, what bin should I put it in?

_____

Assistant Editor Checklist

4 Audio Passes

What curse words are bleeped for this show? (Each show has a specific list.)

_____

When bleeping curse words, is the curse word replaced with silence, tone media, or a sound effect?

_____

5 Titles

When are lower thirds supposed to appear within the episode?

_____

Is there a particular font I should use when creating temporary titles?

_____

6 Outputs

What is the naming system for internal and external outputs?

_____

When performing an output to tape, what timecode should the first frame of video begin at?

_____

What are the durations of color bars, tone media, slates, and filler within the output?

_____

What timecode type should I use: drop-frame or non-drop frame?

_____

What information should the slates between the acts of the episode contain?

_____

7 Exports

What are the export settings for QuickTime movies or Windows media files?

_____

What are the export settings for AAF/OMF files?

_____

Should AAF/OMF files be exported as acts or by tracks?

_____

When creating an EDL, what tapename truncation should I use to preserve the important tape naming information?

_____

8 Onlining

How should I set up the online project for the online editor?

_____

Figures and Tables

CHAPTER 3: FILE-BASED MEDIA

Chapter 4: Multigrouping

CHAPTER 5: ROUGH CUTS

Chapter 6: Audio Passes

Chapter 7: Backgrounds and Effects

CHAPTER 8: TITLES

CHAPTER 9: OUTPUTS

CHAPTER 11: ONLINING

APPENDIX 1: CAPTURE TOOL

APPENDIX 2: DECK CONFIGURATION

APPENDIX 3: KEYBOARD SETTING

APPENDIX 4: MULTIGROUPING HELPFUL HINTS

APPENDIX 5: MARK IN AND OUT

APPENDIX 6: TITLE TOOL

Appendix 7: Digital Cut Tool

ABOUT THE AUTHOR

KYRA COFFIE, AN EDITOR for over a decade, has worked for companies that produce programming for TLC, MTV, VH1 networks, and the Discovery Channel.

A native of Washington, D.C., Ms. Coffie took positions as an assistant editor while breaking into the Los Angeles market, and her editing background allowed her to make assistant editing processes more standardized, efficient, and easy to learn.

The Avid Assistant Editor's Handbook is a product of her time in L.A., and it's her hope that any individual wanting to learn Avid will be able to do so with her book. Check out her website at www.AvidAsstEditor.com.

INDEX

406

THE AVID ASSISTANT EDITOR'S HANDBOOK

Video Output tool, Options tab, Sync Lock option, Internal vs. Reference (note), 243
Video Output Tool, Tools menu, 243
Video Placement tool, Title tool, 354
Video Quality Menu button, Timeline, 15
video, timecode of first frame, 223
Video Tool button, Capture tool, 308
video tracks
cameras, number of vs. video tracks in a sequence (note), 89
creating
keyboard shortcut, 4
number, default for sequences, changing (tip), 156
mark clip
mark clip with all video and audio tracks selected (task), 349
mark clip with one video track and two audio tracks selected (task), 347–348
mark clip with one video track selected (task), 346–347
mark clip with overlapping video and audio tracks selected (task), 349–351
multigroups, switching a multigroup's audio or video tracks (task), 165
syncing, locators (note), 111
See also tracks
View Menu button, Timeline, 15
View Name dialog box, 46
Volume Level displays (tip), Audio Mixer tool, 180
volume levels
adjusting the volume level of one audio track (task), 178–179
adjusting the volume level of two or more audio tracks simultaneously using ganging (task), 179–180
Volume Level sliders, Audio Mixer tool, 178–179
Volume Mounting tab, AMA Settings dialog box. See AMA Settings dialog box: Volume Mounting tab

waveforms
marking IN/OUT points, draw waveforms between points on each track, 109–110, 329
Show Marked Waveforms (option), Display tab, Timeline Settings dialog box, 78
syncing, 110
matching waveforms vs. locators (note), 112
website tease, 234
When mounting previously mounted volumes, do not check for modifications to the volume (option), Volume Mounting tab, AMA Settings dialog box, 39, 54
windows
Audio Mixer Tool window, 179
Audio Project Settings window, Output tab, 243
Avid Media Composer window, default setup, 9
Bin window, 18, 21
Composer window, description, 14
Deck Configuration window, 314–318
EDL Manager window. See Avid EDL Manager
Locators window, 81
Project window, 9, 10, 11–12
Timecode window, description, 90
Timeline, description, 14–15

windows (continued)
See also entries of specific windows
Windows Media®, 254
Window tab, Composer Settings dialog box. See Composer Settings dialog box: Window tab
work, colorist's vs. assistant editor's, 276
workflows
AMA, XDCAM discs, 54
finishing the output process, 249
rough cuts script, 154
Wrap Around (option), Timeline Fast Menu settings, 79

X

XDCAM
batch importing graphics into the sequence at full resolution, 298
bringing XDCAM footage into Avid using AMA (task), 55–61
bringing XDCAM footage into Avid with AMA disabled (task), 61–68
Clip folder, 65
consolidating clips, 60
discs, 38, 54
labeling, default, 59
ingest options (table), 55
.MXF, 66
Sub folder, 65–66
transcoding clips, 60
.XML, 66
XDCAM tab, Import Settings dialog box. See Import Settings dialog box: XDCAM tab
.XML, XDCAM, 66

Y

yellow-highlighted clips, 42–43
YRB components, deck hook-ups, 18

Z

zoom in and zoom out, keyboard shortcuts, 4